The Revival of Banned Dances

The Revival of Banned Dances

A Worldwide Study

Reneé Critcher Lyons

McFarland & Company, Inc., Publishers
Jefferson, North Carolina, and London

LIBRARY OF CONGRESS CATALOGUING-IN-PUBLICATION DATA

Lyons, Reneé Critcher, 1961–
 The revival of banned dances : a worldwide study
 / Reneé Critcher Lyons.
  p.   cm.
 Includes bibliographical references and index.

 ISBN 978-0-7864-6594-1
 softcover : acid free paper ∞

 1. Dance — Social aspects — Case studies. 2. Dance — Moral
and ethical aspects — Case studies. 3. Dance — Political
aspects — Case studies. I. Title.
GV1617.L96 2012
793.3 — dc23   2012028775

BRITISH LIBRARY CATALOGUING DATA ARE AVAILABLE

On the cover: *foreground* Apsaras dance taken from the 12th
century Bayon temple at Angkor in Cambodia; *background*
Ghawazee dancers at Cairo, Egypt (lithograph circa 1846 by
David Roberts, Library of Congress)

Manufactured in the United States of America

McFarland & Company, Inc., Publishers
 Box 611, Jefferson, North Carolina 28640
 www.mcfarlandpub.com

For my mother, Anna Belle Holder Critcher Dyer,
who gave me the dance

Acknowledgments

Here in the Appalachian Mountains, one call for our square dances involves forming a large circle and, hand-in-hand as the music plays, stepping inward towards each other, meeting a neighbor face-to-face after a few steps and shouting "ya-hoo," "yip-pee," or "yee-hah." Each time the circle moves inward, another neighbor is encountered, acknowledged as a partner in revelry. Similarly, for this instant scholarly dance, I have many "yip-pees" to deliver!

First, I wish to thank my forever-there mother, Anna Critcher Dyer. Mom, you are a treasure, fast on your feet, too! And, of course, thanks to my beautiful daughter, Faith. Woo, you are the heart of my personal faith, why I believe in myself (and I know why you love to dance, too)! To my boyfriend, Michael, thanks for the constant push up the hill, the cuddles and hugs, and all the meals that sustained me! Thanks also to my sister, Janet Greer, and brother, Chad Critcher, for their inquiries as to how the book was progressing, and for their support.

To my clogging team, Country Magic Cloggers, especially our leader, Mariette Winkler Lisk, thanks for the weekly inspiration (and exercise)! Thanks to the Worldview staff at UNC-Chapel Hill for expanding the "worldview" of educators across the state of North Carolina, and to Caldwell Community College and Technical Institute for allowing me to serve the Global Diversity Committee as part of my employment. To my precious mentor, friend, and colleague at Appalachian State University, Dr. Linda Veltze, I just wish to say, "Where would I be without your encouragement, friendship, and wisdom?" To my friends, Sara Palmer and Helen Kampion, thanks for sending such positive vibes into the universe on my behalf!

A special thanks to the academic institutions which have nourished me: Vermont College of Fine Arts Creative Writing Program (especially David Gifaldi); Appalachian State University for the mind-boggling wealth of information found in their library; and Caldwell Community College and Technical Institute for scholarly access, a livelihood, and a bit of supply!

Calling all students and scholars out there: come join us in your educational adventures, in our dance, everyone!

Table of Contents

Preface   1

Part I. Ritual

1. Rekindling the Flame: The Revival of the Sadir Katcheri
   (Bharata Natyam)   5
2. "It Is a Strict Law That Bids Us Dance": The Kwakiutl
   Hamatsa Dance   17
3. Poetry in Motion: The Hula   29
4. We Are All on This Earth Together: The Plains Indians Sun Dance   39
5. The Churning of the Oceans: The Survival of the Khmer
   Classical Dance of Cambodia   48
6. Of Two Worlds: The Whirling Dervishes of Konya   58

Part II. Revival

7. A Better Way of Life: The Ghost Dance of the Plains Indians   71
8. "The Only People Can Shout Is Right Here": The Unbroken
   Chain of the Ring-Shout Dance   84
9. Visca Sardana! The Astronomical Dance of Catalonia   96
10. Capoeiristas: Righteous Avengers   104
11. The Raqs Sharqi (Belly Dance) Faces Trouble   118

Part III. Revelry

12. Bringing in the May   133
13. All's Well That Ends Well: The English Morris Dance   145
14. Feet on Fire: Irish Dance at the Crossroads   157
15. Sacred, Yet Profane: The Afro-Brazilian Batuque and Samba   177
16. It Takes Two to Tango!   192

Bibliography   205
Index   212

Preface

On with the dance! Let joy be unconfined. — Lord Byron

This dance began in a new century. In the fall of 2006, I attended UNC-Chapel Hill's Worldview conference: South Asia: Cultural Traditions, Contemporary Dilemmas. I spoke with Professor Purnima Shah of the dance program at Duke University about the revival of one of the oldest art forms found on the globe, India's *bharata natyam*. (As a clog dancer myself, a tradition of the Appalachian Mountains with Scotch-Irish roots, I was intrigued.) I learned of Rukmini Devi and her incredible story of courage as she embarked upon a quest in the early 1900s to save the dance of her native land. Fitting that this introduction to India's icon was the "seed" for this present work on banned dances from around the world (and their subsequent revival and/or attempts at revival), as the oldest language known to man, Sanskrit, provided the very first word describing dance, *tanha*, meaning "joy of life." A phrase worth repeating. *Tanha*, Joy of Life!

Dance, indeed, contributes to our collective pursuit of happiness. It is healthy for our minds, bodies and souls. An hour of dancing burns between three and four hundred calories, much needed in this age of Twinkies and super burgers. For shapely dancers, dance can help maintain a positive body image and help them delight in their physical prowess. Emotionally, the dancer forgets his or her problems for a bit, enjoying time to regroup and recharge. Dance releases pent-up energy, positive or negative. The ecstasy or intense happiness we experience while dancing is a way to heal after experiencing personal loss or tragedy. Thank goodness we can still stomp a good ol' Irish jig, rumble with the samba, or skip around the May Pole in merrie ol' England.

Returning to the birthplace and time of dance, India or Egypt five thousand years ago, we must honor the most important aspect of the art form, its "transritual" nature, a trajectory to otherworldliness. The transcendent experience enjoyed as one dances, differing from individual to individual and from culture to culture, serves as an avenue, a bridge of connection, to our own personal god, what some call "universal consciousness." Thank goodness that in our search for inner peace, contentment, and strength, hula chants point out directions, sun dances test our core, and dervishes exemplify a means of connection! Additionally, as citizens of the ancient cradles of civilization knew, dancing revives and recycles life. (Five thousand years ago, people did not survive as easily, of course. In fact, they were always concerned with finding enough food and enhancing survival by increasing the population.) Men and women participated in dances honoring their gods, believing these deities would bless them with food and children. When these blessings were delivered, dance turned into a ritual of celebration. Or, a group weakened by lack of food or subjection to physical attack danced to re-energize the community, strengthening a sense of solidarity and the group's resolve to survive. In essence, dance was a way to shape events, to insure a proper outcome (the academic term for this belief is *sympathetic magic*). Thank goodness the Khmer classical ballet continues to pay tribute to our oceans and the environment, belly dancers help mothers endure the bodily exertion associated with childbirth, and Ghost dancers remind us to never stop trying!

In early societies, religious rituals also included dances which helped to ease a young person's passage from childhood to adulthood. Dancing provided an opportunity for young men and women to attract a partner (which is still true today). And community dances supported "new" adults as they first shouldered the responsibility of marrying and raising a family. Thank goodness *at least* the boys from Canada's Kwakiutl tribe walk a trail-blazed path to manhood, the tango spurns our yearning for a life-partner, and Morris dancers reveal how adults, too, must take time to play.

Dance not only helps an individual identify with his or her immediate group, it also supports one group's understanding of another. Put simply, it dissolves the differences between friend and stranger. Because it is a spontaneous language of the body rather than a deliberate language of the tongue or pen, it breaks down walls that keep people apart, such as black and white, Christian and Muslim, rich and poor. While dancing, people may live in the present without giving up their past. The art carries the wisdom of our ancestors into present-day life, where meaning, depth and understanding are applied to the character development of both nations and individuals. Thank goodness Bharatynam is a reminder of humanity's need to collectively extinguish the flames of ignorance and destruction, the sardana and the ring-shout teaches humanity to stand together as one, and capoeira reminds us of the flexibility and wit required of healthy interpersonal relationships.

Embarking upon this journey of studying the dances banned throughout history, I found very few collective works regarding the oppression of dance culture. Two works which did explore the concept were *Dancing in*

Sadir katcheri for Hindu worshippers, circa 1914 (Library of Congress).

the Streets: A History of Collective Joy, by Barbara Ehrenreich, and *Adversaries of Dance: From Puritans to the Present*, by Ann Wagner. A journal article of primary note is Susan Reed's "The Politics and Poetics of Dance," found in the *Annual Review of Anthropology* (1998). A multi-media work of note is Rhoda Grauer's *Dancing in One World*. However, these works do not consider, define, or explore each individual dance, its cultural value, history, major players, and repression/revival in depth as I hope the present work does. My research involved piecing together stories through historical works, such as *The Book of Days*, documentaries such as *Khmer Court Dance*, produced in association with the Department of Anthropology at California State University, articles from such journals as *Dance Research Journal* or *Annual Review of Anthropology*, and historical accounts such as Giles Tremlett's *Ghosts of Spain*.

Irrefutably, the chapters which follow illustrate how throughout history our species has used dance as a means of survival, path to joy, and benefit for mind, body, and soul. They tell miraculous stories, confirming a revolving truth: life itself will never be extinguished as long as humans continue to dance! Most of all, they serve as a beacon call. A call for dance in our schools, our workplaces, our churches. A call for dance by our leaders, our artists, our visionaries. A call for dance in our homes, in our communities— across our globe!

Feet, get busy, for as the popular Bees Gees song from the 1970s insisted, "You should be dancing."

PART I. RITUAL

1

Rekindling the Flame: The Revival of the Sadir Katcheri (Bharata Natyam)

Because you love the Burning–ground, I have made a Burning–ground of my heart — that you may dance an eternal dance. — Hindu Hymn

Have you ever watched dancers while attending church? In today's culture, probably not. Yet, over two thousand years ago in India, the dance known as *sadir katcheri* (artistic dance) served as a form of worship. Only women performed the dance, as a means of honoring the primary god of the Hindu religion, Brahma, creator of the universe, as well as the Hindu lord of the dance, Shiva, and his companion, Vishnu.

The dancers were considered the living representatives of female power or energy, known as *shakti.* They personified auspiciousness, empowerment, multi-dimensionality, and luminosity. Their duties involved communicating the many faces of love, such as love between a man and woman, love for a child, love for an unfortunate person, and, most of all, love for their god. Through the artistic interpretation of these stories, dancers became human agents interceding with the gods for the purpose of removing evil (the jealous eye) and averting calamity. Dancers also helped to create a mood of devotion within the temple. Similar to a ritual found in many modern churches, the dancers were the "waivers" of the pot-lamp. At six each evening (the hour when darkness falls), they entered the temple with the sacred lamp. In front of the statute of a particular deity, they waived the pot-lamp in a clockwise circle three times and then in a sweeping gesture from the head of the image to the foot.

Dancers also served the public by creating an atmosphere of comfort and a source of entertainment for temple worshippers. Accordingly, sadir dancers were considered "good luck," purveyors of well-being, and were well-respected, even eating and associating with the wives of kings. Their life-giving touch even "sent the Asoha tree into blossom."

Considered poets of the dance, the women performing during worship services were known as *devadasis*, or devotee of their god. Sadir dancers were chosen for their youth, beauty, and rhythmic abilities and began their training around age eight. Because devadasis enjoyed a high social status, parents took pride in allowing their daughters to leave home and devote their lives to service within the temple, where girls were taught not only to dance, but also how to read, sing, and play music. Additionally, they were allowed to inherit property.

The transformation from young initiate to devadasi required four ceremonies. The first dance lesson was a time of celebration and mirth when gifts (fruit, flowers, incense, and money) and praise were lavished upon the teacher (on behalf of and to support the student). The guru in fact picked up the dancer's foot at the first lesson, striking it against the earth as a gesture of faith and awakening. After the dancer's mastery of the first item from her concert repertoire, the dancer participated in the presentation of ankle bells, a ceremony honoring the dance and tradition itself. Third, after years of training, the dancer held an *arangetram*, or debut recital. Finally, the dancer dedicated her art to the service of her god, essentially undergoing a wedding ceremony of sorts. One German visitor to South India in 1711 described the festive occasion:

> When they are taken on as servants to the gods in a pagoda, they have to become betrothed only to the god whom they serve. Then the priest of the gods carries out the full wedding ceremony with them, and binds them to the gods with a golden bridal necklace, which is the sign of all those who are married. Afterwards, all the young maidens who have been married to the gods are given a marvelous procession around the streets, as happens at other weddings [Bor 19].

Dancers told the stories of Hindu heroes and heroines with the use of over fifty-two hand gestures (*mudras*), facial expressions, and fancy footwork, all such movements performed to rhythmical music. The dancer's movements were choreographed to resemble the movements of a dancing flame, as sadir was considered a "fire-dance," a physical act honoring the human spirit. It was the dance of Shiva, the Hindu lord who holds a flame in his left hand, and who is also surrounded by a circle of flames as a reminder that all things are created from fire. (Consider how an explosive volcano eventually forms into a lush, lovely island.)

On his trip to South India in 1786 the Dutch author Haafner stated:

> Their dances are very different from ours. Some of them consist of supple and fast movements of the limbs, which are regulated and gracious; others of light

and ingenious jumps and steps. They are excellent mime artists. With an amazing precision of attitude and gestures, while singing and dancing, they can portray a love story or any other theme, even a fight. Their art to express emotions has been developed to such a height that our dancers and showgirls on the stage, with their cold and meaningless gestures, contortions of the body and breakneck jumps, would compare poorly to an Indian dancer. Their eyes, arms, hands, and even their fingers— all their limbs— move with a wonderful expression, gracefulness and art [Bor 24].

To achieve such mastery, dancers underwent rigorous training in multiple *adavu*, or units of movement. These units included movements of the feet, hands, head, chest, side, and waist. In sadir, each part of the body was split and given definite kinetic functions. Additionally, poses were crucial for aesthetic effect. One such pose is the *soughtavam*, the basic position, in which the knees are flexed, the feet are angled at 45 degrees apart, and the body brought down to half its height. Foot movements include the *naatu*, in which the heel of the foot strikes the ground pursuant to the rhythm of syllabic music (similar to do-re-mi), and *kunchita*, a movement on the balls of the feet. Two examples of hand movements, which can be either one or two-handed, include (1) representing a bee, parrot, wing, heron, or cuckoo by curling the first finger against the thumb, allowing the second finger to rest on the thumb, and lifting the third and fourth fingers in a fan-like manner, and (2) portraying respect, acceptance, or obedience by cupping the palms in front of the chest to where they touch only at the fingertips and the base. The dancers eyes also contributed to *rasa*, or the aesthetic delight described by Haafner, by portraying one of the nine states of being or emotions: love, valor, wonder, compassion or grief, laughter, fear, aversion/revulsion, rage or wrath, and tranquility.

All these movements (poses, footwork, mudras, and facial expression) were concerned with interpreting not only the story, but also the three elements of the accompaniment, i.e., musical notes or scale, rhythm, and lyrics or words. Dance masters or gurus determined the rhythm with chanted syllables and cymbals (*talam*), along with a drummer playing a two-headed *mrdangam*, the slapping of the dancer's feet against the floor, and the sound of her ankle bells. One or more singers conveyed the lyrics (using a drone for pitch), and two or more instrumentalists provided the notes. Instruments included the sitar, bamboo flute, or violin (introduced in the 18th century).

Thus, the dance incorporated five physical elements— the feet keeping to time, the hands expressing gesture, the eye following the hand with expression, the ear listening to the dance master's music, and singing from the dancer or her accompaninests. And as famous twentieth-century dancer Balasaraswati stated: "The inner feeling of the dancer is the sixth sense which

Sadir katcheri dancer with musicians, Calcutta, India, circa 1900 (Library of Congress). Note the **mrdangam.**

harnesses these five mental and mechanical elements to create the experience and enjoyment of beauty" (Balasaraswati 203). (Balasaraswati's grandmother was a temple devadasi. Balasaraswati began her own training at the age of seven, outside of the temple. Her expertise and charisma as a performing artist overshadowed a dark era for the art of sadir, rendering Balasaraswati an international sensation.)

The sadir consisted of several dances. First, the *nritta*, or pure dance, displayed the non-interpretative athletic prowess of the dancer and the beauty of the human body in motion. Second, the *abhinaya*, allowed the dancer to interpret a story through mime (acting), in which "facial expressions and hand gestures in particular are used to convey dramatic, narrative, and spoken language meanings" (Puri 56). Third, the *nrtya* incorporates both pure dance and mime and is closest to the Indian view of dance (*nrtya*) and theater (*natya*). Indians see the distinction between nritta and nrtya the same as that of folk versus classical.

In addition to daily dancing and singing at the hours of 11 A.M. and 6 and 9 P.M., devadasis performed at temple festivals and full-scale concerts honoring deities and, on occasion, kings. The repertoire usually consisted of seven parts. The first was *namashar*, or an introductory bowing and touching of the ground and the eyes, prayer, and offering of flowers in respect of the god or goddess (this ritual in modern performances honors the god, the guru, the musicians, the stage, and the audience). After the prayer, in which the gods were asked to bless the performance, dancers warmed up with an abstract dance intended as a greeting. This opening led into a short dance accompanied by a poem or song of devotion. The main event — a dance that highlighted a Hindu myth (speaking stories of love)—came next. To slow the pace before the ending, a love song and/or an erotic song were rendered in mime. In closing, dancers showed off their fancy footwork and flexibility with an abstract, many times improvised, grand finale. (Today's repertoire is much the same, with the elimination of the erotic element and the consecration of the stage rather than the temple.)

As devadasis were considered perpetual and divine brides of the deities, their costumes were rich, colorful (usually bright reds and gold) and exotic. Modeled by today's dancers, pursuant to temple art, the costume included a pajama like pant with a fan in front, a blouse longer than normal, a veil covering the breast, and a back piece covering the hips (also opening into a tiny fan above the larger pant fan). A waist belt was of polished brass, engraved or studded with figures of the gods and goddesses. The hair was plaited or placed in a large bun. Orange and white flowers highlighted the hair's beauty, and flower droplets were sometimes placed at the end of the braid. A hair ornament, the *rakodi*, was placed on either side of the forehead, one figure upon the ornament being a moon, the other the sun. A long, heavy, gold chain was worn to represent marriage to the deities, along with a nose ornament, bangles, rings, and, of course, the ankle bell bracelets. Makeup was heavy, with eyebrow and eye enhancement (to highlight facial expression and eye movements), a tilak (or red dot) on the forehead, lipstick, and paintings on the hands and feet.

Marco Polo was the first European to provide a lengthy account of the sadir dancers (who were firmly established as professional experts of the arts by the thirteenth century). He noted, "They devote themselves to singing, dancing, leaping, tumbling, and every sort of exercise to amuse the god and goddess and to reconcile them" (Bor 14). A traveler from Rome, Pietro della Valle, wrote in 1623: "Their dancing was high, with frequent leapings and odd motions, sometimes inclining their haunches as if they meant to sit down, sometimes rising very high and causing the skirt wherewith they are cover'd from the girdle downward to fly out, and always holding one arm strech'd out before them" (Bor 17). And, the French, who were the first to witness a traveling Indian dance troupe (these dancers made the trek to ensure that devadasis were not regarded as common dancing girls), adored the dance. The Paris–based *Journal des debats*, on August 8, 1838, printed: "They dance with

Sadir katcheri dancers, India, circa 1922 (Library of Congress). Note the heavy jewelry.

their whole frame. Their heads dance, their arms dance — their eyes, above all, obey the movement and fury of the dance.... Their feet click against the floor — the arms and the hands flash in the air — the eyes sparkle — the bosom heaves — their mouths mutter — the whole body quivers.... It is a mixture of modesty and abandonment — of gentleness and fury ... a religious drama, which a young priestess delivers without pause" (Bor 30).

Nonetheless, in the late 1700s and early 1800s, Britain colonized India, becoming rulers of its people. This colonization was not necessarily forced by any technological or military superiority but rather "by supplying a number of key resources—commercial and military—to the main contending regional states, who thus fell fatally into reliance upon it" (Washbrook 504). Once this destructive reliance became irreversible, India's economy was crushed and its people were impoverished. The control of commerce, and therefore the "power of the sea," belonged to the British, forcing India to turn on itself, relinquish its ties with the rest of the world, and see itself through a British mirror. Of course, "this sea-borne power could not translate itself into state power without the cooperation of many Indians on land: merchants who supplied its products; bankers who helped to finance it; princes who utilized its commercial services or contracted for its soldiers; later, landowners who basked in the security which it provided to their rights" (Washbrook 511).

British colonial rule was committed to manipulating and altering Indian kingships as well as the social order traditionally insured by Hindu temple structure and ritual, for the British did not understand, nor attempt to understand, the Hindu religion. Britons believed all honorable women should be married. They did not understand a woman's right to devote her life to her god and the art of dance and were committed to the belief that women should only be defined by their domestic relationships with men. The goal of the patriarchal British rulers became in time to "usurp the power and authority that the devadasis had built up for themselves over the years" (Hubel 165). Such time-honored dances as sadir katcheri were promoted as immoral and "suggestive."

This philosophy was taught to Indian leaders, by virtue of an English education, a sort of training in which "the world was where European peoples, by virtue of their superior material culture, had subjugated them" (the Indian people) (Chakravorty 111). Eventually, in the 1890s English missionaries, Hindu social reformers (educated by the English), and even Muslim leaders, began an "antinautch" (or anti-dance) movement for the purpose of "purifying" society. The devadasi tradition was viciously attacked, "obliterating in one sweep the history of the devadasi and nautch dancers from the national history of India" (Chakravorty 113).

To understand the intensity of the reform movement, consider history's record of one "educated" English woman, known only as "Miss Tenant," who traveled all the way from England "to persuade cultured and high placed Indians in Madras and elsewhere not to have anything to do with this art" (Ohtani 302), indeed collecting signed promises from Indian peoples dependent upon England for their economic well-being. The indoctrination worked, as revealed in the account of one Indian teenager, who in 1908 wrote of his experience with sadir dancing. While attending a wedding reception at which the dance was being performed, the teenager, P.N. Appuswami, "sternly turned my face to the wall, and did not look at one gesture or one movement of the dancer" (Ohtani 302).

By the 1920s, legal decrees banned dancing from the temples altogether. In essence, the dancers were ordered not to practice their religion. As a result of this law, the devadasis were no longer supported by worshippers and so became extremely poor. They could not publicly teach the ancient dance as a form of religion to young female students. One dancer, Saride Anusuya, remembers: "We became beggars. The temple trustees took all our land. We were born for the temple, for God. We danced for God. But they took our land and made us beggars" (Soneji 36). To add to their disgrace, in certain areas (the cities of Madras, Guntur, and Narsapur) devadasis were forcibly institutionalized in "centers of refuge." The earliest such institution was built in 1922 as a "rehabilitation center," seeing to the "moral, vocational, and literary instruction of the *inmates* to wean them away from their traditional lives ... the vocational part of the instruction consisted of spinning, weaving, basket-making, and gardening" (Soneji 47).

The dance was almost lost, a beautiful art form turned into a condemned social evil, as "the generation that went to colleges founded by the British in the early nineteenth century was isolated from the art traditions of the country. Apparently, the art had died by the twentieth century and what could be seen of it was only a diluted, almost degenerated form of what was known as *Sadir* ... it was like a shadow of a bygone reality" (Meduri 6).

Perhaps Braham, the Hindu god of creation, and Shiva, the Hindu lord of the dance, were displeased! For on February 29, 1904, under a glowing full moon, the primary savior of sadir, Rukmini Devi Arundale, was born. Rukmini was born to a Brahman family, a priestly class high on the social ladder, and her father was a member of the Theosophical Society, an international fellowship organization which encourages inquiry into world religions, philosophy, science and the arts. Yet, as a young girl, similar to Appuswami, Rukmini was forbidden to learn, or even watch, the sadir katcheri.

When just sixteen years of age, Rukmini met George Arundale, an Englishman, at a religious society meeting. Causing a scandal, Rukmini agreed to marry Arundale, despite the fact that such a marriage was "unheard of" within upper class Brahman society. In fact, George and Rukmini left India for a tour of Europe to avoid the wrath of her community.

During her travels with George, Rukmini became a patron of the arts, enjoying theatre, music, painting, sculpture, opera and ballet. While on a ship to Australia, Rukmini met and became friends with famed Russian bal-

Dancing in the streets of New Delhi, circa 1907 (Library of Congress). Note the importance of fanned dresses.

lerina Anna Pavlova. She fell in love with ballet, and asked Anna to teach her this classic dance. Instead, Anna encouraged Rukmini to study sadir, the Indian dance almost wiped out by British colonization, telling Rukmini, "You can learn ballet, but I think that everyone must try to revive the art of his own country."

Since the sadir had been banned, where was Rukmini to learn the art? During the period in which sadir was targeted as "bad," and eventually banned from the temple (the 1850s to 1940s), trained devadasis taught the dance to their daughters within the privacy of their homes. Also, before the ban, most of the teachers, or gurus, were males. Many of these great teachers, some quite old, carried the knowledge of the dance in their heads. These gurus secretly continued lessons in the remote villages to which they retreated after the ban, escaping the wrath of British authorities.

In the 1930s a lawyer named E. Krishna Iyer sought out these former sadir dancers and gurus for the purpose of presenting public performances at the Madras Music Academy, founded by Iyer to help preserve the tradition. Indeed, Iyer "fought with the anti-nautch movement through performing, writing, giving lectures, and encouraging and helping other dancers" (Ohtani 303). Rukmini returned to India and arranged to attend a sadir performance at Iyer's Academy. Two impoverished devadasis danced for Rukmini: the Pandanallur sisters, Rajeswari and Jeevaratnam. Rukmini was enchanted by the dance and immediately began lessons under the direction of Mylapore Gowri Amma, a former devadasi who remained knowledgeable in the expressive traditions of sadir. Eventually, Rukmini also studied under the Pandanallur sister's guru.

Years before India declared independence from British rule, Rukmini Devi Arundale performed the sadir in public. Dancing under a sacred banyan tree, a tree whose roots spread far and grow deep, Rukmini wore a self-designed costume based upon ancient temple sculptures (Rukmini's first dance was held at the 1935 Diamond Jubilee celebration of the Theosophical Society). Many of the followers of her father's religion praised Rukmini's performance, calling it "beautiful, aesthetic and spiritual," while members of the elite society asked her to stop her "antics." Like her marriage, Rukmini's decision to study and perform sadir, renamed *bharata natyam* (bharata meaning India, itself, and also referring to the second century sage who composed a treatise regarding the aesthetics and staging of sadir; and Natyam, meaning dance, drama, and music), to revive the respect owed to the art form, was unheard of in 1930s India, especially for a woman of her social rank.

Rukmini not only continued to perform this dance herself, but also taught it to others, founding Kalakeshetra, the Institute of Fine Arts. (Classes were held in a grove of trees in open air.) The first student was Rukmini's niece, Radha, who became president of the Theosophical Society in the 1990s. Other initial students were daughters of members of the Theosophical Society, or daughters of family friends.

Rukmini re-instilled a sense of elegance to bharata natyam, steadily lost during the period of British colonization. She invited the finest musicians and dance gurus in India to join the Institute. Musicians no longer followed the dancer around on stage, but remained seated at all times. Non–traditional instruments, used during the British reign and before the ban (clarinets and bagpipes), were replaced with traditional flutes and sitars.

Rukmini also choreographed dance-dramas, twenty-five altogether, which spoke to traditional Hindu myths. A special theatre was built at the Institute with state-of-the-art lighting techniques and backdrops. She wrote:

> When it is perfectly expressed through gesture, movement or facial expression, the dancer becomes something beyond and unfolds another great art into her-

self—the art of natya or drama. She becomes the storyteller or the actress ... [Arundale 193].

As a result of Rukmini's innovations, enrollment in dance classes grew (beyond daughters of acquaintances), especially among middle class families. Within just a few years, the dance's status as a respectable and dignified art form returned. Even women from the upper classes gradually began pursuing dance instruction. A South Indian journal, *Triveni*, in 1940 featured an article on bharata natyam, stating:

Shiva, Lord of the Dance, stomping out ignorance and creating new life.

> Another unique feature of music that South India has preserved through all the vicissitudes of time and tide is Bharata Natya. Even our children have caught this new spirit so much that almost every child that attends a girl's school is a danseuse. The culture, refinement, and world-wide influence of Adyar (the place where Kalakshetra was situated) should be sufficient to ensure the future of dance as a national expression of art [Ohtani 306].

Indeed, Kalakeshetra is now a fully operational school of the arts sponsored by the Indian government.

Rukmini's courage changed her country for the better in many ways. As in ancient days, dance became a prominent art form and part of the education process. A sense of pride spread among Indian people subjugated for over a century by British authority. Most of all, Rukmini's determined spirit lit the fire for a cultural and spiritual rebirth which coincided with, and likely fueled, India's struggle for independence. Just eleven years after Rukmini's first performance under the banyan tree (1947), India once again became a free country.

Today, bharata natyam is lauded and respected all over the world. Modern dancers are interpreting issues related to femininity (appropriately, since the dance honored shakti) such as gender inequality, as well as global issues such as war, human greed, and destruction of the environment. Additionally, dancers are incorporating elements of ballet, jazz, yoga, and modern dance as befits the traditional movement patterns and philosophy of the dance. As one famous South Indian musicologist wrote in 1973, "*Bharata Natyam* awoke one morning to find itself great" (Allen 94). Both Brahma and Lord Shiva must be pleased! For bharata natyam dancers still mimic Shiva's song:

> He danced, and all the eight directions shook
> The head of the cosmic snake Sedan trembled,
> the whole earth shivered.
> Water drops from the Ganges splashed over the land,
> and the gods celebrated.
> He sang lovingly for Shiva's dance.
> Shiva's matted locks swayed in the air while the cobra danced
> with its hood spread.
> He danced about, giving all assembled his blessings
> with the sound "tontom tantom"
> And he danced: "tam, takita takajam takanam tari kundari..."
> [He danced so beautifully] [Allen 81].

2

"It Is a Strict Law That Bids Us Dance": The Kwakiutl Hamatsa Dance

The Cannibal spirit made me a winter dancer.
The Cannibal spirit made me pure
I do not destroy life, I am life maker— Kwakiutl song

Similar to the South Indian bharata natyam, prior to European contact the indigenous peoples of the Northwest Coast of Canada, specifically the Kwakiutl (or, written in the Native language, Kwakwaka'wakw) of Vancouver Island, also performed a dance steeped in theatrical renderings. Imagine a dance so dramatic and intense that whistles are blown, masks are donned, onlookers are deceived by means of trapdoors and tunnels, and twine-secured figurines are flown above the floor. Anthropologist Helen Codere described the distinct dance in this fashion: "The theatrical character of the winter ceremonials is apparent ... in a mere listing of their prominent features: performances polished by rehearsal, costumed dancers in carved and painted masks of wood, songs and song leaders, an impressive variety of musical instruments, and elaborate stage devices such as trap doors" (Raibom 178). Such is the *hamatsa* dance of the Kwakiutl, hamatsa referring to a person who has crossed the line into the spirit realm.

For hundreds and perhaps thousands of years before Europeans discovered the area known as the Northwest Coast (located in what is today the Canadian province of British Columbia), young Kwakiutl "initiates" (males between the approximate ages of fifteen and twenty-one) participated in this dance-drama. The purpose of the hamatsa was to "tame" malevolent aspects of the psyche, in an extremely non–Western, alternative manner, by projecting the subconscious, forbidden desires and anti-social aspects of the human

Alert Bay, British Columbia, circa 1914 (Library of Congress).

experience through the mediums of dance, song, and role-playing. It allowed the initiate to develop a deep sense of self, the ability to trust and control his inner psyche, and an intense respect for his community and its socialization process. It was a ceremony "much like the ball that marks a debutante's coming out into society or the bar mitzvah that heralds a Jewish boy's elevation to manhood ... celebrating a change of rank or status with dancing, feasting, and gifts" (Cole 51). In other words, the child becomes an adult, the raw animal a human.

Although one theme of the dance ritual was coming of age, the major theme, overcoming death, was acted upon and experienced by means of the dance ritual, in that the young man was "possessed by a supernatural cannibal spirit, tamed, and reintegrated into the community" (Raibmom 162). Taming, for the Kwakiutl, "was a ritual act of restoring a person to the human realm after that person had been transformed into an other-worldly supernatural being" (Goldman 205). In a way, the dance was similar to European tales of dragon slayers: a young man travels through the forest to face and kill the fiery beast (symbolizing the self-actualizing task of becoming increasingly humane by journeying through a spiritual aperture). Upon his return, the hero is afforded all the luxuries of home and community, including, many times, a lovely princess.

Likewise, hamatsa dancers first enter the forest to take on the spirit of Baxbakalanuxsiwi, known as Man-Eater or the Cannibal at the North End of the World. "Hap! Hap! Hap!" (Eat, Eat, Eat), the dancer cries when he encounters the Cannibal's earthly slaves, Raven (the ravenous bird who plucks out and devours the eyes of humans), Hokhokw (the bird with a massive, extended beak who cracks open human skulls with his powerful beak and eats the brains inside) and Crooked Beak. These dark spirit birds serve much the same purpose as the candy house of Hansel and Gretel fame; they lure the young man into the "dark realm," where he lives alone, or in the company of previously initiated hamatsa dancers (who prepare him for the dance with a period of fasting, praying, instruction in the multi-dimensionality of the human spirit, and access to secrets known only to the hamatsa), for a period of two to four months. Only male initiates who have inherited the right to enter the prestigious hamatsa society through their maternal lineage (in Kwakiutl society, men were considered the "great devourers," and, while women procured, they did not consume) may inherit the myth of an ancestor who, before the initiate's birth, met the Man-Eater. Thus, the privilege to enter the realm and perform the dance was based upon an inherited social rank and privilege of limited supply, not material wealth. Nonetheless, the inherited myth was not activated automatically, only by means of the initiation, as "the dancer was establishing himself as the heir to the dance, the possessor of the spirit's mystical force" (Woodhead 111).

Similar to the story collected by the Brothers Grimm, the Kwakiutl myth surrounding the dance introduces youthful male initiates ignoring adult warnings and sneaking into the forest, encountering a house puffing red smoke from its chimney, the mark of the Cannibal at the North End of the World. When they enter, a woman sitting on the dirt floor says, "I am rooted to the floor. I will help you." "Rooted Woman," as she is known, explains into whose house the young men have stumbled and how to kill him. They must dig a fire pit, fill it with hot coals, and cover the pit with boards as a trap. When Baxbakalanuxsiwi, whose name translates "eating humans at the river mouth" (Berman 59), returns home, he crashes through the boards and faints. The youth seize ornaments, paraphernalia, masks, whistles, and a cannibal pole (each such ritual item representing a soul or vital component of being). Before they leave, Rooted Woman teaches the young males the songs of Baxbakalanuxsiwi, whose insatiable appetite is symbolized as a figure covered with mouths (Goldman 96). Though Rooted Woman attends to Man-Eater as his slave, "her role of provisioner is only incidental to her human destiny as the persistent enemy within Man-Eater's house. She teaches men how to overcome devouring death" (Goldman 111). (In fact, one of Man-Eater's names is "Wishing to Be Tamed").

Based upon this myth, as winter approached (the Kwakiutl method of counting a year was one summer, the productive, food-gathering, Earthly time, and one winter, the ceremonial, social activity, Other-worldly time), Man-Eater kidnapped the initiate and carried him into the forest. Drama was important at each stage of the ceremony, thus a bundle of torn and bloody clothes marked the spot of abduction. (In actuality, the initiate was blind-folded and taken into the forest by members of the society, who taught him tricks which aided the manifestation of supernatural powers, the province of Man-Eater.) This "disappearance" could last up to four months, during which time the initiate did not work, gamble, or enter into sexual intercourse. Sup-posedly, while under the "tutelage" of Man-Eater, the Cannibal spirit (devourer of man) entered the young man, possessing him, causing "excite-ment," and converting the whole community into an assembly of spiritual beings, for, according to the Kwakiutl, "ritual was by function the reshaper, the subduer, and the tamer of all raw states" (Goldman 112). The dancer became the actual impersonator of frightening and formidable supernatural spirits and powers. The adjective which described him was *laxsa*, the state of having gone into the home of the Man-Eater to receive powers and dance instructions.

Due to the nature of these forces, the recapturing and taming of the young male required the "strenuous efforts" of the entire community. The duties were divided into two parts, that of the Seals (or the hamatas), creatures of the sea inhabiting a world opposite in time orientation than that of human beings; and that of the Sparrows (shamans), former Seals who are charged with officiating and managing the ritual, bringing the Seals back into the realm of secular safety, and controlling the voracity of beings within the spirit world. Females served in the role of Rooted Woman, for taming "required the force of the shaman, an expert in the orphic voyage, and of a woman, whose sexual nature as progenetrix and as partner in coitus introduced and also restored persons to the secular world" (Goldman 205).

Symbolically, "the sea, source of salmon and copper, is the element that finally cures the hamatsa and releases him from a state of possession ... as wealth satiates the voracity of Man-Eater" (Goldman 117). The members of the community did not view these duties as a burden, but instead believed the wild (portrayed as cannibalistic) nature of the initiate brought "mystery" into the village, a state in which the young male is actually productive and creative, for, having died to society, he may recreate and/or improve upon societal values and patterns. As his alienated state (portrayed symbolically when the initiate is swallowed or overtaken by the dark face of Cannibal at the North End of the World) was indeed considered a gift to society, the community's role, in return, was to help the initiate integrate his subconscious and conscious states (in essence helping the Seal return to Earth) and "lure him in and tame him sufficiently to be able to perform his duties" (Reid 271), for "only in dance is every individual part totally itself, and by being itself contributes to the whole" (Reid 271).

Hamatsa emerging from the woods, circa 1914 (Library of Congress).

Approximately one month before the dance commenced, the young man reappeared near the Kwakiutl community, seemingly emaciated and desirous of human flesh (but in actuality thinner due to fasting). The dancer began running along the beach crying the terrifying words of Cannibal at the North End of the World, "Hap, Hap, Hap." He returned "full of the power that destroys man's reason" (Benedict 177). At times, he hung upside down or climbed the cannibal pole. He sang the cannibal songs taught by Rooted Woman. Attendants tried to capture him, but in a frenzy the hamatsa would faint (seemingly at any sign of human imperfection). Finally tied to a pole in the dance house, attendants would revive the young man by blowing water over his body, chanting, shaking rattles (carved in the shape of human skulls), and performing other procedures, such as the destruction of faulty masks. While on the pole, hemlock boughs were placed on the dancer's head and around his waist and wrists as a sign of his untamed state. Alas, the initiate always escaped during the late night hours!

Near the time the community dance commenced, the hamatsa crashed through the roof of the ceremonial "Big House," the Kwakiutl's version of a recital hall, an elaborately constructed structure fashioned from huge red cedar logs and beams. He ran back out the door again, but not before encircling the fire and biting people's arms to remove bits of flesh. The villagers also witnessed him, during this period, breaking into grave boxes, stealing mummified corpses, or cutting bits of flesh from the body of dead slaves. Whether flesh was actually consumed by the initiate during these ceremonies is a subject of much unresolved debate. We do know, however, that the Kwakiutl (1) "felt an unmitigated repugnance of eating human flesh" (Benedict 177); (2) the "performances involved much dramatic tension and much show of violence, for it was a wild and destructive group of supernatural beings that was portrayed" (Codere 6); (3) the "masks, whistles, the ornaments, the dramatizations of mythical events simulate a hidden reality, a reality that does not literally exist on this side of the cosmos, belonging only as the Kwakiutl always say, 'on the other side'" (Goldman 102); and (4) "there was so much sleight-of-hand involved in the Winter Dance that it is uncertain whether human flesh was actually swallowed or simply hidden somehow" (Jonaitis 97).

The initiate's hunger seemed so overwhelming that he continued to return to the village and near to the dance hall. Enticing him into the hall was Kinqalatlala, a woman symbolizing the slave of Man-Eater, Rooted Woman. She carries a corpse, maybe the body of a relative prepared for burial, or a substitute, such as a skinned bear or a mannequin (the hamatsa could only be "caught" with human bait). Her dance proved slow and restrained, and she sang: "I am the real tamer of Baxbakualanuxsiwae. I pull the red cedar bark from Baxbakualanuxsiwae's back. It is my power to pacify you when you are in a state of ectasy" (Goldman 97).

For three nights, the community beckoned the hamatsa into the hall, always in a state of "excitement," crouching low, outstretched arms trembling, poised to attack the congregation. On the third night, he dances only for society members. Finally, on the fourth night, the hamatsa completes his dance, amidst a ceremonial potlatch (P!Esa'), a celebration in which "one person bestowed traditional names, ranks, and privileges upon another" (Cole 51), and for which property distribution, dancing, and feasting were primary components. (In fact, one present-day Kwakiutl has described the potlatch as their "Constitution" [Spirit].)

Potlatches were held by village chiefs, who distributed surplus or luxury items (such as furs, canoes, mats, and meats) to members of his community or kinship group, known as a *numina*. Respected members of the community received the first and finest gifts, not for material gain or prestige, but as "symbols to bind potlatch participants to a hereditary system of titles and to each other" and to "bring family groups together for the purpose of identifying individuals as members of the group, establishing their relation to the whole" (Ringel 352). Village members expected chiefs to "die poor but rich in rank and honor, giving the privileges associated therewith to their heirs" (Cole 51). In other words, unlike European society, which determined status by material wealth, the Kwakiutl determined status in terms of social respect and/or the individual's association with the supernatural, "confirming the links between resource rights, social hierarchy, and supernatural ancestory" (Raibmon 162).

The first stage of the hamatsa community dance (4th night dance) involved setting up a screen of cedar boards, the *mawil*, to provide a separate "dress" room for the initiate and his attendants. Preparations also involved the erection of a large pole behind the screen and the painting of a face with a wide-open mouth on the screen. To begin the performance, the initiate, dressed in a cape with long cedar-bark fringe, bark fringe on his knees and ankles, and a blackened face, climbed the pole and emerged from the screen-painted mouth. As the dancer emerged, he also wore the hemlock branches around his waist and forehead, beginning the dance in a squatted position with his trembling arms extended. He danced one foot before the other, fists clenched, and thumbs pointing upwards, moving with long leaps.

Suddenly, a singer uttered a taboo word (for the hamatsa) and the dancer's responding antics required restraint once more. Participants in the dance pushed the hamatsa to the ground, burned the hemlock branches, and re-attired the initiate with red cedar bark rings around his head, neck, wrists, and ankles. (The rings represented the magic circle of souls and spirits encased within the containers of power, the sun and the moon. The knots, flaps, and braids weaved into the cedar rings told their own story, referring to events heralding the hamatsa's acquisition or inheritance of the dance prerogative.)

Once dressed in rings, the hamatsa danced again, upright this time as he drew one knee up to his chest while lowering the other, encircling the fire four times (counterclockwise). Singers uttered another taboo word, and the hamatsa disappeared behind the screen. Suddenly, the audience heard a loud "clack, clack" and a dancer moving backwards emerged wearing an enormous raven mask, the great beak clacking as it opens and shuts pursuant to the manipulation of the mask's strings and moving parts. Raven is followed by the Crooked Beak mask dancer, and Huxwhukw. These three dancers, imitating the servants of Cannibal at the North End of the World, dance four counterclockwise circuits around the fire, the rhythm of the music changing each turn. As the tempo changes, the avian dancers squat on the floor and snap their beaks, click, clack, and shake their heads from side to side (as a bird searching for food), then resume circle dancing.

As the avian dancers retire, the hamatsa makes another appearance, wild as ever. Nevertheless, his "taming" is almost complete. He is contained and dressed in a blanket, lead to the dance by a female relative, and followed by male attendants continuing to shake their human skull rattles. In his final appearances, he dances calmly. An older female relative may dance with him, offering a "copper," a decorative breast plate of embossed copper or metal, to the hamatsa, as a means of "feeding" and taming her male relative. (Coppers carried the names and histories of all owners, serving as a diplomatic accounting of sorts.) Finally, women dancers danced around the hamatsa, honoring him with an eagle or thunderbird headdress (presented by a female relative also sporting such a headdress).

The transformation of the male youth is complete. He is now spiritually balanced. He receives a rightful name and membership within the hamatsa society, which he may pass down from generation to generation through his daughter's line. The society member, once possessed and under the tutelage of Man-Eater (and considered a Man-Eater himself), is now Man-Eater's conqueror. The community triumphs in the knowledge that "if Man-Eater can die and return to life, death, it must be assumed, cannot be final" (Goldman 111). And, life lessons are, once again, confirmed (1) He who eats must be eaten (life is full of sacrifices); (2) The natural law of give and take, nestled deep within the human psyche, requires a sense of balance and a degree of control; and (3) Individuals must identify with and participate in a collective existence, "an association of the free" (Reid 271).

During the spring, summer, and autumn months, the Kwakiutl worked hard to catch, preserve, and store the abundant food sources found in the British Columbia area: shellfish, seaweed, berries, roots, salmon, herring, and sea mammals. They fell huge cedar trees, hollowed into canoes or fashioned into totem poles, cooking utensils or masks. Nevertheless, during the time of the winter ceremonial, tribe members devoted themselves to spiritual ceremonies and ritual. After George Vancouver discovered their island in 1792, the Kwakwiutl were left to these same practices until around 1849, as European contact was infrequent prior to this date. The Hudson Bay Company established a trading post at Fort Rupert on Vancouver Island at this point in time, however, introducing European traders who were interested in the fur and salmon trade, material goods easily supplied by the Kwakiutl. While happy to trade with Europeans, yet aware of the superior military force of the British, the Kwakiutl refused to adhere to the European Protestant "values of progress, industry, thrift, and sobriety; they seemed fundamentally opposed to the accumulation of wealth and the workings of capitalist markets" (Raibmom 163).

Plus, Europeans seemed horrified of the Kwakiutl ceremonial dances and practices. Specifically targeted was the hamatsa dance, in actuality a "spectacular complex of dance, drama, art, potlatching, and community interaction with the spirit otherworld" (Berman 53). The great paradox of this reaction was "in spiritual terms, the hamatsa vividly demonstrated the danger of disrupting the careful balance between human desire and socio-moral requirement. In material terms, it secured a young man's inherited social rank and publicly acknowledged his entitlement to the accompanying material resources. Thus, a rite that spoke to non–Aboriginal society of social chaos, uncontrolled depravity, and savagery was, in fact, premised on the exorcism of these same destructive, anti-social traits" (Raibmon 159).

Missionary and government forces mounted a joint assault on the Kwakiutl lifestyle, attempting to covert both cultural and religious practices, most likely as a way to establish a dependent workforce (an 1872 report by the Indian Agency Superintendent considered the potlatch a "tendency" that "encourages idleness"). They wanted to obliterate all vestiges of Kwakiutl culture in order that the tribe would no longer wish to live close to and from the land. Indeed, if the Kwakiutl could provide for themselves, who would punch the clock for "near-to-nothing" wages at the newly-established salmon canneries? By 1884, the Canadian government, supposedly as a means of improving the economy, passed the Indian Act which legislated: "Every Indian or other person who engages in or assists in celebrating the Indian festival known as the Potlatch ... is guilty of a misdemeanor, and shall be liable to imprisonment for a term of not more than six nor less than two months" (Jacknis 284).

Bureau Indian agents attempted to use the law as a means of quieting the hamatsa dance (and its venue, the potlatch), but charges against individual Kwakiutl members did not occur until 1919. In fact, one agent wrote circa 1890: "I am sorry to say that I cannot report any improvement among these Indians; they seem to have given themselves up again to the Potlatch, which has absorbed the whole of their time and energies during the last 10 months, and, in consequence they have earned very little money, though they could all have obtained renumerative employment at the different canneries had they chosen to work" (Codere 83). And in 1912, Indian agent William Halliday reported: "There is no decrease in the number of potlatches held nor is its influence apparently less" (Cole 52).

Nevertheless, when fellow aborigines were employed to "rat-out" natives who continued to practice traditional rites, the last great potlatch was "busted." On Christmas Day 1921, Canadian officials entered a potlatch being held by Daniel Cranmer on Alert Bay, arresting eighty of the attendees and confiscating hamatsa dance regalia, including masks, valued at over

Hokhokw and Crooked Beak masks, made circa 1914 (Library of Congress).

$35,000.00. (Over 300 guests attended this potlatch, one in which 24 canoes, four gasoline boats, blankets, violins and guitars, sewing machines, and gramophones were distributed, a far cry from furs, canoes, and dried meats!) Fifty-one guests were actually charged, and twenty-two were given suspended sentences. At the sentencing, agents illegally blackmailed the tribe into giving up even more masks and regalia in exchange for suspended sentences. Twenty tribal members were sent to Oakalla Prison near Vancouver, serving sentences of two to three months. (The confiscated masks were sent to museums all over the globe, some of which were only recently returned to the Kwakiutl.) A majority of the masks, however, were returned to the Kwakiutl from the National Museum of Man on the condition a museum be built for their storage and preservation. The Umista (return of something important) Cultural Centre opened its doors in 1988, becoming the "storage box" for these treasures. The masks were not encased, for, according to Daniel Cranmer's granddaughter, Gloria, they had "been locked up for so long in strange places. They should not be locked up again" (Box).

Forced underground in 1921, the Kwakiutl began a pattern of evasion. First, they transferred the potlatches to inaccessible villages, such as Gwayi at Kingcome Inlet. Any approach to this location, "two miles up a shallow, snag-ridden river that froze over in the winter" (Cole 52), could be seen for miles, day or night. Second, they organized private give-aways. For example, when Kwakiutl Charlie Nowell's daughter married in 1927, he bought movie

Kwakiutl masked dancers, circa 1914 (Library of Congress).

tickets for the bridal party. When everyone gathered at the movie, he distributed candy, cakes, and fruit. Third, the Kwakiutl held disjointed potlatches in which they separated dancing from gift-giving. Agents could not prove gifts given on any certain day were actually part of a dance held six months earlier. Fourth, they used traditional European days of festivity, such as Christmas or birthdays to participate in potlatching and dancing.

The Kwakiutl's insistence on retaining their cultural patterns worked, for in 1934, an official reported: "We are about as far away from doing anything really effective toward the supression of the potlatch system as we were when actions against the Indians were started years ago" (Cole 52).

One child who witnessed the trial of the dancers arrested at Alert Bay was James Sewid. The arrested *Hamasta* dancers were tried in James' own schoolhouse while chained to a pot-belly stove. As an adult, James became a member of the Native Brotherhood, an organization promoting native fishing rights. Continuing to pursue his tribe's economic rights, Chief Sewid also began lobbying for the return of regalia taken by officials during the raid on Chief Cranmer's potlatch, as well as legislation designed to lift the unreasonable ban on potlatches. To further his cause, Chief Sewid began performing the hamatsa dance for tourists and organized the Kwakwala Arts and Culture Society, displaying the fine arts of his people, including the art of the dance masks. As a result of Sewid's activism, and due to the now archaic and obsolete nature of the original law, the ban on potlatches was lifted in 1951.

The first legal potlatch hosted within the 20th century occurred in 1952 in Victoria, British Columbia. This potlatch was hosted by Chief Mungo Martin, an internationally renowned totem pole carver (one of his poles stands in Windsor Park in London). In addition to carving totem poles, Chief Martin also designed and constructed a traditional Kwakiutl Big House. The 1952 potlatch was held to dedicate this communal "dance" hall.

The hamatsa dance, once again, became a community affair, helping young adolescent males gather the love, strength, and courage necessary for life as an adult. Today, the hamatsa is performed at traditional potlatches, social events, and as a means of entertaining and educating tourists and the general public, though in an abbreviated form. The hamatsa dancer is only isolated overnight, does not enter from the roof, is not tied to a pole, and pretends to eat a copper instead of human flesh. Also, the hemlock is not burned, and only one night of dancing occurs.

The tradition and spirit of the hamatsa survives, captured and preserved, not in the forest, not inside the Big House, but by brave Kwakiutl people who lived between the years of 1884 and 1951. As the Kwakiutl teach us, the "past and present are indissolubly tied, and fearful and wondrous powers lie just a few steps away, waiting" (Woodhead 113). What a gift, for as Picasso noted: "Masks are weapons to keep people from being ruled by spirits. If we give form to these spirits, we become free!" (Spirit).

3

Poetry in Motion: The Hula

The fires of the goddess burn!
Now for the dance, the dance!
Bring out the dance... — Hawaiian chant

Since the fifth century, Hawaiian natives have performed a dance in which their hands, body movements, and accompanying chants tell a story. The dance is called the *hula,* a term meaning movement and gesture. Its stories tell legends and speak to the exploits of kings or the beauty of the islands. It was and is performed at births, feasts, weddings, funerals, and for sheer entertainment. The Hawaiians believe the dance began when Hi'laka, the adventurous sister of the volcano goddess, Pele, danced to calm down her fiery sister. Hi'laka gently swayed her hips back and forth to imitate trees swaying in the breeze. Her hands waved like the ocean. Her feet stomped like the rumble of the rocks in the rivers. (On the northern coast of Kaua'I lies a peak beneath Mt. Makana, Kaulu-o-Laka, which continues to serve as an altar for Hi'laka.) Hence, the graceful hula is steeped in religious tradition. Before Europeans discovered the islands, the dance was held in temples and dedicated to Hawaiian gods. Hawaiians believed in a magnificent power that guarded and protected the islands' craters, forests, and flowers. This life force was known as *mana,* or spiritual power. The hula honored and invoked this force as a means of incantation. As Nathaniel Emerson wrote, "The hula was a religious service, in which poetry, music, pantomime, and the dance lent themselves, under the forms of dramatic art, to the refreshment of men's minds" (qtd. in Solberg 43).

The hula also served to honor the nobility, or *ali'i,* and the history of the race. It was "the history of a people without a written language. Its main purpose was to keep up the relationship between gods and mortals through dance. But, importantly, it also preserved the greatness of the senior chiefly lines of rule. The hula honored the race and told of its continuance through procreation. It described the beauty of their natural environment. And, finally, with all its rules and stratifications, the hula forced the dancer to achieve perfection in the dance" (Topolinski qtd. in Solberg 45).

Ritual and prayer were included in all aspects of the dance. *Mele*, or chanted poems, essentially expressed prayers, served as the "backbone" or root of the dance and spoke to the mystery of life, our relationship to both nature and each other (physical and spiritual), the link between past and present, present and past, and to the "spontaneous emotional response of an individual to a specific instance of a physical or spiritual experience" (Topolinski qtd. in Solberg 45), for as the Hawaiian proverb "I ka 'olelo no ke ola; I ka olelo no ka make" teaches, in the word is life; in the word is death. Mele could be composed by a person or by a group, or a god or goddess might reveal the song in a dream. As the song honored the god, the composer was soon forgotten, and the song belonged only to the particular god or goddess. Composers usually wrote in "couplets in a rhythmic setting of an even number of beats in four counts to accommodate the movements" (Kaeppler 39).

Mele inoa (name chants), the preeminent mele, honored a god or a specific chief. Pele, the fire goddess of the volcano, figured prominently in these chants, Aia la o Pele being the most famous:

> *Pele is at Hawai`i*
> *She is dancing at Maukele*
>
> *She surges and puffs this way*
> *Devouring the land of Puna*
>
> *It makes Paliuli beautiful*
> *Fire tongues leaping at the cliffs*
>
> *It is heard at Maui*
> *Land of Kaulula'au*
>
> *Where will we find peace?*
> *Oh, how we yearn on the road*
>
> *The end of my song*
> *A name song for Hi'iaka*

Another example of a mele is the *mele ho'oipoipo* or song of a less formal nature which spoke to people, places, events, or things in an endearing way. An example is the chant Na Pua Lei 'Ilima, which proclaims the beauty of the 'ilima, the orange-yellow flower found throughout the islands, considered the official flower of the island Oahu:

Beautiful is the wreath of 'ilima blossoms
An adornment of Kakuhihewa that is cherished

My thoughts are forever captured by
The blossoms of lei ilima, so famous

Outstanding, regal and elegant
It is magnificent to the eye

Famous are the blossoms of lei ilima
That represent the capitol of our islands

Honored guests are bedecked (with leis)
Famed is the beauty, never to be forgotten

Tell the refrain
Of the famous wreaths of ilima.

Mele singers (*ho'opa'a*) used their voices to portray the sounds of the natural world, such as the wind, ocean, birds, (common style —*koi honua*) or volcanic eruptions (bombastic, guttural style). Also, the singer might use the *hoaeae* or sentimental style for love songs and the *olioli* for ceremonial wailing (a vibratory trill upon the vowel sounds i and e). Correspondingly, the

Hula dancers in the Crater of Punch Bowl Mountain, circa 1901 (Library of Congress).

hula dancer expressed the metaphorical or symbolic meaning of the mele by means of hand and arm, hip, and foot gestures. These gestures were understood on both a literal and metaphorical level, which only native Hawaiians understood, a type of "double symbolism ... both subtly mimetic but also metaphoric. So complex and indirect was the communicative and aesthetic code of hula that by the end of the nineteenth century very few Hawaiians were capable of appreciating the textual richness of the chants" (Balme 237). An example follows:

A certain plant, the *noni* is used to produce a red dye: so, when the unsuccessful suitor of the volcano goddess wishes in revenge to ridicule her inflamed eyes, he sings about a woman pounding *noni* [Beckwith 412].

The poetry was introduced during a hula performance with a call (*kahea*). Percussive instruments set the rhythm of the chant and dance. Each of the two-line couplets was performed twice, once to the right, once to the left. Between couplets (or stanzas), one dancer recited the next line in order for all dancers to remain together in rhythm, verse, and step. Finally, a short instrumental break again confirmed the rhythm, and a final call honored the god or goddess who was the subject of the mele. Intriguing poetic devices, untranslatable, were sometimes included in the final call, such as *la ea*.

As rhythm is the essence of great poetry, music, and dance, the musical instruments used for the hula determined the classification of the dance. Musicians used a drum (*pahu*), made from the trunk of a coconut tree and covered with a sharkskin membrane, for *Hula pahu*. A smaller drum, *puniu*, tied to the knee, was used on occasion for seated dances as well. Additionally, "the *hula pa ipu* was accompanied by a gourd idiophone that was thumped on the ground and struck with the hand. Other instruments included a gourd rattle (*uli'uli*), rhythm sticks (*ka la'au*), tradleboard (*papa hehi*), stone castanets (*'ili'ili*), slit bamboo rattle (*pu'ili*), bamboo stamping tubes (*ka'eke'eke*), a three-gourd or three-coconut rattle (*'ulili*), and, finally, the human body itself was used as an accompanying instrument by striking the chest and legs (*pa'I umauma*)" (Kaeppler 40). Traditional costuming included a skirt made of kapa (cloth made of bark), anklets, leaves, flower necklaces (lei) and a hand-held rattle.

Dancers were responsible for acquiring knowledge of the mele hula (dance set to poetry) at schools (*halau*), for "the hula was an accomplishment requiring special education and arduous training in both song and dance, and more especially because it was a religious matter, to be guarded against profanation by the observance of tabus and the performance of priestly rites" (Emerson 13). Hula masters (*kumu hula*), holding one of the most prestigious positions in Hawaiian society, were responsible for the construction of the temple or dance-house dedicated to a particular goddess who would inspire the company's performances (no one entered the halau without a call-and-response password song and a sprinkling of sea water and red earth), the recruitment of dancers and chanters, the repertoire, choreography, and performances.

The *kuaha*, or altar, was a frame lavished with greenery and flowers, constructed with the observance of formalities such as song chants and prayer recitals. Approved decorations included "the fragrant maile and the star-like fronds and ruddy drupe of the ie-ie and its kindred, the halapépe; the scarlet pompons of the lehúa and ohi'a, with the fruit of the latter (the mountain-apple); many varieties of fern, including that splendid parasite the 'bird's nest fern' (ekáha), hailed by the Hawaiians as Mawi's paddle; to which must be added the commoner leaves and lemon-colored flowers of the native hibiscus, the hau, the breadfruit, the native banana and the dracæna (ti), and lastly, richest of all, in the color that became Hawaii's favorite, the royal yellow ilíma" (Emerson 20).

Supported by a chief or king (all roads led to the king's court), masters were chosen on a democratic basis, as anyone who mastered the technique and ritual could organize a dance company and seek patronage (company numbers could climb into the hundreds). Also, though constricted by technique, the

Hula dancer at Festival of Nations, Cherokee, North Carolina, 2008 (author's photograph).

master could introduce fresh choreography. (The Hawaiians structured a proverb: *Aohe pau ka iki I kau halau — Think not that all wisdom lies in your dance house.*)

Dance recruits (who offered a prayer at the altar when joining the company) were subject to the hula master and followed a strict regiment (during rehearsal) of abstinence, frequent bathing, and dietary mandates, for, during training and rehearsal, the dancer was considered sacred (*kapu*). (A dancer's début ceremony was known as a *uniki*). In fact, as the time for a dance appearance approached, dancers went about with heads covered, speaking to no one, for "the goddess was now taking possession of the worshipper to inspire him in all his parts and faculties—voice, hands, feet, whole body" (Beckwith 410). On the night before the ceremony, all bathed and rehearsed. On the morning of the performance, a black pig feast was held (the eating of the brain of the goddess), the dance hall decorated with flowers, and the altar consecrated.

Performers were divided into *'olapa*, the dancers, and *ho'opa'a*, the chanters and drummers. Naturally, dancers also had to learn movements, as "the body of hula dancers hold a body of knowledge, a complete philosophy with its own epistemology, its own vision of reality, and an ethic based on the virtues of sharing, responsibility, reciprocity, and humility ... hula dancers were the moving archives of the cultural knowledge of the Hawaiian people" (Rowe 37). In the hula's basic stance, the dancer achieved full contact with the earth. Known as *aiha'a*, the dancer's knees were bent and feet flat in order to feel the rhythm of, and connection with, the earth. The dance steps, whose rhythm followed the beat of the mele call and chant, included *kaholo* (stepping side to side), *'uwehe* (stepping in place, then lifting and dropping heels) and *'ami* (circular pelvic shifts and tilts mirroring the movement of the wind and waves). Hand and arm gestures interpreted the chant, examples being:

Pua (Flower)

Place the hands palm down. Slowly turn the hands over, bringing all fingers together, touching the middle finger to the thumb.

Moana (Ocean); Kai (Sea)

Arms are extended and out in front with hands at waist level or below. Hands are flat. Push down with the fingers, then up and down again. This motion crosses the body, either the side or the front.

Kuahivi, Mauka (Mountain)

Begin at one side and bring both hands up and to the other side with both arms straight and one hand lower than the other ["Hula Gestures"].

Cultural facial expressions also interrupted the "story" of the chant, such as a lifting of the eyebrows or a grimacing of the nose. But, as with all dances, "many of their gestures, like the rhetoric of a popular orator, were mere flourishes and ornaments" (Emerson 181).

Unfortunately, upon European arrivals, the death of Kamehameha II in 1819, and the accession of his wife, Ka'ahumanu, global interests and missionary conversion tactics significantly altered Hawaiian culture, and therefore the hula, in a period of no less than seven months. First, the world seemed to converge upon the Islands, for, once they were discovered by Captain Cook in 1778, they began serving as a global geographic crossroads. Kaahumanu, influenced by European wealth and gifts, and the ability to use funds reserved for religious ceremony to establish foreign trade in the sandlewood, fur, and whaling industries, abolished the *kapu*, the sacred taboos, such as the prohibition preventing men and women from eating together, undercutting the traditional Hawaiian religion, hierarchy, and social order.

Calvinist missionaries from Boston and other areas arrived soon thereafter. A captain of the Russian Imperial Navy, Otto von Kotzebue, noted at the time: "The missionary Bengham found means to obtain such an ascendency over the imperious Kahumanna, and, through her, over the nation, that in the course of only seven months an entire change had taken place ... singing is a punishable offense; and the consummate profligacy of attempting to dance would certainly find no mercy" (Buck 107). Bengham in fact found "the whole arrangement and process of their old hulas designed to promote lasciviousness" (Buck 15). Christian hymnals were introduced on April 23, 1820, when newly arrived missionaries sang for the Hawaiian court, "which profoundly affected the nature of Hawaiian music, and, to some extent, the lyrics" (Solberg 47).

Missionaries also created an orthography, designed to transcribe the Hawaiian language to written form. This emphasis on the written word quickly eroded traditional religious beliefs and practices (such as hula), as well as the culture's oral tradition. With Queen Kaahumanu's support, hula was denounced and banned as "pagan, sinful, and a breeding place for lust." A lengthy period of "mission rule" and legislative edicts ensued. Dancers performed only in private or in rural areas for over fifty years.

The hula was nearly a lost art by the time King David Kalakaua came to power (1874). Thankfully, Kalakaua was a patron of Hawaiian arts, especially music and dance. He almost single-handedly restored the myths, legends, and dances of the Hawaiian peoples, soliciting a hula master from Kaua'i, Nama-elua, to assist in his efforts to initiate a revival of Hawaiian arts, music, dance, and, of course, poetry. At the time of his coronation in 1883, over the objections of both Hawaiians and non–Hawaiians, this brave king invited dancers from around the islands to perform. For hula was "an important vehicle for expressing Hawaiian royalist sentiments about Hawaiian nationalism during the 1880s and later the overthrow of the monarch and annexation of Hawai'I by the United States. Because *hula ku'I* was so closely associated with Kalakaua and his supporters, its performance was criticized by antiroyalists" (Buck 113). Both the ancient form of hula *(kahiko),* and a new Europeanized version complete with ukulele and guitar *('auana),* were publicly acknowledged. On his fiftieth birthday in 1886, at the King's Jubilee, hula events were held for over two weeks. And when Kalakaua returned from a trip around the world in 1887, hula festivals were held in his honor.

Hula hand gestures, Festival of Nations, Cherokee, North Carolina, 2008 (author's photograph).

Two other people worked wonders in preserving the hula tradition. First, Mary Kawena Pukui, born in 1895 in Ka'u, learned the chants, lore, and movements of the hula dance from her grandmother, who spoke only Hawaiian. As an adult Mary helped preserve the mele tradition by co-authoring a Hawaiian dictionary, later described as the "bible of the language." She also wrote *The Echo of Our Song*, a translation of old chants and sayings, as well as lyrics to over 150 mele.

By starting her own halau (hula school) in 1948, another woman who helped save the dance was Ma'iki Aiu Lake. During her thirty-eight years as a teacher, Ma'iki trained two generations of hula dancers and teachers, also reviving the traditional participation of males. Describing hula as "life," she also gave free lessons to tourists interested in the art form.

The question for Hawaiians in today's modern world is: "How do we teach the meaning and tradition of hula to a world that is not Hawaiian?" The answer seems to be: festivals and competitions. The first festival in modern times to highlight the dance tradition was the Merrie Monarch, organized in 1964 to honor King David Kalakaua, at a time when "young adult Hawaiians spoke out against the encroaching development that alienated them from the land and other natural resources" (Stillman 360). Founded by hula master George Naope, and held the week following Easter, the festival draws together many important figures in the world of hula: instructors, masters, researchers, and students. Since 1971 dancers compete at this festival in both ancient and modern styles. The 5,000 tickets available sell out in a matter of days, and the event has been televised since 1984.

Another festival which began in the '70s is the King Kamehameha Chant and Hula Competition, commemorating Kamehameha Day, "a Hawaiian holiday observed each June 11th since 1872, honoring Kamehameha I, the chief who united all of the Hawaiian islands under one rule by 1800" (Stillman 362). This festival is complete with pageantry, hula performances, and a colorful Hawaiian women's equestrian unit. The event is sponsored by the State Council on Hawaiian Heritage, "a private nonprofit organization that sponsors short hula workshops led by master teachers" (Stillman 362).

Private dance schools also flourished in the '70s, "particularly noteworthy is the resurgence of interest in hula by male dancers ... following decades in which hula dancing was considered to be feminine and the few male dancers who pursued study were frequently perceived to be effeminate. Such perceptions dissipated with the emergence of a vigorous men's style of dancing" (Stillman 360). Hula also became a multiethnic event, and schoolchildren were offered courses at the elementary and secondary levels.

Hula has not chosen to stay at home. The World Invitational Hula Festival, held in Honolulu since 1992, "aims to provide a venue in which performers from all over the world compete alongside the best performers in Hawai'I" (Stillman 364). Competitions are also held on the U.S. mainland, the two strongest events held in California, a state supporting over 50 halau, or dance schools (memberships climbing to the hundreds). In this state, hula masters are "cultural resources, not only in dance, but in everything surrounding the dance, including history, legends, Hawaiian language, plant lore, lei-making and other crafts" (Stillman 59). Indianapolis, Indiana, has sponsored a hula workshop called the "Dancers' Dream Weekend" since 1988.

Hula is also popular in Japan, first offered as a course for housewives in the 1980s, and quickly sought out by younger dancers. Japan contributed its hierarchical tradition to the art form to the point that some master teachers have as many as 25 assistant instructors spread throughout the country. Also, the Merrie Monarch Festival organized a "satellite" festival in the town of Ikaho, Japan, held each August. Europe and Mexico have joined in the fun, Europeans having entered in the World Invitational Hula Festival competition since 1992. As the organizer of the King Kamehameha Hula Competition, Keahi Allen, stated, "Hula lives around the world, and if we've got other people from other countries who respect it, and want to learn it, and they're hungry for it, it'll just make it live more" (Stillman 63).

Because of the *mana*, or spiritual power, found in the Hawaiian islands, hula has survived the test of time. One of today's famous hula teachers, descended from the Pele clan, a family linked to the very beginnings of the

dance, is Pualani Kanaka'ole Kanahele. For her, the traditions associated with the hula teach both performers and observers "how to respect family, appreciate natural phenomena, memorize lengthy chants, love the land, understand hierarchy, recognize life and death cycles, and acknowledge and honor the presence of life" ("History of Hula"). With so much to learn at stake, it's no wonder the Hawaiian people reclaimed their sacred dance, hula, a form of poetry in motion which "evinces a deep and genuine love of nature, and a minute, affectionate, and untiring observation of her moods ... an inexhaustible

King David Kalakaua, circa 1882.

spring of joy, refreshment, and delight" (Emerson 263). Nature (*laka*) no doubt responded to the call of hula in the same manner as Boki (governor of Oahu during the ban), who predicted: "Dance we will — no taboo!"

4

We Are All On This Earth Together: The Plains Indians' Sun Dance

here am I
behold me
I am the sun
Behold me—Lakota Sun-Rise Greeting Song

A poster announcing a call for performers of the Sun Dance of the Plains Indians of the Americas should read: ONLY THE ENAPAY NEED APPLY! (Enpay is Lakota for "brave.") For this dance, as performed by male members of the Plains tribes of the Americas long before the arrival of the Europeans, required complete mastery of mind over matter, each participant exhibiting unbelievable courage and a complete disregard for physical pain "to insure that the energy of this world and life will be renewed so that the cycle may continue" (Brown 78). Ironically, however, the Plains Indians see the dance not as a way to prove a man's bravery, but as a way to "prove his great spirituality through his ability to be unconscious of and to transcend pain" (Highwater 153).

In its original form, Sun dancers offered themselves as a sacrifice for their community (tribe), therefore the dance was considered a collective prayer. Dancers thanked their god, *Wakan Tanka*, for saving a relative's life or granting supernatural aid in war or other trials, or asked that in war "no evil shall befall them, but that they shall be the ones to bring evil to the foe" (Deloria 389) or "to recover from a mortal wound, for a dear one's life to be spared, or for a raging pestilence to cease" (Deloria 388). Sometimes the dancers simply asked for a personal vision to learn how to best serve others, for "only in sacrifice is sacredness accomplished; only in sacrifice is identity found. It is only through suffering in sacrifice that freedom is finally known and laughter in joy returns to the world" (Brown 80).

The dancers also demonstrated their awesome respect for Wakan Tanka, whose name means "all that which moves" or "the Great Mystery." One of the prayers still in existence today reveals this respect:

> Oh Holy Powers, we honor You this day that we may live. Have pity on me.
> Accept my suffering this day in reciprocation for all You have given us.

The Sun Dance of the Lakota, Blackfeet, Arapaho, and Mandans was actually a dance-drama in four acts: capture, torture, captivity, and escape. Not only a drama, it allowed tribes to communicate with their god through other sacred arts: music, dance, and painting. It was known by many names across the Plains: "The Utes, Shoshonis, Plains Crees, and Plains Ojibwas call it Thirsting Dance. Cheyennes and Arapahos call it Sacrifice, Offering, Medicine Lodge, or Medicine Dance. The Cheyennes also refer to it as New Life Lodge, or Lodge of the Generator (Creator). The Assiniboin term was Making a Home, signifying the Thunderbird's nest in the fork of the sacred tree" (Laubin 275). Depending on the tribe, festivities lasted eight to fifteen days.

As practiced among the Lakota, the dancer, sometime in the spring, asked a holy (medicine) man for a sponsorship. Generally, each medicine man accepted five to six candidates. A public declaration, in which the declarant and the medicine man stood side-by-side facing the sunrise, occurred shortly thereafter. In this ceremony, the medicine man presented a speech:

> O Day's Light-Giver, listen kindly to me. When these sprouting grasses change their appearance, these youths of proper age promise to meet you face-to-face. It is so. But, also, they say they would meet face-to-face with the animals of the land. And, in the next battle whatever brings annoyance shall be easy for them to control, and, in fact, all annoyance and trouble shall go out from them, they say. But as for me, they say, let me return to my people without meeting with any mishap. Then those winged beings who live at the starting points of the Four Winds; and beneath these, all animals; and fowls, the eagle, the hawk, the crane, the loon: To all of you, these youths promise to present the pipe. A day with blue sky unmarred by clouds; a warm, calm day without heat; on such a day, they will meet you face-to-face. So they promise [Deloria 390].

The pledged dancers thereafter entered a period of consecration in which they refrained from all worldly pleasures, and, if married, lived apart from their wives. During this period, the dancer assembled his costume, which included (1) four hair ornaments decorated with porcupine quills to part his hair; (2) a pendant necklace made of rawhide and painted blue, from which dangled a single eagle feather; (3) rabbit skin strips, two tied to the ankles, two to the wrists; (4) a tanned deer skirt; (5) paints of all colors; and (6) a whistle of eagle wing bones from which was attached a *wa' cinhi*, a fluffy plume from the tail of a golden eagle. The dancer also assembled the dance paraphernalia (1) a long braided rawhide rope; (2) two sharpened sticks for piercing; and (3) a figure of a man and buffalo cut from rawhide. Before sitting up the dance camp, the medicine men held another ceremony in which they implored Wakan Tanka: "With my people I would live without misfortune. Prepare for me a pasture for the buffalo bull, his wife and young ... so that by means of them, I and my people may keep alive.... All the people say 'Hayé' and then they sing — So saying, I am arrived (repeated three times), I am related to all spirits the world over" (Deloria 394).

Preparations for the dance began, held when the berries ripened (June-July), or when the cherries blackened (July-August). A site for the dance was selected, the whole tribe broke camp, and the journey to the selected site began. Upon arrival, a council tipi was erected in front of the main circle of tipis (a consecrated buffalo skull placed on a bed of sage behind the tent), and to the east, the tipi of preparation where the candidates met for instruction.

Appointees were determined over the next several days. For instance, children were informed who would undergo ear piercing, chaste women received an announcement regarding selections in association with the cutting of the sacred Sun Dance Pole, scouts were gathered to select the tree, and musicians were organized. A cottonwood tree, "about eight to ten inches in diameter at its base," had to be selected, for it was considered a sacred tree, "growing where no other large tree will grow. It can always find the life-giving water. Its rustling in the slightest breeze represents continuing prayer to the Great Spirit, and its fluffy white down looks like the sacred eagle down so important in many ceremonies" (Laubin 279).

The scouts dressed for war carrying shields and weapons. They simulated stalking and capturing an "enemy" as they searched for the tree. When arriving back in camp, they rushed at a bundle of boughs, life-size, another effigy of the "enemy." The first to arrive at the effigy was considered the greatest warrior. The four chaste women were shown to the tree. The first struck the tree on the west side, the second on the north, the third on the east and the fourth on the south. From the time the tree fell (of course other tribal members actually finished cutting the tree), the dancers could not eat or drink until the dance was complete several days later. The tree was purified in this fashion: "An incense of sweet grass was made, and all the branches were trimmed off close to its trunk except for the large fork at the top, twenty to thirty feet up. Sometimes a little tuft of leaves was left at the tip of the tree also. The priest rubbed red paint in the wounds of the tree and from then on the tree was regarded as sacred. No one dared touch it or step over it" (Laubin 281).

Next, this pole was erected straight towards the Sun and became the central focus of the dance. The rawhide images of the buffalo and man were tied to the pole and a bundle of tobacco placed at the top as a sacrifice. Six cloths of differing colors were also tied to the pole: red, yellow, black, and white represented the four cardinal directions (South, North, East, and West) as well as the four stages of life (childhood, young adult, adulthood, and old age). Green and blue represented the Heavens and the Earth. Once decorated in this fashion, this pole was considered the *axis mundi,* the center of the world. Braided rawhide ropes were attached to the pole, and it was lifted by sling into a pre-set hole (the digging of which was considered an honor) filled with buffalo fat and red paint. Tribal members cheered and danced as the pole was erected, and "it was said by some to represent the morning star, the symbol of wisdom and the patron of warriors, but One Bull said it represented the Four Winds" (Laubin 282). The Lakota fashioned an arbor supported by twenty-eight posts (representing the days of one moon) around the pole and performed a "smooth the floor out with their feet" dance around the pole.

After the site was prepared, participating dancers were isolated for instruction and contemplation. Medicine or holy men instructed the dancers in sacred prayers, songs, and spiritual practices. The men fasted, going without food and water, attending a sweat lodge ceremony as well. The dancers painted their hands and feet red and their trunk in contrasting designs, such as sunflowers (who turn their face to the sun all day), buffaloes, eagles, hawks, the moon, or the morning stars, and the "emblems were painted in green, yellow, blue, and black. The colors used in this case had symbolism relating to the heavens. Red, in addition to being the tribal color, also symbolized the red of clouds at sunset; light blue represented a cloudless sky; green, earth and the power of growing things; yellow, the forked lightning; white, the light; and black, the night" (Laubin 285).

The entire camp then escorted the dancers to the Sun Pole, the capture portion of the drama. A select Holy Woman carrying a sacred pipe escorted the inductees. Tribe members shrieked and cried during this journey to represent the great weight of their sins, to be absolved by the sacrificial dancers. On the first day of dancing, the dancers prayed around the Sun pole: "Wakan Tanka, be merciful to us. We want to live. We sacrifice ourselves that our people may live" (Laubin 284). Withdrawing to the West to face the sun, dancers, to the rhythm of a drum or dry hide, raised their toes slightly and from this position bounced the entire body in time with the beat. He blew his eagle-bone whistle in time with the drum as well, and "the whistles, all being closely registered but no two exactly of the same note, have an eerie, pulsating quality, reminding one of the bell-like chorus of the peep frogs we hear in early spring" (Laubin 285).

The *axis mundi:* Sun Dance in progress with created lodge, circa 1910 (Library of Congress).

Dancers continued this step until someone lay exhausted, at which time a brief rest upon a buffalo robe was allowed. Paint was renewed around noon, and except for a few brief breaks, dancing continued all day and night, stopping just before dawn. Dancing at night represented the darkness of men's minds (ignorance), while the fire built toward the East symbolized the coming light of knowledge and understanding.

On the second day of dance, once again escorted by Holy Woman, the dancers rejoiced for the wisdom they were soon to receive. Wearing wreaths of sage upon their heads, they danced first to the south, then west, north, and east, faces upturned. Finally, the dancers were attached to the pole, the piercer "holding the flesh out far, piercing the chest down to the quick through the muscle under the skin, and running a sharpened stick through the holes like a pin" (Deloria 405). A rawhide string was tied on one end of the skewer and then attached on the other side to the Sun Pole itself. Now a part of the Pole, and thus all of creation ("individual participants are reconnected to the sacred through a vertical axis ... at the same moment that they are reconnected to each other in the circle of coparticipation they inscribe with their bodies on a horizontal plane") (Lincoln 6), each participant began dancing with various movements to loosen the string. The steps taken by the dancers recreated stories associated with the cosmos: the fury, straining and jerking of time, space, and energy. Release usually came within an hour, and the dancer was administered to by a medicine man who rubbed healing herbs into the wounds (Laubin indicates a case of injury or permanent infection was never reported). While seemingly cruel, this stage of the dance "did not imply that Wakan Tanka was a cruel god, For Wakan Tanka was the power in everything, largely impersonal, and yet concerned with the welfare, proper balance, proper relationship, of all his creation" (Laubin 292). The men felt liberated from ignorance and selfishness, having insured the welfare of their tribe by means of personal sacrifice "that all the world and humankind may continue on the path of the cycle of giving, receiving, bearing, being born in suffering, growing, becoming, returning to the earth that which has been given, and finally being born again" (Brown 80).

In the 1850s, unfortunately, the white man's cultural encroachment arrived in the lands of the Plains Indians. Multiple clashes ensued, and many tribes were forced onto reservations, dependent upon the federal government for food and supplies. Many settlers were cruelly indifferent, such as Indian trader Andrew Myrick: "So far as I am concerned, if they are hungry let them eat grass" (Dunn 59). Despite courageous attempts to regain control of their homeland, such as the Battle of Little Big Horn, the Plains Indians were ultimately defeated, for as the *Dallas Daily Herald* reported in 1876, "Killing a mess of Indians is the only recreation our frontier rangers want" (quoted in Dunn 71), despite the fact that Ulysses S. Grant told *The New York Herald*, "I regard Custer's massacre as a sacrifice of troops, brought on by Custer himself, that was wholly unnecessary" (quoted in Dunn 71). By 1871, Congress had even ended their original recognition of sovereign Indian nations. Of course, as a result of this mindset and the forced reservation system, "reformers and Indian haters alike agreed it was no longer possible for Indians to follow traditional practices and that Native Americans should be assimilated into American mainstream life and culture. The best way to do this, according to U.S. policy makers, was to abolish what remained of traditional Indian ways, creating an indigenous population of English–speaking Christians who farmed for a living" (Dunn 78).

Government officials and missionaries from both the United States and Canada frowned upon the dance because of its bloody features. Famous anthropologist and folk song collector Frances Densmore wrote, "Strange as it may seem, the element of pain, which ennobled the ceremony in the mind of the Indian, was a cause of its misunderstanding by the white man. The voluntary suffering impressed the beholder, while its deep significance was not evident" (Laubin 275). This misguided belief led to the Canadian government's banning of the dance in 1874. The U.S. government followed suit with its own administrative ban in 1881. According to Indian historian Little

Rock Reed, "Indians who maintained tribal customs were subject to imprisonment, forced labor, and even punishment by starvation. Indian dress, ceremony, dances, and singing were forbidden. Sacred instruments, medicine, and pipes were confiscated and destroyed. Even Indian names and hairstyles were forbidden by law" (Reed 48).

The last original Sun Dance was held at the Standing Rock Sioux Reservation in 1882 and was broken up by U.S. troops. This governmental ban was prosecuted with vigor until the late 1920s, as "convinced that dances and their associated rituals posed a fundamental threat to the government's assimilation goals, officials waged an intensive campaign between the 1880s and the early 1930s to suppress what one Baptist minister on the Southern Plains called the 'moral curse' of Indian dancing. Missionaries, reformers, and philanthropists alike joined the chorus, placing their combined influence behind policies designed to destroy every ritual, ceremony, and dance that reinforced Indianness and thus stood in opposition to federal aims" (Ellis 548).

At first, troops were called on to force the end to the dance; in 1877 amongst various tribes, 1888 to curtail the Kiowa Sun Dance, and again in 1899 when troops were used to "peremptorily end the Sun Dance." Thereafter, agents tried every means to control the Sun Dance, or any Plains Indian dance, such as promising to provide rations on the land and game-poor reservations, to which one young Kiowa recounted: "We don't want your rations, we want this dance" (Ellis 550). Other sanctions included fines, imprisonment, and forfeiture of annuity payments, to the point that "dancers found themselves increasingly hemmed in by agents determined to quash dances" (Ellis 552).

Agents even had to provide specific information on dancing in their reports. In 1914 Commissioner of Indian Affairs Sells stated: "Both the Indians and the public should be made to realize that these old customs retard the onward march of civilization" (Ellis 557). Commissioner Charles Burke (1921–29) called dancing "vicious" and wrote the notorious "Circular 1665" in 1921, denouncing dances for their "acts of self torture, immoral relations between the sexes, sacrificial destruction of clothing or other useful articles, reckless giving away of property, use of injurious drugs or intoxicants, and frequent or prolonged periods of celebrations which bring the Indians together from remote points to the neglect of their crops, livestock, and home interest" (Ellis 554). Burke limited dances to "once a month in the daylight hours of one day in midweek, made them off limits to anyone under the age of fifty, abolished them completely in April, June, July, and August, and urged 'a careful propaganda be undertaken to educate public opinion against the dance'" (Ellis 554).

The Plains Indians, amidst this repression, attempted to maintain the meaning and symbology of their dances through reinterpretation at other social gatherings, such as the Gourd Dance. For example, the Kiowa "transferred crucial ritual and spiritual actions from a dance that was banned to another that was not ... mediating the new social and cultural realities of the early twentieth century" (Ellis 567). In the end, the Sun Dance was more resilient than troops, agents, regulations, or imprisonment, becoming "part powwow and part annual fair" (Carlson 120). Indeed, "Indians who maintained dance traditions were spokepersons for the right of Indians to be themselves. They survived the contest.... They were never destroyed" (Moses 177).

In 1935, Sioux Chief One Bull revived the dance at a place called Little Eagle on the Standing Rock Reservation. While recovering from an illness,

For strength and visions: *The Piercing*, circa 1908 (Library of Congress).

One Bull had a vision of riders from the early days, war bonnets flowing in the wind as they rode white horses across the sky. To One Bull, this was a symbol that he should repay Wakan Tanka for allowing him to recover. He did so by performing the first public Sun Dance since 1882. This particular performance, while not as long as the dances of the past, was powerful because One Bull prayed for an end to the drought that had plagued the Dakotas since 1932. Shortly after the dance, it rained so hard that flooding forced One Bull and his family to higher ground. In another Sun Dance held by One Bull in 1942, at a time when our nation was in the middle of World War II, the Chief asked Wakan Tanka for a U.S. victory, which of course came to fruition in 1945.

In 1955, performances of the dance began in Pine Ridge Village in South Dakota. Natives also began promoting the Sun Dance as thoroughly Christian, equating the sufferings of the dancers with the Christian concept of penance.

A major revival occurred in 1972 at the Sioux Rosebud Reservation in South Dakota. Native Americans from many different tribes participated in the dance. Today, the dance is held on one of the Lakota reservations each summer since 1979 by visionary medicine man Francis Strong Bear, who was instructed in a vision quest (hanble eya) to "become a religious practitioner, to stage the Sun Dance, and to help all people for 'we are all together on this earth ... by the middle 1980s two white dancers had joined the circle and a handful off

One Bull and Sitting Bull hold a calumet, the Sacred Pipe, circa 1884 (Library of Congress).

others came as spectators ... of the 150 who entered the circle on the first day of dancing in 1991, more than thirty were white, and there were also two black dancers" (Lincoln 10). The Sun Dance, despite assimilation efforts, was never destroyed. One of the most authentic sun dances held today takes place each summer in Northern California at a school for Native American and Mexican American studies. In Canada sun dances are held on over half of Saskatchewan's seventy-four Indian reserves. Indeed, "where a people's vision speaks of life, sacrificial means for recurrent renewal of all life, and suffering for the identity with the source of life — such vision can neither be destroyed, denied, nor ignored" (Brown 77).

5

The Churning of the Oceans:
The Survival of the Khmer
Classical Dance of Cambodia

"We ought to dance with rapture that we might be alive ... and part of the living, incarnate cosmos."—D.H. Lawrence

Travel back to the 800s, into the far away realms of Southeast Asia and into the throes of the Khmer Empire of Cambodia. A powerful monarch (the god-king, *devaraja*) oversees and nourishes all forms of art. His power is believed to emanate from his spiritual prowess or abilities. The major city is Angkor Thom, the "Great City," home to vast temples, elaborate waterways and bridges, and fantastic myths. Rocks, trees, and temple structures enshrine the essence of ancestral spirits by means of elaborate, artistic type carvings. Dancers, musicians, and singers are considered "slaves of the gods" whose purpose is to honor and communicate with these spirits according to a strict schedule. The dancers' particular purpose is to embody the spirits, in order that all creation will remain balanced and blessed. (For example, the monsoon rains will only fertilize the land, not destroy the villages. The land will produce great fruit, and will never become barren.) Indeed, the dancers' dedication to the temple is considered a high calling, thus, they are bestowed such names as "Adorable," "Gifted in the Art of Love," or "Spring Jasmine." In fact, "it seems fairly certain that ritual dance has been intimately connected with ancestor communion and fertility rites in the area of Cambodia from the most ancient times" (Cravath 182).

Such a lifestyle did exist for the Royal Cambodian Ballet dancers (known as *lakhon lueng*) from the sixth century to 1970, a period of fifteen hundred years. In fact, the period from 802 to 1432 is considered "the most culturally and politically sophisticated age in Cambodian history" (Cravath 184). The number of dancers who graced the temples was tremendous. For instance, during the reign of one monarch, King Jayavarman VII, the following dancers were initiated into the temple: 615 dancers dedicated to the spirit of the king's mother, 1,000 dancers dedicated to the spirit of his father, and 1,622 dancers in other temples throughout the kingdom. Surely, "the extent to which dance and dancers were integral to the social and religious fabric of Cambodia is perhaps unequaled in world civilization" (Cravath 184). On the stone reliefs of the temple ruins of Angkor, dancers appear in the thousands. To this day, "Cambodians view dance as one of the most powerful temple offerings to obtain assistance from the spirits" (Cravath 181).

Next, imagine the Cambodian court in the year 1432. Dancers perform the *buong suong*, a ceremonious offering given in exchange for the gift of rain. The dancers transform themselves into divine beings through the use of costume. They wear silk skirts (sewn-in) with beautiful patterns and elaborate high, gold-studded headdresses. They don gold-painted jewelry and portray bejeweled princes, princesses, giants (antagonists) and monkeys (benefactors). They paint their faces white to represent beings in touch with the spiritual world, and "unquestionably the thick white powder gives her the appearance of a dissociated, otherworldly spirit" (Cravath 197).

The troupe is accompanied by a pin peat, a formal orchestra that includes three singers, two bamboo xylophones (*roneat*), tuned brass pots suspended in a frame (gong), a kettle drum, and a quadruple reed oboe (*sralay*). Traditionally, "Khmer music was performed as an offering to the spirit world and was considered to be an ancestral heritage and, hence, sacred.... The high-pitched blend of the chorus leader's chant with the *sralay* is one of the distinguishing features of the genre" (Cravath 189). The tempo begins slowly, increasing to a "frenzied climax, both musicians and dancers keeping perfect time to the accelerated tempo of the music. There is an intoxication in the monotony of the plaintive cadences that almost sends the listener into a trance; the insistent throbbing of drums, now muted and now swelling, produces a feeling of tenseness and excitement, and one is carried away on waves of sound" (Strickland-Anderson 269).

The dancers' choreography requires complete muscle control, begins with one hand and arm, and uses "comparatively large movements of arms or legs, together with various forms of turning, walking, and kneeling, alternated with long periods of standing in a single spot performing very small movements of the hands, feet, and head, often in delicate interaction with a partner. The elbows are continually away from the body, one or both arms are usually extended at shoulder height, the fingers are always taut with energy, the knees are bent, and one foot is often raised for long periods—all

8. - Visite de S. M. Sisowath aux ruines d'Angkor - Les ballerines du Roi dansant en l'honneur des invités.

A visit to Angkor Wat, Royal Khmer dancers, circa 1875.

of which contributes to a hypnotic balance of movement and stillness" (Cravath 190). Toes are also flexed upwards and held for the duration of a pose (there are over 4,500 positions) or sequence.

The dancers strive to embody the tension between female and male, offerings, and the concern for social and sexual harmony. Standing positions imitate rippling water, music flows from the sounds of animals and nature, and movement mirrors the sway and bend of trees. Pierre Loti observed, "The Apsaras, how pretty and smiling they are, in their coiffures of goddesses, yet always with that expression of reserve and mystery, which is so little assuring. Richly adorned with bracelets, necklaces, head-dresses of precious stones, tall tiaras either pointed or surmounted with a tuft of plumes, they hold between their delicate fingers, sometimes a lotus-flower and sometimes an enigmatic emblem" (qtd. in Stickland-Anderson 273). Figure-eight patterns, the symbol of infinity, trace the movements of a giant *naga*, the sea serpent bridge to the divine, across the floor (see below). The connection between heaven and earth is affirmed, balance is achieved, and justice triumphs, as the "body of the female dancer becomes the narrative container of the cosmos, a microcosm of myriad nuanced interrelationships between the physical and the spiritual" (Hamera 78).

Dancers are trained almost from infancy: "Their limbs are made flexible and supple; their ears attuned to the rhythm and beat of the music they interpret; and they are taught to perfect the intricacies of spectacular ballets"

Apsaras, Bayon Temple, Angkor Wat, Cambodia. The carvings date to around the 12th century.

(Strickland-Anderson 268). They are selected on the basis of beauty, talent, and, occasionally, family/artistic lineage.

Dancers became such an important part of the Khmer civilization because of the mythological beliefs of its citizens. Most important to this belief system was the story known as "The Churning of the Sea."

> At the bottom of the ocean lives a giant serpent, or *naga*, whose length stretches forty-nine yards. On top of this *naga* lies a second serpent, just as long. To the left of the *naga*, ninety-two ogres (*yakkha*) pull on his head. To the right, eighty-eight gods (*deva*) pull on his tail. The *naga*, day-in and day-out, winds himself around a stone, becoming one with the forces of the earth. As a result of all the pulling and coiling, the ocean gurgles, waves and churns. From the resulting foam, thousands of flying dancers emerge. These celestial dancers, *apsaras*, (angels), are responsible for the welfare of all people; they bring fruits and flowers and flourishing life to each and every soul. Each time the ocean churns, a dancer is born, to move over the earth in harmony with the spirits of nature.

In this worldview, not all people are equal, yet all are involved in the maintenance of social order and harmony. Some are kings and some are ogres. Some are female and some are male. Some are old and some are young. Some pull and some tug. Yet together, the people dance in spiritual harmony to create one society, peaceful, balanced, and happy. As Cravath notes, "It is no wonder that at Angkor there were myriads of dancers both in art and in human form. The king was surrounded by thousands of women as concubines, dancers, and even guards. His central position in this feminine world was believed to create the welfare of the kingdom" (Cravath 185).

As in other dances around the world, such as the Polynesian hula, the hands of Cambodian dancers express the essence of nature (bent backwards at the wrist until the fingers are nearly parallel to the forearm). Famed dancer Sophiline Shapiro describes the following movements:

- Point the first finger to represent a tree, and the other fingers are leaves.
- Place your thumb and index finger together, then spread the other three fingers to represent a flower
- To represent fruit, form a circle with your thumb and middle finger. Put the other three fingers backward.
- Drop the three fingers to represent the fruit dropping the seed into the ground, and, thus, the growth of another tree, or tendril (point again).

Shapiro says, "These are just the four basic hand gestures that embody the meaning of the circle of nature, the circle of life. And that's the theme that classical dance usually focuses on" (Shapiro 2).

The repertoire consists of two types. The first is the *roeung* (dance dramas), involving literary elements, such as plot, characterization, and dialogue, "chanted by a female chorus of former dancers. The dramas originate from about forty stories; in some cases single episodes have remained popular, while in others the entire story is telescoped into a flexible series of episodes. While many of the dramas concern events in the lives of protohistorical kings, the pervasive theme of the dramatic repertoire is the eternal struggle for control of the Feminine" (Cravath 188) in order to insure regeneration. Staging techniques eliminate a void of space and represent palaces, forests, skies, and the human realm. The second branch is the *robam* (pure, or sacred), ritual dances hastening the return of the rain (seven types of robam, consisting of sixty dances, are included in this repertoire). The dancer's space is sacred and thus void of props, furniture, or sets.

The dances are always performed at the annual *sampeah kru* ceremony as an offering to the spirit of the dance, kru. The word *kru* means "teacher," and "the essence of the ceremony is receiving the teachers' empowerment to perform the dance" (Cravath 198). The leader of the dance, the *tep robam*, one of the few men who perform with the female dancers (in addition to the monkey and clown) plays the role of the hermit, "placing the mask of the *eysei* (or hermit) on his head ... taking each of the masks and headdresses in turn, placing it on the head of the dancer who had learned that role, and removing it" to insure each dancer is indeed "possessed," taking on the persona of the mask itself (Cravath 198).

An awe-inspiring performance of artistic elements, Khmer Royal dance incorporated "music as an offering to the local spirits, choreography to reflect fundamental and ancient Khmer social values, and hand gestures representing natural forces" (Cravath 193), from ancients who "conceived vast dreams, complicated cosmogonies, and prodigious speculations on the origin of man and his destiny" (Strickland-Anderson 274). How could such beauty, such synchronicity ever be questioned or extinguished?

Ironically, similar to a Cambodian myth portrayed by the royal dancers for centuries, sometimes a "Thunder God" enters the drama, wielding his magic axe, jostling the followers of the "Goddess of the Water" and the "King of the Divinities." Such was the case when the Marxist regime of Pol Pot came to political power in Cambodia in 1975, "calling for an elimination of class distinctions and the creation of a uniform population of unpaid agricultural laborers answerable only to an amorphous higher revolutionary authority" (Shapiro-Phim 305). Pol Pot's forces, which became known as the Khmer Rouge, set about on a course of destruction, wielding the axe by attacking anyone who questioned the new regime and attempting to erase all of Cambodia's past, including the artistic Khmer civilization. Specifically targeted were "potential traitors," teachers, students, bureaucrats, technical workers, dancers, and professionals, even those who wore eyeglasses. Each citizen was required to "wear identical black garb, cut their hair short, adopt stereotypical patterns of 'appropriate' speech and behavior, and divest themselves of individualistic traits that precluded a proper revolutionary consciousness" (Hinton 824). From 1975 to 1979, approximately two million people were tortured, executed, starved, forced into eighteen-hour-a-day labor camps, and exposed to fatal disease. One survivor, Dith Pran, noted: "They forced all Cambodians to live in labor camps and work fourteen to eighteen hour days. They fed us one daily bowl of watery rice; they separated families; they destroyed all Cambodian institutions and culture; they systematically tortured and killed innocent people" (qtd. in Hamera 65).

Prior to Pol Pot's rise to power, 380,000 artists and intellectuals lived in Cambodia. Despite this rich manifestation of culture, Pol Pot's Khmer Rouge "came to power through a series of self-serving maneuvers and miscalculations by Cambodia's leaders and foreign nations; again, largely Vietnam and the United States" (Becker xv). These included the decline of the Angkor empire, feuds in the royal family which allowed foreign invasion, 90 years of French colonialism and the French belief that Cambodia was "unfit for the modern era," the "grabbing" of territory by Siam and Vietnam as the result of corrupt princes, an idealogical war with communism, and the devastation associated with the Vietnam War.

Between 1975 and 1979, ninety percent of the classical dancers of the royal court were murdered! The University of Fine Arts was shut down, and dance and music were forbidden. One surviving dancer, May Sem, explained, "You dancer, play music: killed. We are strong, we run and walk to camp. Old, dance long time, look like dancers: killed. And I hear in camp, you know, so many did not get out. Dancers and teachers from the school. I see and I hear. They did not get out. All dead. Before I get to camp" (qtd. in Hamera 72). Minister of Culture Chheng Phon remarked, "Khmer culture was the most refined, the most gentle of Indo-china. The most beautiful. It lasted 1,000 years. Now Khmer can't add, just subtract. Can't multiply, just divide" (qtd. in Hamera 75). Ben Sem noted, "Khmer culture so beautiful. Artist and dancer live well because they are like jewels. Live like jewels. My teacher say, 'Every dancer a book. Every great dancer a library. Khmer Rouge kill the dancers, kill the books. All the books are killed'" (qtd. in Hamera 75–6).

Thankfully, in relief camps found on the Cambodian-Thailand border during this period, Cambodians continued their arts as an undertaking free from the control of the Khmer Rouge and/or international aid agencies, and "the pride in mastery of a subtle manipulation of energy and of intricate patterns of movement was theirs to strive for and to claim ... statements against the precariousness of their existence" (Shapiro-Phim 308–9). In the camps, "anybody who wanted to, anybody dedicated enough to keep practicing, was welcome to dance in the camps. Performances, as well, were open to all" (Shapiro-Phim 321). Nevertheless, when Pol Pot's reign of terror (known as the "killing fields") ended in 1979, very few dancers had survived. Many dance students not in the camps had survived by feigning their identity. Monkey dancer Proeung fooled his captors into thinking he was a simpleton. Pen Sokhuon worked in the fields as a peasant. Chea Samy escaped to a farm where she was put to work collecting manure and compost for fertilizer. Eight-year-old Sophiline Cheam left her home for the countryside, pushing a cart up and down hills, only to arrive at a location where she "worked from sunrise until sunset, breaking only to eat. Our two daily meals consisted mostly of one watery cup of rice porridge.... We were productive, but where was the rice going? There was no democracy. There was no glory. There was no laughter. There was no happiness. By 1977 there was no more singing, and there was certainly no peace" (Shapiro 2). Even the Vietnamese, who took over the reins of power in 1979, proposed to ban Khmer court dance because they believed it "no longer suited and served the country's new political thrust."

Thirty-two surviving dancers fought back. They gathered costumes and instruments that had been buried in haste in 1975. They reviewed films and sound recordings. They formed troupes and colonies and finally reopened the Royal University of Fine Arts in 1981, enrolling over one hundred students, one such student being Sophiline Cheam (Shapiro). They transformed the story of the dance, for instance, instead of illustrating the difference between ignorance and enlightenment, "stories and dances were revised ... and new themes were imposed to reflect the differences between communism and capitalism" (Meneses 2). Few dances were recovered 100 percent, some 70 percent, others 40 percent.

The American government also helped out. The State Department allowed ninety former student dancers to settle in the Washington, D.C., suburb of Wheaton, Maryland. The National Council for the Traditional Arts took these dancers under their wing. The Vietnamese–backed government eventually asked fifty-seven-year-old Chea Samy to assist in the revival of the nation's classical dance, for the purpose of returning a sense of pride and identity to Cambodian citizens (Samy had served as a dancer for King Sisowath Monivong, teaching the dance from the time she was 30). "I survived because I hid my biography," Samy says. "I told them I had been a vendor in the market" (Spragens 1). At the Royal University, Samy asked students to aspire to perform "even better than the dancers under the old regime.... We will preserve this kind of dance forever," she vowed.

One of Samy's students was Sophiline Cheam (now married to an American and living in Los Angeles as Sophiline Shapiro), the eight-year-old wanderer mentioned above. Sophiline mastered the intricate movements of the dance during her residency at the university. She began traveling worldwide to preserve the integrity of the dance form. In 1984, she toured Cambodia to perform in remote villages. Former followers of Pol Pot were still at large, and travel was dangerous. Shapiro performed her art on the back of a flatbed truck, in the middle of a rubber plantation, and in villages full of dangerous "double-faced people." According to Shapiro, an older man in ragged and torn clothes approached her and asked "if she was a human being and if she ate rice and went to the bathroom, because he couldn't believe that anything associated with his miserable life could be so lovely" (Meneses 3). This encounter taught Shapiro "what art can do, how it can change the negative into positive" (Meneses 3).

In 2000, she returned to Phnom Penh, Cambodia, for a victorious, emotion-filled performance. Later, she and her husband launched the Khmer Arts Academy in Los Angeles, providing classical dance instruction to a new generation of Cambodian-Americans. In 2004, Shapiro spoke to the UCLA Center for Southeast Asian Studies on "The Two-Headed Naga: Cambodian Classical Dance as a Symbol of Cultural Rebirth and as a Tool for Political Propoganda." Perhaps the ultimate savior, Shapiro has "devoted herself tirelessly to the preservation and public performance of classical dance; her company, Dance Celeste, and her Arts of the Apsara foundation and school" (Hamera 78).

Shapiro has pondered: "Every time I think about the tragic events that happened to me, to my family and to my people during the Khmer Rouge, I have to think about something that is beautiful about my culture and about

Khmer classical ballet, 2007.

my country. And one thing that is beautiful is the dance and music" (Shapiro 2). And, indeed, today's dancer recreates the traditional spiritual beauty, "beginning with meditation; dancers light incense, bow and kneel.... Prior to each dance, the performers stand still, palms in prayer, with feet together and only big toes lifted" (Stein 128).

A third individual assisted in the revival of the Khmer classical ballet, Minister of Information and Culture Chheng Phon. During his service, the number of students at the University of Fine Arts increased, as students were provided free room and board and government subsidies. The university began presenting performances not only all over the country, but also around the world, averaging twenty performances per month! Correspondingly, "*apsaras* remain one of the most common icons among Cambodian people anywhere, painted with spired crowns and golden jewelry on billboards, stamped on organizational letterheads, sketched on restaurant menus, and cast in cement or metal ... seen as precious repositories of Cambodia's past and as such, the guarantors of her future" (Shapiro-Phim 306). And, in 2003, UNESCO proclaimed the Cambodian Royal Ballet (*robam kbach boran*) a masterpiece of oral and intangible heritage, a distinction which honors remarkable examples of cultural expression across the globe. Today, visitors to Cambodia may attend dance rehearsals at the University of Fine Arts, a performance on the grounds of the Royal Palace, or the nightly dance held at the east gate of Angkor Wat (limited to 1,300 by the Angkor National Park World Heritage site administrators and sold out every night)!

In the Khmer myth of the Thunder God, after the magical axe is wielded, the Goddess of the Water enters the drama. She throws her magical ball (representing lightning) into the air three times, blinding the Thunder God and knocking him to the ground. Perhaps the Goddess is not just a myth, for indeed she has struck three times, in the form of three extraordinary individuals, whose light "burned and blinded" Pol Pot's plot to destroy art and artists. These individuals have succeeded in throwing evil "to the ground," thereafter dedicating their lives to the restoration and revival of the Khmer Royal classical ballet.

The oceans still churn!

6

Of Two Worlds: The Whirling Dervishes of Konya

"Draw near, draw near!
I'll whisper in thy ear
His name, whose radiance
Maketh the spheres to dance." — Rumi

The Christmas season in Istanbul, Turkey: a Europeanized Turkey celebrates Christ's birth, enjoying many of the same customs found in England or Germany, no longer considering itself "the sick man of Europe." Yet the prime minister of the Republic of Turkey does not attend, introduce, and herald a national Christmas celebration, but rather the annual Mevlana celebration (December 17), commemorating the death, and therefore nuptials (now at one with Allah or God), of prophet, poet, dancer, musician, and mystic Mevlana Jalalu'ddin Rumi. This is ironic in itself considering the Turkish government, in 1925, banned the sacred rituals of the Sufi order began by the mystic in 1273 (the Mevlevis, commonly known as Whirling Dervishes). In modern times, the dance of the dervishes is a symbol of Turkey itself, though performances are still primarily restricted to tourist-oriented performance venues, such as auditoriums or even the Istanbul train station, despite the fact UNESCO (United Nations Educational, Scientific, and Cultural Organization, whose motto is "building peace in the minds of men and women") declared 2007 the "Year of Rumi" and placed the dance of the Whirling Dervishes on the "Intangible Cultural Heritage of Humanity" list. Rumi himself (who will be referred to as Rumi and Mevlana, interchangeably) would not be surprised by the transformation which occurred from 1925 to 2007, or the journey ahead, the road back into Islamic temples, for, as he taught, "enlightenment is in the beginning of every movement as well as the end."

At the 2010 Mevlevis Festival, the dervishes entered to the sound of chanting, singing, and a musical ensemble. Music, to Rumi, was the catalyst drawing the soul of the devotee to God, to the dance. Music symbolized the opening of the Gates of Paradise. The Sufis believed in the "religious power of music which, so to speak, oozed not only into the bodies of the Whirling Dervishes but also into their garments" (Schimmel 12). And the handbook of Sufism reads:

> Music does not give rise, in the heart, to anything which is not already there. So he, whose inner self is attached to anything else than God is stirred by music to sensual desire, but the one who is inwardly attached to the love of God is moved, by hearing music, to do his will.... The common folk listen to music according to nature, and the novices listen with desire and awe, while the listening of the saints brings them a vision of the Divine gifts and graces, and these are the Gnostics to whom listening means contemplation. But finally, there is the listening of the spiritually perfect to whom, through music, God reveals Himself unveiled [Schimmel 12].

The Sufis also say when God asked the souls in the spirit world, "Am I not your God?" the sweetness of His breath penetrated their soul to the point that now, when they hear music, the memory of the sweetness stirs within, causing the body to move.

One of the instruments used for a Mevlevis ceremony is the reed flute, known as the *ney*, which cannot reveal its secrets unless the musician breathes into it, a metaphor for man's relationship with God, the Beloved. Can a man be moved, act, speak, or think without the creative breath of God touching upon the holes in his heart (resulting from the pain and suffering of life)? On the contrary, unless separated from his primordial roots, just as the reed is separated from the reed bed (or the flute from its player), can man tell the story of eternal longing, for the time "when it was as it was before it was," before the dawn of creation? Does not the longing for God, and our actions associated therewith, enable humans to speak, and thus create? Does music not motivate the soul to find the breath of God, the movement of love, the creative force (producing all that is and shall be, the sound of the flute)?

As a sidenote, other instruments used in the Dervish ceremony include the *rabâb*, an ancient Oriental three-stringed violin with a body made of coconut shell; the tambourines, for without the touch of beloved fingers there is silence; the *kudum*, a small double drum used for rhythm and played with drumsticks; the *kanun*, a zither-like instrument with seventy-two strings; the *tambur*, an ancient form of the lute; and, in modern times, the violin-cello. Of course singers and chanters are important to Turkish religious music, and the three elements of rhythm, voice, and melody combine to create what some might call monotonous music whose purpose is participation and meditation, not listening, the music of the Creative Divine.

Illustration *La Danse des Deruis* from the book *Levant* (1705).

Does not the Creative Divine music of God, the Beloved, eminating from the spheres, intoxicate the listener, inspiring the "Not-Being" "to dance, to whirl around, so that out of this dance, stars and suns, atoms, animals, and flowers emerge" (Schimmel 15)? In essence, our response to the breath, the music of the Divine, the first song of the cosmos, elicits response: the dance of creation. Everything, under the spell of primordial music, must dance: "the atoms spin around their centres, the plants turn around the sun; the soul leaves its normal orbit and enters higher spheres. It — the soul — whirls around a spiritual sun and receives strength from it. Nature dances: "Flowers and birds, dragons and djinns dance, and the garden is involved in constant dance; the nightingale — the imam of the birds — sings, and while all flowers listen to him, they grow as though they were dancing." Even non-beings dance: "The child dances in the mother's womb as the dead dance in their shrouds when they hear the name of the Beloved" (Schimmel 15).

Again, a favorite metaphor of Rumi explains humanity's need to dance: in spring, the breeze dances and quickens the trees and branches, seemingly dead after winter's tyrannical rule, "and every twig, touched by this breeze, dons a green dancing-gown and begins to move joyfully. Only those not touched by the breeze of love (the dance) are dried up" (Schimmel 15). Rumi writes:

The trees, donning their dancing gowns
Supplicate in love
The image in me: is a different image
How many stars fall into my interior dance!
I whirl and I whirl, the skies whirl as well...
Roses bloom out of my face.
The trees in the garden, in sunshine...
"He created Heaven and Earth"
...the serpents listen to the song of the reed
In the trees donning their dancing gowns.
The meadow's children, intoxicated...
Heart, they call you.
I look, smiling, at suns
Which have lost their way...
I fly, I fly, the skies fly...

Clearly, with wisdom inspired by the music of the Beloved, in the spirit of the reed flute, whose tone mimics that of a fine soprano, Rumi invites all to the whirling dance, his Mevlevis order to the *sema*, a ceremony of sacred music, chanting, prayer, and the recitation of poetry, a spiritual concert:

O come, o come! You are the soul
Of the soul of the soul of whirling!
O come! You are the cypress tall
In the blooming garden of whirling!
O come! For there has never been
And will never be one like you!
O come! Such one has never seen
The longing eye of whirling!
O come! The fountain of the sun
Is hidden under your shadow!
The whirling, see, belongs to you
And you belong to the whirling.
What can I do when Love appears
And puts its claw round my neck?
I grasp it, take it to my breast
And drag it into the whirling.
And when the bosom of the motes
Is filled with the glow of the sun:
They enter all the dance, the dance
and do not complain in the whirling!

Rumi began whirling himself subsequent to the loss of his spiritual instructor, Shams-I Tabrizi, to political exile, and, eventually, to death at the hands of Rumi's jealous students "forgetting all about his scholarly pursuits—

Photograph dated 1905 from the book *East and War*, published by Sytin, Moscow. Note the reed flutes and hand positions.

at least for some time — and instead listening to music and whirling around while dictating poetry in a state of near unconsciousness" (Schimmel 13). (Indeed, many of Rumi's poems compel the reader to get up and turn around, such as "The man of God is a king beneath dervish-cloak; The man of God is a treasure in a ruin; The man of God is not of air and earth; The man of God is a boundless sea; The man of God rains pearls without a cloud; The man of God hath hundred moons and skies; The man of God hath hundred sun. The man of God is made wise by the Truth; The man of God is not learned from book"). Rumi (Mevlana) refused to see anyone and often whirled around an architectural pole in his garden. In his mourning, he experienced both annihilation and glorification, for, as the legend goes, "the angels removed the thin shell that remained over his heart. They removed the last bit of ego that remained within him and filled his heart with Love. As this was happening, Mevlana ... experienced the highest initiation he would know until his 'wedding day.' Re-entering the world, one day he came upon his dervish brother, the goldbeater, Salahu-d-Din Zer-Kub. As the hammers beat the gold into precious objects, 'Allah, Allah' became every sound he heard, and he began to whirl in ecstasy in the middle of the street. He unfolded his arms, like a fledgling bird, tilted his head back, and whirled, whirled, whirled to the sound of 'Allah' that came forth from the very wind he created by his movement" (Friedlander 56).

I see the waters which spring from their sources,
The branches of trees which dance like penitents,
The leaves which clap their hands like minstrels.

Mevlana instructed: "Dance where you can break yourself to pieces and totally abandon your worldly passions. Real men dance and whirl on the battlefield; they dance in their own blood. When they give themselves up, they clap their hands; when they leave behind the imperfections of the self, they dance" (qtd. in And 86). Thus began the Mevlevi order of Sufis known as the Whirling Dervishes.

The sema ceremony, as devised by Rumi's followers, allows the participant to perceive the mysteries of God, to open the eyes of the heart, through the heavens of divinity, represented as infinity and eternity, as found in the cosmos. The dancer's aim is to transcend awareness, to reach a higher plane of consciousness, "to be the work (or medium) of God manifesting itself through their bodies ... to discover love, feel the shudder of the encounter, take off the veils, and to be in the presence of God" (And 84). (The veils represent the pull of the lower soul, the *nafs*, and the shudder the finding of God, *wajd*.)

Dressed in the dervish costume, long black cloaks called *cübbe* (symbolic of the grave and/or the box of man's actions), high, conical-shaped felt hats, *sikke,* pulled over the ears, originally white but now of any color (the tombstone), soft, black slippers, and a long white robe, *tennure*, which bellows into the form of a bell as the dancer whirls (representing a shroud), Mevlevis dancers filed in the assembly hall (*semahane*) as the musicians took their places. The dance leader, *sheykh,* whose taller hat also carried a green turban, or *destar,* and who also wore a girdle (*eliflamet*), advanced to the center of the room, placed a red sheepskin (*postnisin* or *seyh*) in the middle of the floor. The red color represented (1) the color of the sky at sunset; (2) Mevlana's death; and (3) the color of union and ceremony.

Next, a prayer and chant was read by an older "turner," and the roll of the kettle drum represented "the roll-call after creation, when God first called every creature by its name, and it replied, 'Here am I,' and the last trump, when, once again, every being will be called, the dead standing up from out of their graves, to answer to the judgment" (Fremantle 331). The dervishes slapped the floor to represent the bridge Sirat, crossed to journey from this world to Paradise, a bridge supposedly as thin as a hair and as sharp as a razor.

The dervishes then circled the room three times in a counter-clockwise position, bowing each time near the sheepskin, looking between the eyebrows of the dervish opposite them, contemplating the divine within the Other. (The rotations represented mineral, vegetable, and animal life and/or the knowledge of God, seeing God, and the state of transcendence, the truth of Unity with God.) With one simultaneous movement, the dervishes threw off the black cloaks, symbolic of the resurrection, then one-by-one walked past the dance leader in file, stooping to kiss his hand or maybe bowing to the right and then the left of him. In turn the *skeykh* kissed the hat of each dervish as a signal to begin the dance. Arms crossed across the breast, right over left, with hands on opposite shoulders, each dervish walked simply into the dance space and began turning like "men moving into pleasantly warm water and beginning to swim" (Fremantle). As they turned, eyes closed or downcast, they slowly uncrossed the arms, lifting them slightly above shoulder height, the right palm turned upward to receive God's grace and wisdom, the left downward to share God's influence, His gifts, with the world. The head was inclined to the right (the highest point of the body), and the pivot was performed on the left foot (*direk*), "with the right foot crossing over the top of the left instep after the manner of a paddle to keep up the motion" (And 90). (The dervishes underwent an arduous "1001 days of penitence" in preparation for whirling, learning the ethics, codes of behavior, prayers, poetry, music, and dance of the Mevlevis Order. To learn the dance "step," whirlers practiced with nails on the ground, placing the big toe and second toe of the left foot between the nail and spinning around this pivot. These nails can still be seen in Konya, Turkey, where Rumi lived and worked and the location, prior to 1925, of hundreds of *teekes*, or Sufi monasteries.) The dancers repeated and remembered the name of God over and over as they whirled, a type of mantra known as a *dhikr*. In the background could be heard the "lulling melody of the reed flute, the sweeping harmonies of the zither, the steady beat of the small drums, and the hymns of the chanters" (Barber 330).

Some dervishes moved in the outer orbit, some in an inner orbit, "whirling round and moving onward" in a counter clockwise manner, turning "from the west of non-existence to the east of God's sole existence" (Fremantle 332) for a first period (the going forth of creation from the Unity) of approximately fifteen minutes. After resting on the sidelines for three minutes, upright with no swaying, bowing again to the *sheykh*, the dancers began the eight-minute second period (man's ascension to God by means of mystic exercise). Another rest followed, preceding the faster, jerkier tempo, eighteen-minute third period (annihilation in God: in dying you have freed yourselves from death; by annihilation you have found God again). Another rest, and during the fourth and final period (eternal order is restored; God himself is turning), no one is admitted to the inner orbit and the *shekyh* himself takes part in the sema. He represents the sun, the dervishes the planets rotating about him. (Note: After each period, when the music stopped, the dervishes also stopped, as if on a dime, bellowing skirts whipping about the legs.) The dancers returned to the side, in a seated position. To end the ceremony, a singer cited from the Koran, and cloaks were returned to the dancers (they have returned to their earthly tomb, yet in an altered state). Dervishes kissed the floor, rose and joined in sounding "Hu," the sound of all the names of God in one.

The processes of this ceremony were laden in symbolism: "The room in which the dance was performed symbolized the year, the leader himself the sun, the life-giver of the earth, and dancers turned around him like the planets and the moon. The whirling itself symbolized the celestial motions—as the earth turns on its axis as well as revolving round the sun, so the dervishes pivot on their feet while making a revolution of the hall, which was considered the hall of celestial sound. The four dances symbolized the four seasons born of the twelve months. They are represented, no doubt, by the twelve tonalities of music from which the four dances were born. The four dances were linked not only to the four seasons but to the four elements, and to the four ages of men" (And 93). (Some scholars speculate that individual dervishes turned to the ratio of the particular planet within the universe they may have represented. If so, this theory has not been passed on to those who turn today.) Additionally, the right half of the dance hall is the visible world, the left the invisible (world of the angels). One end represents divine nature, the other human nature. The right semi-circle symbolizes the descent from the divine nature to human nature, the left semi-circle, the ascent from human nature to the Divine.

The Sufi religion and belief system itself is believed to have evolved from Zoroastrian times ("Some Sufi holy places were venerated even before the advent of Islam; Islam just 'recycled' them into its own sanctuaries" [Arabov 346]). The likely derivation of the word *Sufi* is "one who wears wool," the term applied to those whose ascetic inclinations led them to wear coarse clothing (other scholars believe the term to have derived from the Greek term *sophos,* wisdom). The term eventually came to refer to a group differentiating themselves from other Muslims. Basically, Sufis strived to rise above the worldliness of established religion, and Islam's rise to power, rendering their entire life a prayer, an example of *how* to love, again, rising above religious directives (such as love one another). Sufis believed something larger and more profound dwelt within each individual, nurtured and released from within, where the "paint is mixed that colors the world." Generally, they have "looked upon themselves as those Muslims who take seriously God's call to perceive His presence both in the world and in the self. They stress inwardness over outwardness, contemplation over action, spiritual development over legalism, and cultivation of the soul over social interaction" (Chittick 19).

Your cure is within you, but you do not know,
Your illness is from you, but you do not see.
You are the "Clarifying Book"
Through whose letters becomes manifest the hidden.
You suppose that you're a small body
But the greatest world unfolds within you.
You would not need what is outside yourself
...if you would reflect upon self [Gnostic Ali ibn Abi Talib].

Founded in Konya, the Mevlevi Order of the Sufis established by Rumi eventually established branches in many of the major cities of the Ottoman Empire, each order with its own tekke. Above the doors of the tekke was written, "The raw ones come here to ripen." Raw men were those interested in the external nature of life; ripened men were those concerned with the internal spirit. Rumi said, "I was raw, then cooked, and now I am burnt!" Seven levels of authority manned the monastery, all important to the stages of initiation: the *sheikh* of the order himself; the *ahchi dede*, assistant sheikh; the *neyzenbashi*, in charge of the musicians; the *kudumzenbashi*, who lead the drum section; the *semazenbashi*, dance master; the *kazandji dede*, who maintained the tekke; and the *dandji dede*, secretary to the *sheikh*. Men of all ages participated in the whirling dance (those under eighteen required parental permission), the speed of their turns many times dependent on their age (whirling was considered a means of remaining balanced while moving, yet another wise metaphor for use in daily life). Married men always returned to their homes and family after the 1001 days of penitence, but single men lived within the tekke, supported by the government, meditating, teaching and providing service to the community.

Less frequently, women entered the Order as well, the great saint Rabia of Bashra noting on her pilgrimage to Mecca: "I see only bricks and a house of stone; what do they profit me? Tis Thou (God) that I want" (qtd. in Friedlander 23). They even served as *sheikhs*, the most famous Destine Hatun, daughter of Sultan Divani. (Legend says that when Destine held the post, the tekke at Afyon burned to the ground. Destin prayed to her father for help. He appeared in a dream and told her to go to the fountain where the dervishes gathered to find a silver vessel filled with water. He instructed her to pour the water out and reach within for gold coins, which would forever replace themselves within the vessel.)

By the early seventeenth century, Western travelers were writing accounts of the dervishes. An English author known as Miss Pardoe gave her account in 1836:

The number of those who were "on duty" was nine; seven of them being men and the remaining two, mere boys, the youngest certainly not more than ten years old.... So true and unerring were their motions that, although the space which they occupied was somewhat circumscribed, they never once gained upon each other and for five minutes they continued twirling round and round, as though impelled by machinery, their pale passionless countenances perfectly immobile, their heads slightly decline towards the right shoulder, and their inflated garments creating a cold, sharp air in the chapel from the rapidity of their action. At the termination of that period, the name of the Prophet occurred in the chant, which had been unintermitted in the gallery; and, as they simultaneously paused, and, folding their hands upon their breasts, bent down in reverence at the sound, their ample garments wound about them at the sudden check [qtd. in Friedlander 90].

From the middle of the seventeenth century until 1925, and the enactment of Atatürk's suppressive laws, the Grand Master of the Order played an important role in the enthronement of the Ottoman sultan, i.e., tying his belt, the Turkish equivalent of a coronation. The Mevlevis enjoyed wealth, a high social status, and political power in the Ottoman Empire, acquiring land and serving as the sultan's chief officers. They were well-educated, artistic, and bi-lingual in Arabic and Persian. They indeed fulfilled the roles noted in one of their axioms, "To be publicly with men, privately with God" (Fremantle 333). Turkey aligned with Germany during World War I, becoming a defeated nation, a "ruined and decrepit" Ottoman state. The sultan came under the control of the victorious Allies. Europeans held a dim view of the resistance from the Turks, a name traditionally applied to peasants, stereotyping them as "cruel and violent conquerors," "the Terrible Turk," or "the Sick Man of Europe." The Turkish people themselves were confused about their identity, for "they had been Ottomans, rulers of a vast empire that embraced the whole Near East, North Africa, and much of Europe. They were also Muslims, and their sultan headed all Islam as the caliph, successor of the Prophet. Now the empire was gone, the Arab territories lost" (Foss 11). One "peasant," Mustafa Kemal, or Atatürk as he came to be known, traveled to Asia Minor in 1919 and there formed a nationalist movement resistive to the Sultan, with headquarters in Ankara. He elicited the help of the Soviet Union, entered an agreement with France, and defeated the Greek forces which had advanced into Asia Minor.

The treaty of Lausanne (1923) recognized the independent Turkish Republic, whose leader was Atatürk. He "embarked on an astounding series of reforms that disestablished Islam, introduced Western laws, and increasingly obliged the Turks to act and think like Europeans" (Foss 11), even replacing the Arabic alphabet, introducing a compulsory Latin alphabet in 1929, the year he became "firmly in control of a one-party state, essentially a dictatorship" (Foss 11).

One such Western reform was the December 13, 1925 Law #677, "which prohibited and abolished the profession of tomb-keeping, the assigning of mystical names ... closing the *tekkes*, dervish lodges, *zavi-yes*, central dervish lodges, and tombs ... service to the title of dervish and the wearing of dervish costume prohibited ... those who give temporary places to the orders or people who are called by any of the mystical names mentioned, or those who serve them, will be sentenced to at least three months in prison and will be fined at least fifty Turkish liras" (Friedlander 677). On that day the military police entered the tekkes, ordering them closed. (Dervish life in Istanbul was pervasive at that time, and, alone, hosted more than 250 tekkes, as well as small centers for the gathering of brotherhoods.) As the dervishes wept at the tekke in Uskudar, Sheikh Ahmed Remzi Dede spoke of another such closing during the reign of Sultan Murad IV (1618–1640), "who feared the dervishes and their practices could turn against him with a great power. Those close to his ear whispered of the strange occupations of these madhoubs (God-intoxicated men) and warned the sultan of the danger their freedom held. All the tekkes were ordered closed and all dervish practices forbidden. The doors of the Mevlevi tekkes were bolted for eighteen years before their rusted hinges creaked the sema prelude. The tekkes were closed before and they opened. Perhaps the day will come when these doors will again open" (qtd. in Friedlander 111). On that cold December night in 1925, citizens throughout Turkey placed burning candles on the military police locks now barring entry to the tekkes.

As Sheikh Ahmed Remzi Dede prophesized, the door hinges did rust. Unfortunately, they have yet to creak open. In 1927, the tomb of Mevlana (Rumi) was opened as a museum. Tourists today can travel to the tomb, which lies behind a "silver-encrusted gate and beneath a deep arch that is smothered with green, red, and gold floral motifs and with selections from the Koran, themselves a calligraphic jungle of rippling serifs, shimmering golden whorls and arabesques. The mystic's coffin is shrouded in cloth of gold thread, with an enormous green turban to symbolize his religious authority, and surrounded by the lesser tombs of the sheiks and dervishes who led the Mevlevis until the early 20th century" (Bordewich 13). The museum also houses a hair from the beard of Mohammed, Korans lush with labyrinthine calligraphy, prayer rug collections, and even the dark blue and white pinstriped robes worn by Rumi himself. The tomb of Rumi's father and son are also encased in the mausoleum, all topped by black stone turbans encircling the white stone dervish hat atop each tomb.

Another organization outlawed by Atatürk was the freemasons. Due to pressure from the international freemasons, they were reinstated, and based upon this decision, the Mevlevis petitioned for and were allowed a small cer-

Top: Rumi's tomb in Konya, Turkey (courtesy Georges Jansoone). *Bottom:* Sema ceremony at Sirkeci Railway Station, Istanbul, Turkey, 2006 (courtesy Shioshvili).

emony in 1953. The former drum leader of a tekke in Istanbul at the time the monasteries were closed, Sadettin Heper, approached the mayor of Konya with this argument, also noting the dervishes could dance independent of religious organization. He noted, "If the *tekke* is closed, then you must become the *tekke*" (qtd. in Friedlander 112). The revival started small; held at a local cinema in Konya, only two dancers in street clothes dancing to the sound of the reed flute. By 1956, the ceremony was performed at the Konya library, drew large crowds, and was thereafter moved to a large auditorium. (Those who had been dervishes passed on their art, despite the fact police monitored whether they prayed as they turned in the public ceremonies.) The government began welcoming public, though not sacred, performances, benefitting the tourism industry. In 1973, the Turkish government authorized performances in London, Paris, and America to mark the 700th anniversary of the death of Mevlana.

An annual commemorative sema ceremony (*Sheb-I Arus*) is held in Konya each December 17, on Mevlana's "Wedding Day," or the day of his death and unity with God. The Mevlana annual festival itself begins on December 2, lasting sixteen days and attracting people of all nations, creeds, and colors. Each summer, the Mevlevis participate in the Istanbul International Festival, whirling in the Yildiz Gardens beneath the rococo palaces from which the Ottoman sultans ruled their Empire.

Yet the gates of the tekke remain closed. Perhaps in the 21st century, the Mevlevis' calling is to demonstrate to humans worldwide the importance of considering and nourishing each internal tekke (as noted by Sadettin Heper in 1953). Peaceful and tolerant Rumi, "never heard to utter one bitter reply," would understand (for the Sufi is one who accepts all things):

> I have seen that the two worlds are one.
> One I seek. One I know. One I see. One I call.

Likewise, he would recognize the phoenix-like return of the international Whirling Dervish:

> Every night flowers blossom in the sky,
> The universe is at peace, so am I.
> Then hundreds of sighs break out in my heart
> Where in cold darkness...
> ...flames rise with each sigh.

7

A Better Way of Life: The Ghost Dance of the Plains Indians

"Those who dance are thought mad by those who have not heard the music."—unknown

Costumed dancers seem to transcend life, swapping this world for another one. Such was the case for the Plains Indians who tried to recapture the freedom, pride, and happiness they lost upon the arrival of the Europeans. In 1890 these tribes donned special hand-painted shirts and dresses of leather and muslin to practice a religious ceremony known as the "Ghost Dance." They believed the dance and its costumes would bring back their old way of life. Among the Lakota, the shirts and dresses created for the dance were even believed to carry protective bullet-proof powers, for, according to the vision of one of their own, "if the high-priests would make for the dancers medicine-shirts and pray over them, no harm could come to the wearer, that the bullets of any whites that desired to stop the Messiah Dance would fall into the ground without doing any one harm, and the person firing such shots would drop dead" (Andersson 64).

Why did the Plains Indians, at this particular point in history, need bullet-proof clothing? Around 1850, forty years before the Ghost Dance became popular, the way of life they enjoyed for centuries came under attack as "settlers took their lands, miners desecrated their holy places, railroads and telegraph lines criss-crossed the countryside" (McCann 33). White settlers demanded more and more land and claimed the gold found in South Dakota's Black Hills as their own. "In 1889, the Sioux surrendered 11,000,000 acres, about half of the dwindling land they had left. But payments for the ceded lands did not arrive. Seed and rations promised never came ... chickens were stolen ... against express promises, beef rations were halved by Congress, two million pounds being withheld at Rosebud Agency, and one million at Pine Ridge" (Le Barre 231).

The natives' food stock and cultural emblem, the buffalo, reached extinction as the white man slaughtered this powerful and proud animal by the hundreds of thousands, obliterating a culture, for "the Plains Indians' entire life revolved around the buffalo. It was the focal point of his religion, his folk-myths, societies and economic life. His home, clothes, fuel, tools, weapons and medicines all came from the shaggy beast. Its disappearance brought want, hunger, confusion, and despair" (McCann 33). Non-indigenous cattle provided to the Lakota developed "black leg." Crops were a failure due to drought in 1889 and 1890, and epidemics of measles, influenza, and whooping cough decimated the population.

The U.S. military forced Native American adults onto reservations, taking young children from their parents, compelling them to attend boarding schools that demanded assimilation into white culture. Food rations on the reservations decreased to the point that many of the residents became ill from malnutrition. Involuntarily immersed into such an existence, the Plains Indians naturally believed if the white men left, their life would again be at peace. Therefore, "from the 1850s through the 1870s, the Lakota tried to get rid of the whites by war; in 1890 they tried ritual dancing and prayer" (DeMallie 392). As one famous Lakota chief, Red Cloud, related: "We felt that we were mocked in our misery.... There was no hope on earth, and God seemed to have forgotten us" (qtd. in DeMallie 393).

Into this climate of suffering entered a ray of hope, the ritualistic Ghost Dance, first taught by a prophet out of Nevada. The prophet, whose Indian name was Wovoka, the Cutter (known to the white ranchers for whom he worked as Jack Wilson), was born around 1858 near the Walker River in Mason Valley, Nevada, a full-blooded Pauite. His father before him, Tavivo, was also a prophet or "dreamer," a significant influence upon Wokova. According to anthropologist James Mooney, "The prophetic claims and teachings of the father, the reverence with which he was regarded by the people, and the mysterious ceremonies which were doubtless of frequent performance in the little tule wikiup at home must have made early and deep impressions on the mind of the boy, who seems to have been by nature of a solitary and contemplative disposition, one of those born to see visions and hear still voices" (Mooney 5).

When in his teens, Wokova's father died, and he began work at the ranch of David Wilson, who renamed him Jack Wilson, teaching him Christianity. Wokova later named his wife Mary, to honor Mary Wilson, the wife of David.

Upon marrying, Wokova apparently traveled through Washington, Oregon, and California, meeting Shaker missionaries and Mormons. Thus, by early adulthood, Wokova had been introduced to Pauite mysticism, the teachings of Jesus of Nazareth and Joseph Smith, and the Shaker movement.

Around 1887, Wokova began hearing "voices." On New Year's Day, 1889, he lay ill with fever on a day when the "sun died" (an eclipse of the sun). According to his account, on this day, he died and journeyed to heaven. He saw God "with all the people who had died long ago engaged in their oldtime sports and occupations, all happy and forever young" (Moses 338). During the journey, God told Wokova to "tell his people they must be good and love one another, have no quarreling, and live in peace with the whites; that they must work, and not lie or steal; that they must put away all the old practices that savored of war; that if they faithfully obeyed his instructions they would at last be reunited with their friends in this other world, where there would be no more death or sickness or old age" (Moses 338). Apparently, Wokova also received a dance to share with his people as well as command over the element of water (rain, mist, snow, etc.) during the visit to heaven.

Wokova's vision revealed that only Indians were to survive the great transformation to a new world, described as a sort of earthquake. While the white race was to be destroyed, no ill will or violence was to be directed toward Caucasians by the natives, especially any sort of fighting. Non-violence, truth, faith, and prayer were essential to the lifestyle of those who hoped for the return of the life enjoyed on the Plains before the encroachment of the white man. Supernatural powers would intercede during the spring to create the new world if all natives lived a clean life, just as nature recovers from winter. As Wokova began sharing his message amongst the Pauite, it spread like wildfire amongst the oppressed tribes, "southward to the Hualapais and eastward to the Bannocks, Shoshones, Arapahos, Crows, Cheyennes, Caddos, Pawnees, Kiowas, Comanches, and Sioux. To learn more about the doctrine, tribal delegates traveled westward to Mason Valley to sit at the Prophet's feet" (Moses 341). Though straightforward, the message changed from tribe to tribe, and "each explained it according to its own cultural tradition. The lack of a common language among the different tribes led to transformations and misrepresentations of the original message. Thus the earthquake was replaced by flooding among some tribes, and others wanted to give even the whites a place in the new world" (Andersson 28). For example, in the Lakota version, the landslide caused by the earthquake "was to be accompanied by a flood of water, which would flow in to the mouths of the white and cause them to choke with mud" (Mooney 30). And, for the Lakota, buckskin was to be used for costumes, no metal or knives could be carried, and silver could not be used in earrings or belts.

Similarly, the dance became known by different names amongst the tribes. As Mooney wrote:

In its original home among the Paiute it is called Nänigükwa, "dance in a circle" dance, to distinguish it from the other dances of the tribe, which have only the ordinary up-and-down step without the circular movement. The Shoshoni call it Tänä'räyün, which may be rendered "everybody dragging," in allusion to the manner in which the dancers move around the circle holding hands, as children do in their ring games.... The Comanche call it A'p-anêka'ra, "the Father's Dance," or sometimes the dance with joined hands. The Kiowa call it Mânposo'ti guan, "dance with clasped hands," and the frenzy, guan â'dalka-I, "dance craziness." The Caddo know it as Å'å kakí'mbawi'ut, "the prayer of all to the Father," or as the Nänisana ka au'—shan, "nänisana dance" from nänisana, "my children," which forms the burden of so many of the ghost songs in the language of the Arapaho, from whom they obtained the dance. By the Sioux, Arapaho, and most other prairie tribes, it is called the "spirit" or "ghost" dance (Sioux, Wana'ghi wa'chipi; Arapaho, Thigû'nawat), from the fact that everything connected with it relates to the coming of the spirits of the dead from the spirit world, and by this name it has become known among the whites [Mooney 35].

Wokova wrote "Messiah letters" to the tribal leaders upon their visits. Thus, tribal leaders returned to their people with instructions for the dance of hope, which came to be known, at least amongst the Lakota, as the Ghost Dance. One such letter was recovered by James Mooney from the Cheyenne, and reads:

When you get home you must make a dance to continue for five days. Dance four successive nights, and the last night keep up the dance until the morning of the fifth day, when all must bathe in the river and then disperse to their homes. You must all do in the same way. I, Jack Wilson, love you all, and my heart is full of gladness for the gifts you have brought me. When you get home, I shall give you a good cloud which will make you feel good. I give you a good spirit and give you all good paint. I want you to come again in three months, some from each tribe there in Indian territory. There will be a good deal of snow this year and some rain. In the fall there will be such a rain as I have never given you before. Grandfather says, when your friends die you must not cry. You must not fight. Do right always. It will give you satisfaction in life. Do not tell the white people about this. Jesus is now upon the earth. He appears like a cloud. The dead are all alive again. I do not know when they will be here; maybe this fall or in the spring. When the time comes there will be no more sickness and everyone will be young again. Do not refuse to work for the whites and do not make any trouble with them until you leave them. When the earth shakes, do not be afraid. It will not hurt you. I want you to dance every six weeks. Make a feast at the dance and have food that everybody may eat. Then bathe in the water. That is all. You will receive good words again from me some time. Do not tell lies [Moses 341].

Also, dancers, according to Wovoka, were to wear two sacred objects while dancing: first, a feather "which would transform into a wing that would lift the wearer up in the air when the earth was trembling" (Andersson 28), and second, dancers were to wear red paint given to delegates by Wokova (a bright-red ocher procured from the Paiute's sacred place, Mount Grant, ground and made into cakes), believed to ward off illnesses, contribute to long life, and assist in mental visions.

As instructed by Wovoka, the dance began with prayers and songs. Believers then danced for five successive nights to hasten the return of social order, health, and peace. Many of the songs spoke of hard times, such as this prayer by the Arapahos:

> *My Father, have pity on me!*
> *I have nothing to eat,*
> *I am dying of thirst–*
> *Everything is gone!*

Or this song by the Lakota:

> *Father, I come;*
> *Mother, I come;*
> *Brother, I come;*
> *Father, give us back our arrows.*

Amongst the Lakota, the "ghost stick" was waved over the participants' heads during the prayers, a stick of a peculiar shape wound in red cloth and red feathers, an antler or half-moon shape made from bone affixed to the top. Women held pipes skywards toward the sun and to the West, from which direction came the Messiah. Women also shot four arrows to the four directions, symbolizing the Lakota, Arapaho, Crow, and Cheyenne.

Most notable amongst the Lakota, "ghost shirts" were painted and worn during the dance, even sometimes under their clothing as they went about their daily routine. The shirts and dresses were covered with symbols of hope and renewal. Each individual who participated in the dance created their own shirt based upon messages received in personal visions or dreams. In many of these dreams, the dancers claimed to visit with their ancestors.

The symbols painted on the shirts or dresses did in fact represent other worlds. These included crescent moons, stars, multi-colored lines representing Earth's mountains, rainbows, and dragonflies. Sometimes, eagles and hawks with wings outstretched and lightning bolts zigzagging from their bodies were also included in the patterns. Multi-colored lines were usually painted at the bottom of the shirt to represent yesterday, the known life. The central area of the shirt denoted the present day and portrayed animals, people, or corn

... while the stars and crescent moon adorned the top of the jacket, symbolizing a new world — tomorrow.

The idea for the shirt may have come from the vision of Pretty Eagle, who while experiencing a vision heard someone say: "Look at this, make shirts in this way and give them to them. So when I looked there an eagle was flying off spreading his wings and on both sides there were stars. And a sun was attached to the back of the eagle. And it was flying off. And it said 'make four in this manner: two for men and two for women ... I woke up ... and, then, right there two young men and two young women came and they wanted to wear them.. And there I painted the shirts and the dresses: on the upper part of the back I painted an eagle; and then on both shoulders I painted stars; and on the chest I painted the moon" (qtd. in Andersson 70).

The men also wore leggings painted in red, some stripes painted up and down, others around. Women and men tied feathers into their hair, and men also wore stuffed birds or squirrel heads in their hair. Faces were painted in red with a black half-moon on the forehead or one cheek, circles, stars, crescents. Additionally, a line of yellow or red was painted where the hair parted.

To begin the Ghost Dance (which amongst the Lakota was held around a tree or pole decorated with feathers, the four retrieved arrows, a gaming hoop, stuffed animals, and strips of cloth), participants formed a circle of alternating men and women holding onto one another's shoulders or clasping hands (fingers intertwined) and singing, "lost in the world as the deep voices of the men and shrill notes of the women mingled in earnest harmony" (McCann 25). (Men and women dancing together was an innovation; in traditional Plains dance rituals, men and women danced in separate concentric circles.) In contrast to most other Native dances, drums and rattles were not used in the Ghost Dance, only singing. The Lakota opening song was:

> *The Father says so, The Father says so, The Father says so, The Father says so.*
> *You shall see your grandfather; You shall see your grandfather.*
> *The Father says so, The Father says so, The Father says so, The Father says so.*
> *You shall see your kindred, You shall see your kindred.*
> *The Father says so; the Father says so.*

Another, the form of the Lakota verb indicating a woman talking, was:

> *This is to be my work, all that grows upon the earth is mine.*
> *I love my children; I love my children.*
> *You shall grow to be a nation; You shall grow to be a nation.*
> *Give me my knife, Give me my knife.*
> *I shall hang up the meat to dry, says grandmother.*
> *When it is dry, I shall make pemmican, says grandmother.*

Of course, all of the prayers and songs used spoke to the Plains tribes' yearning for a better life.

The dance itself then began, with dancers first stepping slowly from right to left, hardly lifting the feet from the ground, following the course of the sun with faces turned upward, to form a needle's eye. (A needle's eye is shaped when a large line of dancers walk round and round and round to create a spiral of progressively smaller circles. Think of a sea shell.) They also cried out the names of their dead relatives, and threw dirt into their hair to signify their grief. As one Lakota, George Sword, described, once the circles were formed "they danced around in the circle in a continuous time until some of them became so tired and overtired they became crazy and finally drop as though dead.... When they 'die' they see strange things, they see their relatives who died long before ... they see an eagle come and carry them to where the messiah is with his ghosts" (Mooney 42). As described by a teacher on the Lakota Pine Ridge reservation, Mrs. Z.A. Parker, "They would go as fast as they could, their hands moving from side to side, their bodies swaying, their arms, with hands gripped tightly in their neighbors,' swinging back and forth with all their might.... The ground was worked and worn by many feet, until the fine, flour-like dust lay light and loose to the depth of two or three inches. The wind ... would sometimes take it up, enveloping the dancers and hiding them from view" (qtd. in Mooney 181).

As alluded to by Sword and Parker, the participants did indeed enter what seemed to be a trance, as they stepped, swayed, and waved. A young Lakota who participated in the dance related:

> Waking to the drab and wretched present, it was little wonder that they wailed as if their hearts would break in two with disillusionment. They danced without rest, on and on.... Occasionally someone thoroughly exhausted and dizzy fell unconscious into the center ... seeing their dear ones and a time of no sorrow, only joy, where relatives thronged out with happy laughter. The people went on and on and could not stop, day or night, hoping ... to get a vision.... And so I suppose the authorities did think they were crazy–but they weren't. They were only terribly unhappy [qtd. in DeMallie 399].

As an example, in Little Wound's vision "broad and fertile lands stretched in every direction, and were most pleasing to my eyes ... God called my friends to come up to where I was. They appeared, riding the finest horses I ever saw, dressed in superb and most brilliant garments, and seeming very happy. As they approached, I recognized the playmates of my childhood, and I ran forward to embrace them while the tears of joy ran down my cheeks" (qtd. in Andersson 63).

After the dance, those who entered a trance related their visions. Any members who wore blankets as they danced shook them "clean" to drive away

An example of a slanted depiction of the Ghost Dance of the "Sioux" (English for Lakota) Indians. The *London Illustrated News*, 1891 (Library of Congress).

any evil spirits that had settled within. All members also bathed in a creek, men in one area, women in the other, before returning to their tipi.

Sadly, the White Man (including government agents for the Bureau of Indian Affairs) did not understand the Ghost Dance. According to Mary Crow Dog, one of today's leading advocates for Native American causes, "The Ghost Dance was a religion of love, but the whites misunderstood it, looking upon it as the signal for a great Indian uprising which their bad consciences told them was sure to come."

The Lakota began dancing in earnest in August of 1889, possibly due to the dire drought of the summer and the reduction of rations mentioned previously. Even those who did not participate in the dance began seeking guidance from their chiefs and medicine men, rather than Indian agents, and "even Lakota nonbelievers accepted the religious motivation of the ghost dance" (qtd. in Andersson 47). On October 27, 1890, Major General Nelson A. Miles visited Pine Ridge Reservation in an attempt to convince Ghost dancers to give up the new religion. Little Wound, who saw the vision of the impenetrable ghost shirts, told the general that the Lakota were going to stop living like white men and would dance as they pleased. Even though the principles of the Ghost Dance were extremely Christian in nature, Wokova had asked his followers to farm and receive a Christian education, and only 4,216 Lakota were dancing within a population of 15,329, white agents and settlers began pleading for protection, despite the fact that "there is no indication that the Lakota ghost dancers were hostile toward the whites when the ceremonies were first started on the Lakota reservations. The Lakota ghost dancers became hostile, or warlike, only when the whites tried to interfere in their religious ceremonies" (Andersson 76).

The agent who began asking for military protection was Daniel F. Royer of the Pine Ridge Reservation. On October 30, 1890, he complained that "half or even as many as two-thirds of the reservation Indian population supported the ghost dance and were thus beyond control ... they are tearing down more in a day then the government can build up in a month ... defying the law, threatening the police, taking children out of schools, and harboring wanted criminals" (qtd. in Andersson 109). And, on November 2, at Rosebud, Agent Reynolds followed suit, writing, "The ghost dance is religious excitement aggravated by almost starvation ... the Indians say better to die fighting than to die a slow death of starvation" (qtd. in Andersson 110). As the result of the Lakota killing diseased cattle, Royer again overreacted, sending a memo to Acting Commissioner of Indian Affairs, R.V. Belt: "Indians are dancing in the snow and are wild and crazy. I have fully informed you that employees and government property at this agency have no protection and are at the mercy of these dancers. Why delay further by investigation, we need protection and we need it now" (qtd. in Andersson 111). James McLaughlin, an agent at Standing Rock Reservation, described the Ghost Dance as an "absurd craze — demoralizing, indecent, disgusting."

Newspapers also contributed to the unjustified panic, and "throughout the fall and early winter of 1890, newspaper accounts from the Dakotas sustained the prevalent image of the Indian as erstwhile predator. For all the years the Sioux had huddled around the agency — lulled into submission by rations and gimcracks— they were now portrayed as demonic killers. Mythical stories about treacherous Sioux, joined by other 'hostiles' in a rand Indian conspiracy, overshadowed the actual story of Wovoka and his religion of peace and love" (Moses 342). Similarly, on September 26, 1890, the *Washington Post* and the *Chicago Tribune* reported "stories of disturbing behavior among 5,000 Indians, although neither paper specified who these Indians were. They obtained the information from an officer of the 7th Calvary, who claimed that the biggest Indian uprising ever was ahead; the Indians were expecting a medicine man who would destroy the whites. This had already led to 'incantations and religious orgies.' The officer demanded that the number of soldiers be doubled in all garrisons in the West" (Andersson 197).

Of course, missionaries contributed to the volatile atmosphere: "For them, every Christian Indian who became a ghost dancer indicated that their efforts in pushing the Lakotas toward Christianity were insufficient" (Andersson 181). *The Word Carrier,* a Protestant missionary paper, argued that "all of their heathen dances should be prevented as far and as fast as possible until utterly eradicated, because they are potentially dangerous. We ought not to touch them as religious ceremonials, but, as breeders of riot and rebellion, we must" (DeMallie 396). However, one missionary, Thomas L. Riggs, wrote, "The fact is that not one Indian in a hundred of our western Sioux had any thought of making war upon the whites, of having an 'outbreak' and cutting up generally" (qtd. in Andersson 191). Indeed, Riggs believed the natives were excited about their new messiah, and it was only the arrival of the U.S. Army (noted below) that forced any hostility.

President Benjamin Harrison reacted to these descriptions from agents and settlers by considering the dance a hostile act in defiance of United States authorities, ordering the War Department, on November 13, to take whatever steps necessary to "suppress possible outbreaks resulting from the Indians' belief in the coming of the Indian messiah and the return of dead Indian warriors for crusade upon the whites" (Andersson 133). Between October and December

The earliest likeness of Sitting Bull is this *Harper's Weekly* sketch from 1877.

of 1890, three thousand troops were moved onto the Lakota reservations and land, just to stop ghost dancing!

When the famous chief, Sitting Bull, heard of the troops, he moved some five hundred lodges to a camp on the fringe of the reservation. Two other chiefs, Short Bull and Kicking Bear, led dancers to the Badlands in the northern part of Pine Ridge Reservation, a natural fortress known as the Stronghold. Eventually, dancers from Rosebud and the Cheyenne River gathered at the Stronghold, comprising nearly 3,000 people. Both groups continued their dancing, "growing very intense; the people were planning to dance all winter" (Andersson 82). Sitting Bull was planning to join dancers at the Stronghold, but on December 15, 1890, the Indian police, sent by Agent James McLaughlin, surrounded his cabin for purposes of arrest.

McLaughlin described Sitting Bull as "a man of low cunning, devoid of a single manly principle in his nature or an honorable trait of character" (Johnson 47). As Sitting Bull was led from his cabin, the crowd surrounding the cabin became angry, shouting at the agents and Indian police. A friend came around the corner of the house with a rifle in his hand. The friend fired, the bullet hit Indian police Lt. Bull Head, who, as he was

Chief Big Foot (Spotted Elk), shot and frozen at Wounded Knee, South Dakota, 1890.

falling, shot Sitting Bull. At the same time, Sgt. Red Tomahawk, another Indian, shot Sitting Bull in the head, fulfilling a message Sitting Bull had received a week before: He would be killed by his own people. Some of Sitting Bull's Ghost dancers, under the leadership of Kicking Bear, returned peacefully to the reservation, while others fled to the Stronghold.

On December 24, surrounded and fearing for his people, Big Foot sent messengers to Pine Ridge Agency to inform them the dancers were coming in peacefully. An agent was taken to Big Foot, who said, "We have come to this reservation to avoid trouble and I will take the main road to the agency to join the peaceable people there" (Andersson 90). The weather was cold and the Lakota were starving. During a blizzard that night, many saw a strange light in the sky, believed to be Sitting Bull's spirit. Many of the dancers were wearing their Ghost Dance shirts on the return trip.

As Big Foot's delegation continued on their trek back to the reservation, on the night of December 28, five hundred soldiers arrived, surrounding Big Foot's camp with Hotchkiss guns pointed directly at the dancers. On the morning of December 29, 1890, as the soldiers were disarming the Sioux warriors, medicine man Yellow Bird "started to sing and threw dust into the air. He was wearing a ghost shirt, praying to the Great Spirit and singing about the power of the shirt ... causing restlessness among the soldiers. However, throwing dust in the air was part of the ghost dance ceremony, a sign for the Lakotas to show grief and pity" (Andersson 92). One deaf man raised his gun above his head, not understanding the directive of the soldiers. According to some accounts, the gun accidentally discharged when the soldiers grabbed him. However, Native survivors describe "an officer giving orders, which the Indians could not understand, in a very loud voice. His commands were followed by a sound like a 'lightining crash' when the first volley was fired.... After the first shot, the army responded by opening fire on the Indians. The women and children were caught in the middle of the firing. Big Foot was immediately shot and died instantly" (Andersson 93).

What happened next is one of our country's darkest hours. On this cold morning during the Christmas holidays, almost three hundred men, women and children were murdered by the U.S. Calvary. In the late evening, forty-nine wounded women and children were carried into the Holy Cross Episcopal Church on Pine Ridge Reservation. Ironically, they rested that night under Christmas greenery "looking down in irony and compassion" on the death that claimed most of the patients. Episcopal Bishop W.H. Hare observed the "bleeding, groaning, wounded people underneath the Christmas greenery," saying, 'To one of my moods, they seemed a mockery to all my faith and hope; to another they seemed an inspiration still singing, through in a minor key, 'Peace, good will to men'" (qtd. in Rice 71).

Following what became known as the Wounded Knee Massacre, the cause of the Ghost Dance, suppressed "as part of the historical process of religious persecution led by Indian agents and missionaries against the Lakotas" (DeMallie 54), seemed hopeless. The Plains Indians did not perform the Ghost Dance for many years following this tragedy. In fact, all Native American rituals and ceremonies were outlawed by the U.S. government after the massacre. Fortunately, several small pockets of Native peoples did preserve the tradition of the Dance, including a short revival in 1900 by the Cheyenne chief Porcupine. Around the same time, an Assiniboin native named Fred Robinson taught the dance to a small community of Sioux in Saskatchewan. During his youth, Robinson learned the dance from Kicking Bear (remember: this chief had joined others at the Stronghold). In the 1950s, the Shoshone integrated the dance into their "Father Dance" or dance of Thanksgiving.

One of the most well-known revivals occurred in 1973. Led by the American Indian Movement, a civil rights association containing members from various tribes, Native Americans occupied the Wounded Knee memorial site and demanded the right to practice their religion, including the Ghost Dance. The leader, Leonard Crow Dog, said at the time of the occupation: "Everybody's heard about the Ghost Dance but nobody's seen it. The United States prohibited it. There was to be no Ghost Dance, no Indian religion. But the hoop has not been broken. So decide tonight—for the whole unborn generations. If you want to dance with me tomorrow, you be ready." Once more, the Native Americans were surrounded by U.S. troops for many months.

But this particular incident, which became known as Wounded Knee II, brought positive change. Laws exist today which allow Native Americans to practice the Ghost Dance freely. The most recent gathering occurred in August 2005, when Sioux leader Ed Charging Elk held a public Ghost Dance, reviving the ceremony after years of research and study. He asked non-natives to lend their support, saying, "We need to unite and we need to focus on generations now and generations to come for a better way of life."

Tribal leaders did in fact gather on the steps of our nation's capital on the 500th anniversary of Columbus' landing in America, many proudly donning ghost dance shirts. Their arms swayed like the wind as they danced. Animals and plants, stars and moons, lightning bolts and eagles were painted on their shirts. One hundred years after the Ghost Dances were first performed by their ancestors, these natives of America's Plains were once again dancing for a better way of life.

Standing on the capital steps, high above the crowd, these leaders asked all peoples, all races, to once again practice Wokova's lessons:

> *We stand young warriors*
> *In the circle*
> *At dawn all storm clouds disappear*
> *The future brings all hope and glory*
> *Ghost dancers rise*
> *Five hundred years.*

8

"The Only People Can Shout Is Right Here": The Unbroken Chain of the Ring-Shout Dance

"Never forget the bridge that carries you over..."— Saying of the Gullah people of Georgia's Sea Islands

In the West African tradition, music, singing, dance, and rhythm are the elements necessary for a connection between man and a higher power, and, indeed, an experience with it (spirit possession). They are the physical, artistic avenues which make appeal to supernatural forces for the purpose of shaping events, even contributing to a type of power known in Western society as "miracles." According to African scholar Ivan Karp, "A different view of power is exhibited in African societies than in Western social science. The stress in Africa is not on the element of control but on the more dynamic aspect of energy and the capacity to use it ... African ideas of power ... have to do with engaging power and creating or at least containing the world" (Karp qtd. in Taves 217). Thus, West African societies danced and sang to engage or transform power, or dynamic energy, to "know the Spirit through the body, a dissociative religious experience linking matter and spirit, natural and supernatural" (Taves 222).

This belief system most assuredly compares to a traditional dance known as the ring-shout, the oldest African American performance tradition surviving on the North American continent (despite hundreds of years of suppression). The term "shout" derives from the Afro-Arabic *saut*, pronounced "shout," meaning a fervent dance around the Kabaa in Mecca (Rosenbaum 3), obviously a dance based in religion. (In America, the dance is also known as Rock Daniel, Flower Dance, and the Rope Dance.) The dance has survived intact in North America in only one remote location — the Sea Islands of the state of Georgia — preserving the link between African Americans and their West African ancestors.

Before the institution of slavery disturbed cultural practices (prior to 1500), West Africans connected with their god, Elegba, by means of circle dancing, for circling bodies constituted a type of prayer asking for the spiritual and moral development of individual performers and community members. Further, "the goal for any worship service in African religions is to make a bridge to the sacred, and dance is essential in making contact with the divine" (Washington 18). The West African circle dances held common characteristics:

- Barefoot dancing.
- Shuffling.
- Bent knees and waist.
- Individual improvisation.
- Extensive hip movements.
- Dancing with the whole body, hands and feet included.
- Focus on rhythm, both a downbeat (boom, boom, boom) and a syncopated, "off" beat (boom, boom, boo-boom — boom, boom, boo-boom), rather than melody, encouraging group activity.
- Call-and-response singing, a "dancing-singing phenomenon" in which the song is repeated "sometimes more than an hour, steadily increasing in intensity and gradually accelerating, until a sort of hypnosis ensues" (Lomax).
- A counterclockwise moving circle or ring.

Several indicators confirm the West African connection with the ring-shout of the Americas, as has existed since the days of slavery and into the modern-era in Georgia. First, the "call-and-response singing, the poly-rhythms of the stick and hands and feet, the swaying and hitching shuffle of the shouters, all derive from African forms. The fusion of dance, song, and rhythm in fervid religious possession is an African practice, and it is not surprising that the ring-shout flourished in coastal areas where there are many other documented examples of African, including Afro-Arabic, survivals" (Rosenbaum 4). Second, the bent-knee posture in African dance (as well as art) "signaled the presence of supple life energies" remaining a prevalent dance posture in today's ring-shout dancers. Third, a modern description of Kalahari bushmen dance reveals the correlation: "the ceremonial dance is a religious act, but, although very serious ... is not piously solemn or constrained and it provides occasion for pleasure and aesthetic satisfaction ... the men dance with knees bent and bodies carried with little motion, leaning forward. The steps are very precise. They are minute in size, advancing only two or three inches, but they are strongly stamped, and ten or twenty dancers stamping together produces a loud thud" (Rosenbaum 18–9). This parallels "the movements of the shout as practiced today in McIntosh County (Georgia), especially the small steps and incremental forward motion as well as the leaning stance" (Rosenbaum 19). Fourth, a description of African dance aesthetics from 1673 further establishes the link between African dance and today's ring-shout: "They take the greatest delight in dancing ... if they have the least feeling for religion, it is in the observation of the dance that they must show it ... with their bodies leaning forward, stamp on the ground vigorously with their feet, lustily chanting in unison ... and with a fixed expression of their faces" (Rosenbaum 18). Fifth, in Africa, dances which moved in a counterclockwise position honored the dead and were many times performed around graves to confirm that "life is a shared process with the dead below the river or the sea" (Rosenbaum 20). This practice was known as "marking the point" and caused the power of their god to descend upon the spot. Georgia's ring-shout dancers still "clearly regard the shout as a way of honoring god and of evoking at the very least thoughts of departed ancestors and are thus not far removed from significances deeply embedded in their practices, meanings linking them with African tradition and belief" (Rosenbaum 21). Sixth, anthropologists and visitors from West Africa have noted ties to the African continent. In the early twentieth century, anthropologist Zora Neale Hurston stated, "Shouting is nothing more than a continuation of the African 'possession' by the gods and is still prevalent in most Negro protestant churches and is universal in Sanctified churches" (qtd. in Rosenbaum 45). And, in the early '90s, at the Newport Folk Festival, a group of Ashangi Dancers from West Africa noted that "in their culture, there was a particular name for the rhythm of the Johns Island shout. They were excited by the thought that this rhythm had been brought to the United States and had survived in a contemporary form" (Rosenbaum 49).

Unfortunately, in the 1500s, the African slave trade interrupted centuries-old cultural dance traditions. Millions of Africans were transported by ship to the Americas, Caribbean, and parts of Europe. On the plantations, the ring-shout tradition served as a type of saving grace. It gave a community of people oppressed by slavery, brought together by force, and carried to a foreign land, the hope necessary for survival. Indeed, escape may "be the purpose of all movement among African Americans, starting in slavery times" (Twining 471). Survival in this instance included a chance to hold onto their African culture, beliefs, language, and rituals, for the ring-shout "was the main context in which Africans recognized values common to them — the values of ancestor worship and contact, communication and teaching through storytelling and trickster expressions, and of various other symbolic devices"

The Old Plantation circa 1790, attributed to John Rose (1752–1820). The original is found in the Rockefeller Museum, Williamsburg, Virginia.

(Floyd 50). Additionally, scholar Sterling Stuckey believes the slave ring-shout was "above all, devoted to the ancestral spirits, to reciprocity between the living and the dead" (Rosenbaum 21).

In America, the ring-shout flourished due to the "large slave population, the strong African-derived culture, and the success of the missionary movement in suppressing secular music and dancing ... making the ring shout a widely practiced if not totally accepted form of expression by the time of the Civil War" (Rosenbaum 27). The dance included groups of "players."

- Dancers, who held the honored title of "shouters," danced in a circle, always moving in a counterclockwise direction. They bent their waists and elbows in order to sway the hips or jerk their torsos, shuffled their feet in a double bounce (a "rapid shuffling two-step, the back foot closing up to but never passing the leading foot: step (R), close (L); step (R), close (L)" [Bess qtd. in Rosenbaum 11]), performed various heel stamps according to their own choosing and used their arms to pantomime the meaning or feeling found in the song lyrics. At the end of each song verse, the dancers stopped short, put the trailing foot forward and continued their shuffle as the next verse began. According to Parrish, "The feet are not supposed to leave the floor or to cross each other, such an act being sinful. The shouting proceeds with a curious shuffling, but controlled step which taps out with the heel a res-

onant syncopation fascinating in its intricacy and precision" (qtd. in Rosenbaum 125).
- "Stickers," who initiated the dance, beating broom-handles against the earth or a cabin floor in a rhythmical pattern known as habanera (today identified as the "hambone" or "Bo Diddley" beat).
- "Songsters," the lead singer or singers.
- "Basers," who, in a call-and-response fashion, answered the lead singer's lyrics and set-up syncopated, or "off" beat rhythms by clapping their hands and stomping their feet.

Two rules pervaded the dance: Shouting was only performed to spirituals, and the feet could not be crossed, for "if you cross your feet you were turned out of the church because you were doing something for the devil" (Rosenbaum 2). (As slaves were introduced to Biblical accounts, they made an effort to find scripture to justify their religious activities, such as Psalm 47:1, which speaks to clapping of hands and shouting to God, and Proverbs 4:26, reading: "Keep straight the path of your feet, and all your ways will be sure.") Spirit possession, or communion with God, continued to be the primary focus: "Every part of their bodies danced, from their shuffling feet and bent knees to their churning hips and undulating spines, swinging arms, and shimmying shoulders. Even their necks bent like reeds to balance heads rolling from shoulder to shoulder before pulling upright to reveal faces filled with the joy and the ecstasy of dance" (Washington 65).

The songs accompanying the dance told the story of trials associated with slavery. Lyrics for one such song, "Kneebone Bend," tell the story:

SONGSTER: Kneebone, what's the matter?
BASERS: Oh, Lord, Kneebone
SONGSTER: Kneebone, what's the matter?
BASERS: Oh, Lord, kneebone bend.
SONGSTER: Kneebone in the wil'erness
BASERS: Oh, Lord, Kneebone
SONGSTER: Kneebone in the wil'erness
BASERS: Oh, Lord, kneebone bend.

Lawrence McKiver, a modern-day songster extraordinaire, explains how this song was a prayer of hope for Africans arriving in the Americas:

That's the oldest slave song that ever was sung by black people when they first come over from Africa.... They was going to a place they ... didn't know nothing about, understand? So they would sing "kneebone in the wilderness, kneebone in the valley," they was praying at the time, that's why they say "kneebone bend," they was bending down, they was praying" [qtd. in Rosenbaum 18].

While slaves from Louisiana, Texas, the Carolinas, Georgia, and the

Bahamas tried to continue the performance of the ring-shout dance in the West African tradition, and initially were allowed to gather in groups, slave owners, unjust laws, clergyman, and bigotry soon stood in their way. Hazzard-Gordon wrote, "It is evident that while attitudes toward and regulation of plantation dance varied widely across time and region, dance was very often perceived as a significant threat. In some states, legislation banning dance and drumming was enacted as dances came to be seen as likely sites for plotting insurrections, or even the occasions for the insurrections themselves" (Hazzard-Gordon 62). Many slave owners and their overseers barred any type of dance. Even liberal slave owners followed this lead in 1740, after slaves rebelled at the Stono Rebellion of 1739 in South Carolina. Laws were passed prohibiting slaves from "keeping drums, horns or other loud instruments which might call together or give sign or notice to one another." As Washington states, "The law prohibiting the use of drums was passed in order to place restrictions on the way enslaved Africans worshipped. As a result, the use of the body to replace the drum — hand clapping, body percussion, and foot stomping — became the closest medium that allowed enslaved Africans to achieve rhythmic drive" (Washington 65). Another slave uprising in Haiti in 1793 caused many owners to move Haitian slaves to Louisiana, where owners persuaded the Louisiana legislature to pass laws limiting slave gatherings to certain times (Sunday only) and to areas guarded by overseers.

Initially, slave owners had forbidden Africans to convert to Christianity. This mandate gradually changed, and during the Great Awakening of 1740 and the resulting revivals of the eighteenth and nineteenth century, slaves were forced to display a public loyalty to the Christian religion of their masters. Of course, white European religious ceremonies did not include dancing, and hymns were sung in a hushed, formal manner, with an emphasis on melody rather than a call-and-response style. One account from 1850 by Fredrika Bremer explains the ring-shout dancers' dilemma: "I observed them dancing the 'holy dance' for one of the converted. The dancing ... being forbidden by the preachers, ceased immediately on our entering the tent" (qtd. in Rosenbaum 26).

Not to be brow-beaten, the African American slaves persevered! They incorporated the ring-shout tradition into their new Christian devotion. As Zora Neale Hurston wrote, "The shout is still prevalent in most Negro protestant churches and is universal in the Sanctified [African American holiness and Pentecostal] churches. They protest against the more highbrow churches' efforts to stop it" (qtd. in Taves 219). Albert J. Raboteau has described this fusion: "While North American slaves danced under the impulse of the Spirit of a 'new' god, they danced in ways their fathers in Africa would have recognized. The 'holy dance' of the shout may well have been a two-way bridge connecting the core of West African religions— possession by the Gods— to the core of evangelical Protestantism — experience of conversion" (Raboteau qtd. in Rosenbaum 22). Ethnomusicologist Portia K. Maultsby says, "Slaves, in general, adopted those concepts and practices of Christianity which could be identified with West African religious beliefs and customs" (qtd. in Washington 28).

They also wrote Christian hymns for use during ring-shouts, in keeping with the West African tradition in which songs were used to reaffirm a belief in the presence of God. The slaves used the songs not only as a meaningful spiritual practice, but as a means of coping with daily life, the physical and psychological trauma of enslavement. Many of the songs compared the Biblical account of the slavery of Moses' people with the enslavement of Africans in the Americas. An example is:

> LEADER: *Moses, Moses, lay your rod*
> LEADER AND BASES: *In that Red Sea*
> LEADER: *Lay your rod, let the children cross*
> LEADER AND BASES: *In that Red Sea*
> CHORUS: *Ol' Pharoah's hos' got los,' los,' los,'*
> *Ol' Pharaoh's hos' got los,'*
> *In that Red Sea*
> *They shout when the hos' got los,' los,' los'*
> *They shout when the hos' got los.'*
> *In that Red Sea*

While carrying Biblical messages, the hymns also held hidden messages mocking or satirizing the hypocrisy of slavery.

> LEADER: *Shout my children, 'cause 'yo free!*
> BASES: *My God brought you liberty*
> LEADER: *Call me a Sunday Christian*
> BASES: *Call me a Monday devil*
> LEADER: *Don't care what you call me*
> BASES: *So long Jesus love me.*

In the face of this oppression, shouters met in clandestine, or hidden, locations, usually cabins in the woods, with the threat of danger hanging over their heads. To insure safety, they reverted to a West African custom: They placed a tub or pot full of water in the middle of the dance floor. The slaves believed sound would travel into the water or tub rather than out into the open air toward their masters' quarters. They also pushed the chairs and benches against the walls of the cabin, serving to absorb even more sound. These hidden meetings continued until the Civil War period. Even after slaves were freed by the Northern army, bigoted mindsets continued. Laura Towne

The Negro Dance, Trinidad, 1836, by artist Richard Bridgens (1785–1846). This color lithograph is a good representation of circle dancing (Library of Congress).

described an 1862 ring-shout: "They call it a religious ceremony, but it seems more like a regular frolic to me, and instead of attending to the shout, the better persons go to the 'Praise House.'"

Ministers also attempted to quell incidences of the ring-shout, even African American pastors. In 1860, one South Carolina Episcopal minister described the dance as "Heathenish! Quite heathenish!... Did you ever see such a shout?" Daniel Alexander Payne, an influential bishop and the first black college president in America, wrote, "After the sermon they formed a ring, and with coats off, sung, clapped their hands and stamped their feet in a most ridiculous and heathenish way. I requested the pastor to go and stop their dancing. At his request they stopped their dancing and clapping of hands, but remained singing and rocking their bodies to and fro. This they did for about fifteen minutes. I then went, and taking their leader by the arm requested him to desist and to sit down and sing in a rational manner. I told him also that it was a heathenish way to worship and disgraceful to themselves, the race, and the Christian name" (qtd. in Taves 218). African American poet James Weldon Johnson, discounted the ring-shout as well, saying, "The more educated ministers and members, as fast as they were able to brave the primitive element in the churches, placed a ban on the ring shout" (Johnson qtd. in Rosenbaum 41).

A marvelous account of the ring-shout as practiced on the Georgia Sea Islands in 1862, which carries a striking similarity to that still practiced today (by the McIntosh Shouters), resulted from the Northern army's attention on the "Port Royal" experiment, in which Northern forces overcame the Southern defenses on the island, local whites fled, and the Northern occupiers set on a course of "instructing," and learning from, the freed slaves. It reads:

> From a neighboring campfire comes one of those concerts half powwow, half prayer meeting.... These fires are often enclosed in a sort of little booth made neatly of palm leaves covered in at the top, a native African hut in short; this at times is crammed with men singing at the top of their voices— often the John Brown song was sung, but oftener these incomprehensible negro Methodist, meaningless, monotonous, endless chants with obscure syllables recurring constantly & slight variations interwoven, all accompanied with a regular drumming of the feet & clapping of the hands, like castinets; then the excitement spreads, outside the enclosure men begin to quiver and dance, others join, a circle forms, winding monotonously round someone in the centre. Some heel & toe tumultuously, others merely tremble and stagger on, others stoop & rise, others whirl, others caper sidewise all keep steadily circling like dervishes, outsiders applaud especial strokes of skill, my approach only enlivens the scene, the circle enlarges, louder grows the singing about Jesus & heaven, & the ceaseless drumming & clapping go steadily on. At last seems to come a snap and the spell breaks amid general sighs & laughter. And this not rarely but night after night" [Rosenbaum 28].

As scholar Sterling Stuckey wrote, "By the late nineteenth century it was too late for African religion — and therefore for African culture — to be contained or reversed because its advocates were practically the entire black population in America. The essential features of the ring shout were present in one form or another, and hardly a state in the Union was without its practitioners following slavery. Moreover, the shout continued to be the principal context in which creativity occurred" (Stuckey qtd. in Rosenbaum 17).

The next culprit that threatened the continuation of the ring-shout tradition was acculturation, or the blending of a folk life into the mainstream culture. African Americans were free to live and work as they pleased after the Civil War. The promise of "life, liberty and the pursuit of happiness," not to mention paying jobs, persuaded droves of former slaves to move away from their plantation communities. For better or worse, a change of lifestyle always involves the loss of old values. The ring-shout, which had sustained whole communities of African Americans during the period of slavery, began to evolve into other dance forms, such as tap and jazz. By the 1920s, the shout was in danger of dying out, and, in fact was non-existent in the Carolina Sea Islands by the late 1950s.

Nevertheless, the miracle which saved the ring-shout was a close-knit African American community off the coast of Georgia. The Sea Islands, located "along the coasts of South Carolina and Georgia, extending almost four hundred miles from the southern border of North Carolina to the northern border of Florida" (Twining 1), are separated from the continent. Throughout the twentieth century, access to some portions of the islands still required the use of a boat, particularly Sapelo and St. Simons. Communication with the inhabitants of the islands was not easy. "New" ways of living did not overrun the islands' citizens, allowing the traditional shouters to retain their West African culture and their church-sanctioned social dances. (The members of the McIntosh community on St. Simons Island believed the dance was not only a means to serve God, but also a way to honor ancestors who endured the rigors of slavery.) Plus, the members "very seldom leave from the community.... They maintain homes and families here in the community. They have a sense of home. They don't stray very far away" (Ector qtd. in Rosenbaum 70). Finally, because slaves were allowed to purchase land after the Civil War, the area is economically viable, strong church and family ties sustain the young, and "call-and-response is a ... powerful force for forging group and community cohesiveness while reaffirming the authority of the leader" (Rosenbaum 71), a perfect, isolated, and bonded vehicle of cultural preservation developed on the islands. An indication of the degree of cultural introspection which occurred on the island may be found in modern-day dancer Carletha Sullivan's statement: "I always thought it was something that everyone did. New Year's and Christmas Eve. Until they started going out, and people were just amazed, they had never seen anything like it, and I said, my God, I thought, you know, seriously, I thought it was something everyone did" (qtd. in Rosenbaum 83). Indeed, the tradition became "a unique viable religious tradition in an African American community that continually and specifically references continuity with Africa, slavery, and Emancipation as elements interlocked with worship and oneness with the Spirit" (Rosenbaum 84).

In fact, "in the Sea Islands, dance and rhythmic movement are part of the daily life of the people; it is an expression of life and an important activity, not saved for special times, but flowing out of every possible occasion" (Twining 464). At churches, in family yards, at the gymnasium, and in "praise houses," dance "is a rich expression of the life force and its impetus toward survival" (Twining 477). One of the songs from Johns Island is "You Got to Move," which says, "You may be rich, you may be poor, but when the Lord get ready, you got to move" (Twining 465). "It is a foregone conclusion ... that if you can breathe you can dance" (Twining 477).

In 1942, folklorist Lydia Parrish visited McIntosh County, collected shout songs and published them in a book called *Slave Songs of the Georgia Sea Islands.* She also organized a group called the Georgia Sea Island Singers in

order to preserve and carry on the shout songs by way of public performance, and "she may, in fact, have been partially responsible for its continuance on these Islands after it had fallen out of regular usage elsewhere" (Twining 12). This particular group "moved around counterclockwise while accompanied by a strong syncopated beat, furnished by the late John Davis's feet and his brother Peter's cane held upside down. The resultant beat is exactly the same as one found in a Malian song of the Bambara-Djula speakers called 'Lassa.'" (Twining 12). Today, this group performs worldwide.

Christian Church amidst the oaks, McIntosh County, Georgia — saving the ring-shout for perpetuity (author's photograph).

Wearing costumes their slave ancestors may have worn (the women typically wear matching white and green checked long dresses with long sleeves and matching bonnets or African–style print dresses and head rags; the men wear overalls and straw hats or caps), the McIntosh Shouters, a dance group led by Lawrence McKiver (considered Patriarch of the Shouters), started performing the ring-shout at folk festivals across the country (Rosenbaum 77) in 1980. The group, considered a lifeline between Africa and America, has performed at the Smithsonian Institute and Library of Congress in Washington, D.C., the World Music Institute in New York City, and Emory University in Atlanta. The members have also been featured in *Southern Living* magazine, CNN, HBO, and Oxygen TV. They have recorded a collection of ring-shout songs with Folkways Music (sponsored by the Smithsonian) and assisted in the publication of a book examining the ring-shout.

As mentioned, scholars such as Parrish trace the performance style of the McIntosh Shouters and Sea Island Singers to Africans who stepped off slave ships in Virginia in 1722. As one shouter, Catherine Campbell, states, "The only people can shout is right here! Calvary (Mount Calvary Baptist Church) was the stopping place of the shout because we kept the tradition going. We never did let it go by!" As if by a miracle, the ring-shout has outlasted the darkness of slavery, oppression, bigotry, and indifference. As a result of human perseverance and communion with God by way of artistic expression, the dance remains a living part of American folk life and a shining remnant of West African culture. As Deacon James Cook stated in the early twentieth century, "We are still holding to that yesterday tradition that was taught by our fathers and mothers ... they brought it from our homeland in Africa. They knowed how to shout, they loved to shout — that was one of the ways they gave thanks to God ... someday we'll be shouting the harvest home" (Cook qtd. in Rosenbaum 52).

9

Visca Sardana! The Astronomical Dance of Catalonia

"Visca el poble nostre, Catalunya, las sardana, el germanor; tot ple-
gat!"
Long live our people, Catalonia, the sardana, brotherhood; all
together!— Catalian chant

Heads-up mathematicians and astronomers: A dance based in science does exist in the Catalonia region of Spain and is "the national dance, in which rich and poor, old and young, men and women, participate in one unbroken circle" (Brandes 31). The Catalans perfected and adopted the artistic expression the *sardana* as a symbol of their culture, a dance which follows the rhythm and cadence of the sun and a "communal dance with an almost mystical effect, with trancelike overtones of a ceremony of worship, as in the performance of a rite" (Matteo 222). Indeed, in 1930 scholar Joan Armades speculated on the "ancient astronomical meaning of the dance, posing a hypothesis about the possible relationship between it and prehistoric paint-ings (cave paintings of Cogul in western Catalonia) in which representations of dance can be observed" (Perez 42).

Upon a musical introduction and the drumtap of a tambori, moving in circles (*rodonas*) hand in hand, *sardana* dancers (alternating man, woman) progress to the left (*ampurdanesa*), then to the right (*selvata*), first to the east, next to the west, imitating a compass. They perform eight short, moderate-paced steps called *curts* (a two-measured pattern of point-step-step-cross). These short steps represent (1) the moon and stars; (2) the number of hours we are in the dark each day; and (3) the slow, mellow nature of nighttime. A section (*tirade*) of curts can be 20–50 measures long.

An instrument known as a *floviol* (reed) imitates a cock's crow, symbol-izing the joyful arrival of yet another day. Picking up the pace, the dancers perform sixteen long, running steps called *llargs* (a four-measured pattern of the point-step). Dancers count sixteen llargs to symbolize (1) the sun; (2) the number of daylight hours; and (3) the fast-paced, extended nature of the daytime. A llargs tirade may constitute 50–100 measures. (Before beginning, a sardana dancer must count the measures of the music played for the dance, usually in 2/4 or 6/8 time, converting them to curts and llargs in order to keep in step with all other dancers in the circle and finish on the exact same beat. The typical metronome beat of the music is 112.) Also, dancers alternate lifting their arms during the llargs and lowering them during the curts, similar to sunrise and sunset. A run of curts and llargs is called a *tirtage* (a typical run being 25×79, or 25 curts and 79 llargs), and a typical pattern is: curts, curts, llargs, llargs, curts, curts, llargs, llargs, a 2-measure break called a contra-punt, llargs, contrapunt, llargs.

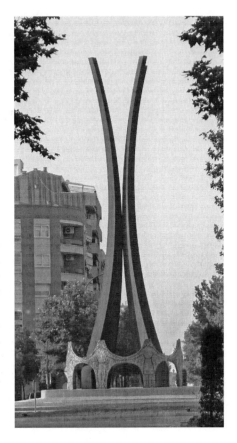

Monument to the sardana, Reus, Catalonia (photograph by Ramon Ferran).

Obviously, the rules of the dance focus on counting, and "in fact, anyone who talks to sardana dancers or reads the sardana scholarship can only come away impressed by the consistent emphasis on quantification. The complexity of the dance and the need for extensive instruction in fact derive from the complicated counting system" (Brandes 33).

While the origins of the sardana are elusive, theories include an Ampurdanese folk belief in the Sartos, or a nomadic Asian race who carried a similar dance to Greece. Conclusively, unearthed Greek vases do depict a dance similar to the sardana, and a dance performed in modern-day Greece, the *kolo*, entails both sexes joining hands, forming circles within circles. Others have related the sardana to a dance of the Iberian culture, the *contrapás llarg*, and documented circular dances known as *ball redon* or *rodó* existed in the 13th century. Finally, Catalan texts from the 16th century mention the cerdanes, serdanas, cardanes and numerous other alternatives (Brandes 28), proving that "the precursors of the modern sardana, which were themselves localized folk dances, existed and evolved over the course of centuries" (Brandes 28). In fact, before industrialization in the mid–19th century, "numerous variants of the dance, generally associated with religious festivals, flourished in the Alt and Baix Empordá, la Selva, el Gironès, and other north Catalonian districts. As Prat i Carós has said, in this period the sardana 'had no special significance and was but one of many dances that could be found in Catalonia'" (qtd. in Brandes 29).

The form and style of the modern day dance, as well as its musical accompaniment, was created (and for the most part fixed) during the twenty-year period between 1840 and 1860, "when the sardana was established as 'dance of the Catalans,' although Catalonia was at that time home to numerous other local dances as well" (Brandes 29). Two men "formulated reforms and gave the sardana the musical and choreographic characteristics which continue to this day" (Dru 231). The dance choreographer was Miquel Pardàs (1818–72), who published in 1850 his *Method for Learning to Dance Long Sardanas*, also opening the first sardana dance school. Pardàs worked in close collaboration with composer Pep Ventura (1818–75), also known as Josep Maria Ventura i Casas. Discerning a nationalist movement was eminent (discussed below), both artists realized the sardana could evolve into a popular national dance spotlighting the culture of the region. (The dance became extremely popular as a result. Even Queen Isabel II noticed. In 1860, a sardana dance was held to honor this monarch.) Due to their collaborative work, in the modern sardana the music and steps are inextricably linked. In fact, the music for the dance is known as "sardana" as well.

The music which accompanies the dance, by reason of Ventura's work, is a twelve piece ensemble known as a *cobla*, the term derived from the Latin *copola*, meaning group or union. Musicologist Delfi Colome notes, "In fact, this word, used to refer to an indeterminate number of musicians, is older than the sardana itself, and was used by the fourteenth century minstrels who played *flabiol, tambori* (the two most ancient instruments used by the cobla), *cornamusa* and *tarot*" (Colome 36). Catalan folk instrument musicians have the honor of sitting in the front row. One plays the *floviol* with his left hand as he drums the *tambori* with his right. A floviol is a pastoral flute made of ebony or wood with five finger-holes and four keys, while a *tamboril* is a small drum hung from the left arm, about four inches high, and three-and-a-half inches in diameter, played with a single drumstick made of ebony. (This musician also introduces the different periods of the music.) The Catalans say, "He who plays the tamborino has not lost the *floviol*" (Sinclair 175). Two musicians play the tibles (a high-pitched oboe-type instrument) and two play

A sardana cobla, 2008. Front row: the *flabiol/tambori*; *tibles* (2); *tenores* (2); back row: trumpets (2); flugelhorns (2); and a double-bass viol.

tenores (a type of English horn which sounds "as much like wood as metal, peculiar, yet agreeable, and very melodious") (Sinclair 176). Composer Garreta said of the tenora, "There is only one instrument in the world which can produce a cry of joy or of pain, in a human voice, and that is the tenora" (Colome 36). On the back row of the orchestra sit two trumpets, one trombone, two flugelhorns, and a double-bass viol, known as a *verra*. Catalonian culture expert Joan Llongueras says, "The tenora suggest melancholy, the tibla, irony, the horns and trombone, severity, the flabiol and the tambori, a joyful stimulation, the trumpets, exultation, and the rhythm of the double bass, continuity ... the resulting harmonious arrangement mirroring the facets of our idiosyncrasy" (Colome 38).

Due to the artistic genius of these two visionaries, *cobla* bands began playing in Barcelona, "corresponding with the period during which Catalan nationalistic consciousness was growing quickly" (Perez 40). Politically active groups founded sardana associations and encouraged "each and every village in Catalonia to have a song association, a library or a sardanes association, and, when possible, all three" (Perez 42). The associations sponsored performances, arranged lessons, and publicized the dance. Dancers became persons who not only enjoyed the dance, but also adopted a social/political movement (Weltanschauung), evolving into *Sardanistas*, those who "believe strongly in what the dance means—music in the service of an idea" (Perez 44).

The dance serves as the national symbol of Catalonia because it is identified with core Catalan values: *harmonia* (harmony); *germanor* (brotherhood); and *democracia* (democracy). In fact, as Josep Miracle explained, the sardana is "living democracy ... the realization of that program which has pervaded the universe with the eighteenth-century triology: Liberty, Equality, Fraternity ... the impact of the sardana is not formed by a portion of the populace but rather by the totality: the people. The people with all their social classes (estaments), with all their differences, in all their forms. The sardana in Catalonia is everybody's, just as the sun that gives us light each day is everybody's" (qtd. in Brandes 30). Similarly, Matorell and Valls believe the sardana to be "almost a rite; the sardana should not be observed, it should be danced, and it should be danced in a spontaneously-formed circle, uniting without distinctions of age or class the female and male dancers" (qtd. in Brandes 31).

Each sardana circle is uniform, and individualization or virtuosity is not encouraged, as "hands should be held at just certain height, feet extended precisely a given distance, the final beat timed by all the dancers as if guided by the same clock ... imposing a mutual interdependence.... Each dancer measures the performance as much by the uniformity of the circle as by his or her observance of the multitudinous, detailed rules by which a dancer's qualities must be evaluated ... implying mutual trust, the confidence that each person's performance will redound to everyone's enjoyment" (Brandes 31–2). Poet Josep Maria Lópex Pico's captures the essence of these strictures:

> Numbered dance, your measure
> is open guarantee of cordiality
> You protect us all, but remain pure
> Because you know the limits of liberty [qtd. Brandes 32].

Another indication of the sense of solidarity and mutual interdependence conveyed by the dance is the practice of placing personal belongings, such as purses, coats, etc., in the center of the circle, protected from abduction. This worldview is summed up in Manuel Capdevila's "Hundred Recommendations."

> He who dances off beat
> Disturbs his companions.
> The circle, neither a little

Nor a lot, should move from its spot.
As much here as in Girona
The dance should be round [Brandes 32].

To explain the Catalan requirement for solidarity, brotherhood, equality, and insular interdependence, consider the history of the region: "In the last 2,000 years, Northern Catalonia has had some dozen changes of rulers, and each occupying power has, in its own way, sought to impose cultural as well as other controls" (McPhee 426). Beginning with the reign of Louis XIV, whose administrators remarked that "it is necessary to extinguish the Catalan spirit" (McPhee 420), France sought to impose its administrative structure and language on Northern Catalonia. "In 1682 knowledge of French became a prerequisite to practicing a liberal profession. After 1700 all public acts had to be written in French, and in 1738 this was extended to cover registers of births, deaths, and marriages kept by priests" (McPhee 403). Despite this *francization* the Catalans retained their language, at the cost of remaining illiterate within the French–based economy. Batlle, a Catalan activist (1848), noted, "The worker is intelligent but little instructed. A very small number understands French, and not one speaks it easily and correctly. Hardly 10% know how to read and write among the men, the women not at all" (qtd. in McPhee 413). The Catalans clung to their culture as well, for a traveler in 1830 wrote: "What he loves above everything is independence and a show of prodigality; he is lively, irascible, and the friend of soft indolence.... He loves dancing passionately; he indulges in it to excess. This movement is truly national in the region, and usually has for its theatre the public places" (McPhee 417).

Yet another "determined re-engineering of the Catalans" occurred in 1925 when Spanish dictator General Miguel Primo de Rivera dissolved the Mancomunitat, a nationalist party. Rivera would "amongst other absurdities, ban the *Sardana*, the painfully earnest ... Catalan group folk dance" (Tremlett 320).

Nonetheless, "none of this prevented the Catalans from prospering economically over the next few centuries. They exported wool and paper. In the nineteenth century the cotton trade was smaller only than that of England, France, and the United States. Barcelona embraced the industrial revolution long before most of the rest of Spain" (Tremlett 313). The protection of this economic viability also elicited the development of a Catalan sense of national identity, and the features of the sardana naturally contributed to an emergence of nationalist tendencies, for "precise measurement of time and money is, after all, a necessary if insufficient condition for the kind of rapid economic expansion that Catalonia achieved in the mid–19th century" (Brandes 33). Further, a "democratic society, open to all those who were willing to learn in order to achieve, is only part of the picture. Also of critical importance, and embodied in the dance (as in so many other aspects of Catalan expressive culture), is the willingness and ability of individuals to cooperate and coordinate efforts toward common goals" (Brandes 39).

Unfortunately, "this impetus given to the sardana was not without cost" (Perez 42). In 1934, a revolt known as the "October Revolution" ensued. Basically, the Catalans upheld a law which allowed winegrowers to buy, rather than lease, their land. The leader of the Catalans, Lluis Companys, declared the independence of the State of Catalonia within the Federal Republic of Spain. The Spanish quickly quelled the revolt, but "reforms were in ruins, the Socialists in prison, regionalist dreams smothered, and a government whose strings were being pulled by fascists and bolstered by the army" led to a political downturn and a resulting civil war between the federalists republic, in power at that time, and fascists supported nationalists, supported in large part by Italy's Mussolini and Germany's Hitler.

Despite their initial declaration, the Catalans remained essentially Republicans during the war (1936–39), though loyal to neither side, resulting in the assassination of over 2,000 priests by the Republicans, 30,000 regional prisoners-of-war, and one million deaths throughout Spain. Due largely in part to the success of the military commander, Francisco Franco, and the financing from Italy and Germany, the fascist left prevailed. By the end of the war, Catalonia was a "traumatized society ... shipwrecked in the abyss of a revolution whose only aim was to scorn and destroy it." (Dowling 19). Indeed, upon Franco's announcement of the end of the war and the beginning of his dictatorship (April 1, 1939), he formed a national council (a political junta) and the *Falange,* whose task was to "establish an economic regime over-riding the interests of individual groups or classes ... to multiply wealth in the service of the state of social justice" (Adams 263). To Franco, any feelings of national pride were considered "insolent, arrogant and a personal affront," therefore the "historic regions were stripped of their autonomy, and a comprehensive and oppressive policy of cultural homogeneity aimed at erasing the distinct linguistic heritage of many regions was implemented. State repression of regional, nationalist cultures was especially intense in Catalonia and the Basque country, where it permeated everyday life" (Encarnacion 64). Straight away, Franco banned the Catalan language, commenting: "Si eres espanol, habla espanol." (Translation: "If you are Spanish, speak Spanish.") The ban was enforced in schools, government offices, and other public places, while parents were prohibited from giving their children Catalan or Basque names. Nationalist symbols, such as flags, were also disallowed (Encarnacion 64).

Franco also targeted the sardana. He felt the dance prompted Catalonians to feel superior to the rest of Spain, exempt from his dictatorial rules.

Described by Franco as "an accursed differentiating agent" one edict "cited the tendency of the sardana to foment false feelings of pride and superiority among the Catalans, justifying the dance's prohibition" (Brandes 34). Visitors to Catalonia during Franco's rule had to cross the border into France to witness the dance, for in Barcelona "the Spanish air was thick with repression" (Lubliner 2).

By the late 1950s, Franco's government "softened," yielding to political pressure from surrounding democratic-based European nations. Coblas and sardana dancers were allowed to return to Catalonia's urban centers, re-emerging with a vengeance and celebrating, circa 1959, a "Day of Sardana.... On this day many diverse activities, all dedicated to the *sardana*, take place throughout Catalonia and one locality is selected to be awarded for their preservation of the dance" (Perez 43). When Franco died in 1975, "the deepening of democracy proceeded at full speed and in spite of the struggle for regional self-rule and even separation from the central state" (Encarnacion 62). Regional home rule was nevertheless reestablished, and Catalonia formed the Democratic Convergence of Catalonia party, which invested "its political capital on attaining ever-escalating degrees of autonomy" (Encarnacion 70).

In twenty-first century Catalonia, monuments honoring the dance are spread throughout the region. Paintings by the great artists Picasso and Dali (who both grew up in Catalonia) depicting the sardana are worth millions and some are housed in the Picasso Museum. The Fundacio Universal de la Sardana promotes the dance on an international level. (A different foreign city is selected each year to help the Catalans honor their national dance.) Also, the government sponsors two official cobla orchestras, and over seventy private coblas are spread throughout the region. Free sardana lessons are offered to children between the ages of six and fourteen, forty-eight sardana dance schools open in the City of Barcelona alone. Finally, more than three hundred sardana societies are spread throughout cities and towns all over the province, and "competent sardana counters, who often with little more than an elementary education, can perform modular arithmetic in their heads in seconds, are national treasures" (Lubliner 6).

Today, on most Sundays in Barcelona, either in front of the cathedral or in the Placa Sant Jaume outside the principal Catalan government building, the dance enlivens a crowd celebrating a brand new week. Sardana dancers regularly cry out "Vicsa!" or "Long-Life" on the final beat of the last dance, for the people of Catalonia "hold firm and without concessions, true to our tradition and to our ancestors ... that robust and candid people who during centuries have known how to endure without capitulation to every kind of invasion, preserving intact their most precious treasure: LA SARDANA" (Albert I Rivas qtd. in Brandes 28).

10

Capoeiristas: Righteous Avengers

"Vamos jogar a capoeira, la na terra de Zumbi.
(Let's go to a capoeira game, in the land of Zumbi)."—from a capoeira
song

Ask any citizen of the South American country of Brazil about a dance-fight game known as *capoeira* (pronounced *ca-prer-a*). The Brazilian would explain: Capoeira is not about fighting. It's about survival ... being smarter and more cunning than the next guy ... sometimes facing the situation, other times running. And, as in real life, always exuding confidence, understanding your enemies and knowing how to win ... and lose.

Such is capoeira: a combination of dance, music, singing, and martial arts born in São Salvador in the state of Bahia, Brazil (and also developed in Recife and Rio de Janeiro). The derivation of the term "capoeira" is intriguing to say the least, relating to the history and origin of the dance. In Brazilian Portuguese, the term may refer to:

• Second-growth brushland, from the Tupi caà (vegetation, forest) and puera (that which has disappeared).
• A partridge-like bird native to Brazil whose habitat is scrubland, the male of the species aggressively resisting any intrusions into its territory.
• The kicking of fighting cocks.
• A large stick basket used to transport chickens.
• The transport of chickens in the large stick baskets.
• An old name for defensive military bulwarks made of interwoven sticks.

Those who attempt to define the dance are running in circles, for, as Lima writes: "Now, to tell you what capoeira is, is really crazy. The people who ask me what capoeira is, right, what is capoeira? It's really crazy, it's the same thing as telling you what is a kiss, what is love. It's a thing you have to be inside to understand" (qtd. in Willson 20). Lima continues: "In reality, capoeira is not a fight, it is a play of a fight, you have to be dancing" (qtd. in Willson 22). It is the ability "to sense with the body, to be able to enter the rhythm of music, of sentiment, to completely lose self-consciousness ... the essence cannot be learned, but is felt. And this feeling comes from the experience of one's self and one's ancestors: from poverty and struggle, from love, joy, and despair" (Willson 23). Nonetheless, when an encyclopedic definition is required, perhaps a definition from the business world will assist: "An acrobatic dance with Afro-Brazilian roots involving fluid movements combined with ritual, musical rhythm and fighting style. Capoeira goes beyond traditional dance as it blends a loose choreography with martial-art-inspired maneuvers, in an interactive game with sequenced movements.... Once prohibited for slaves who disguised their fighting practice as dance, and subsequently banned until the 1930s, it has now become a national sport in Brazil and is fast spreading throughout the world" (Young & Schlie 200).

As the dance begins, two dancers initiate a "game," or *jogo*. Just as capoeira is three-dimensional (a dance-fight-game), so is the jogo. The first side is athleticism: endurance, speed, and action (reflex). The second is a concept known as *malicia,* an intrinsic cunning about the game of life, or "knowing the emotions and traits—aggressiveness, fear, pride, vanity, cockiness, etc.—which exist within all human beings ... recognizing these traits when they appear in another player, and therefore being able to anticipate the other player's movements" (Capoeira 33). Thus, malicia is an elusive concept, belonging to the feminine, for "its power is also of the sort that you don't know exactly what it is. Its power is not to be clear about power itself. It's the power of the void, because malicia is exactly that: to go around what is clear and established. And in that sense it is Feminine" (Capoeira 30). Muniz Sodre also believes malicia is "not only to feign, to pretend that you are going to deliver a blow and do something else, but a system of signs and signals. It is as if you were casting a spell or a charm in order to build a specific reality, a seductive reality, during the game ... and in day-to-day life and in any type of struggle or combat" (qtd. in Capoeira 32). The application of malicia is known as *malandragem,* a "fluid dance of tactics, movements that threaten without ever actually hurting the opposite partner, almost like playing a series of chess moves solely in the minds of the players, without ever making a first real move" (Young & Schlie 201). Finally, the third level is beyond understanding: the mystery, deceitfulness, and joy of life, all combined, a "microcosmos, an imitation of the jungle that we call life, a magic theatre where the interaction between different energies (that happen and then happen again in different contexts with the same basic pattern) is staged and reproduced" ("Roots" Capoeira 15). Within this realm are those who can "cure, curse, or do harm or good for and to others ... *mandingeiros*" (Willson 28). As Mestre Paulo dos Anjos said, "When I truly understand capoeira angola, I will be playing with God, meaning that the depth of capoeira angola, particularly those aspects beyond the physical moves, take longer to learn than the natural lifetime of any single person" (Willson 34).

A *roda*, or circle of singers and instrumentalists, surround the dancers, imitating the world in which we all "play." Within the roda exist three certainties (1) the sensual taste for life and the joy of living (found in the music, singing, and clapping); (2) the bright and dark nature of humanity; and (3) an individual's desire to overrule social laws, moral rules, and conventions. There also exist three spiritual entities from the African *candomblé* religion which represent humanity's (1) aggressiveness—*Ogum*; (2) cunning—*Oxóssi*; and (3) strength/energy/influence—*Pombagira* ("Roots, 45–61). Thus, "when capoeiristas form a circle, they are creating their own world. The roda is closed, and all the energy produced inside it is contained therein, serving to

Women playing berimbau, tambourine, and pandiero (photograph by bk ninja).

benefit all members of the roda. This energy is separate from that outside the roda, and consequently it is vital to keep the circle unbroken ... it is a living and breathing thing. It has a spirit of its own and those within comprise ... organs and body parts" (Essien 10). As noted by Willson, "As a part of this metaphor, the concept of play is paramount; it reflects a control over one's emotions, has religious overtones, and is considered to encompass every part of a player's being" (Willson 12). Within the roda, the dancer finds "a retreat, an insight into what is inside of you, of all your strength, with all that you have ... a part of each person begins to be liberated, a part begins to express itself" (Augusto qtd. in Willson 23).

The music for the roda is vital; it is what the circle feeds from, and "the music of capoeira is what makes it capoeira: without the music, it's just movements" (Essien 11). The soul of the *bateria* (band) is the berimbau, consisting of a hollowed-out gourd to which a wooden bow and metal string is attached. The player holds a stone, coin, or metal washer as a type of slide and plucks the string with a wooden stick. In the plucking hand, a small shaker made of woven straw enriches and adds texture to the sound, either a *gunga* (bass), *de centro* (rhythm guitar) or *viola* (lead guitar) tone. The gunga berimbau is first played by the dance master. But all who participate in the roda must set the pace of the dance by eventually playing the berimbau and also the *pandeiros* (tambourine), *atabaque* (drum), *agogó* (cowbell), and a *recoreco* (a ridged, washboard-like instrument).

The capoeira dancer also learns the call-and-response songs (referred to interchangeably as chants, *ladainhas* or *chulas*) associated with the dance, which tell either the history of the dance, a bit of wisdom, or a story. They are considered "the pure thing within you ... the connection between the capoeirista and the spiritual world of capoeira, where you manage to make a connection between yourself and all those great *mestres* who died and left all kinds of things for us" (Lima qtd. in Willson 30).

Again, three types of chants teach "a code of conduct and the basic premises of a philosophical world view" (Capoeira 46): *Ladainha,* sung by a soloist prior to the start of the game; *Quadras,* four-verse songs, "called" by the soloist and answered by the chorus; and the *Corridos,* one-or-two verse songs, again delivered in the call-response fashion. Many of the chants mention candomblé entities (candomblé honors the cosmic energy of the universe, humanity, and life itself). One traditional chant teaches:

> *You enter heaven on your merits;*
> *Here on Earth what you own is all that counts.*
> *Fare you well or fare you poorly,*
> *All on this Earth is but farewell, comrade.*

Another tells the story of a spiritual encounter, alluding to the diametrical nature of life itself:

> *There I was at the foot of the cross,*
> *Saying my prayer,*
> *When Dois-de-ouro* (famous capoeirista) *arrived*
> *Like the figure of the Dog* (nickname for the devil).

Hence, philosophies are taught, rodas are formed, music and singing determine the energy and the rhythm, and the dance-game begins. One "player" within the roda "calls" an opponent with facial gestures that signal ... come walk with me, come dance with me, come challenge me, as we play, side by side. The dancers then begin their dance stunts, all the while anticipating their partner's next move, which might be a fake attack (kicks, sweeps, head strikes, hand-springs, head spins, or flips) or a defensive move (ducks, rolls, back flips, cartwheels).

These moves "will last from a matter of seconds to as long as twenty minutes [between very fit and experienced players]" (Willson 21). They may be slow, sneaky, and close to the ground (the Angola, or traditional, style) or fast and energetic with high jumps, acrobatics, and spinning kicks (the regional, or modern, style). No wonder capoeira scholar Kia Bunseki Fu-Kiau believes the word "capoeira" derived from the word "kipura," a term used to describe a rooster's movements in a fight, meaning to flutter, flit from place to place, struggle, fight, or flog.

The three basic movements in capoeira are: (1) the *ginga,* the standing swing from which the players (capoeiristas) feign, hide, dodge, or attack, remaining in constant motion; (2) the *negative* and *role* (pronounced ho-lay), the basic movement on the floor in which the player touches only the hands, feet, or head to the ground (never the knees or back), either on all fours like a cat, or one hand, like a monkey, a basically improvised motion which is "part of the web of unexpected movements that dazzle the opponent ... and from which one can quickly recover from a fall or even an attack, or take down his opponent from the floor" (Capoeira 65); and (3) the *alí* (pronounced ah-ooo), or a cartwheel, an upside-down movement of unpredictability which enlarges the spectrum of movement itself, and which helps the player to understand that "capoeira, and life, are not simply a matter of winning and losing; and that if life has many battles and struggles, you also need to learn how to dance, be poetic, have fun, be unpredictable (not always rational and objective), and be slightly crazy and chaotic, if you are to savor the best of life and capoeira" (Capoeira 69). Or, to explain further, "creative chaos is integral to the parties' interaction, and their gradual process of learning and acquiring skill. Each interaction between parties is unique and inspired by improvisation, leading to different sequences of movements with each repetition" (Young & Schlie 200).

Utilizing these three basic patterns of movement, the dancer improvises with regard to (1) defensive movements; (2) sequences; (3) takedowns; and (4) other kicks. An example of each includes:

Defensive: The *cocorinha*— The dancer crouches like a crow, bottom to floor. One hand protects the head while the other touches the ground slightly. A slight hop takes the dancer out of the opponent's range and closer to his legs for a possible takedown.

Painting by English traveling artist Augustus Earle (1793–1838), *Negros Fighting Using Capoeira Steps,* circa 1825.

Sequence: A famous maestre (teacher), Bimba, created eight sequences which help players exercise the dance-game. In one such sequence, the dancers ginga, #1 kicks with the right foot (*meia lua de frente*) while #2 retreats to the cocorinha, followed by #1's kick with the left foot (*meia lua de frente*), #2's cocorinha, #1's spin kick (*armada*), #2's negativa with the left leg stretched, a cartwheel or aú from #1, and a feigned head-butt from #2.

Takedown: The *rasteira* — "falling" downward and sideways while one leg extends to pull the support leg of the opponent, knocking him or her backwards to the floor.

Other Kicks: The *cruzado* — crossing the right leg behind the left followed by a sideways kick with the left leg, coming to rest with wide-spread legs.

As a result of the body's ability to turn, twist, dodge, swing, kick, and spin, "a central part of the play is an intense interaction that keeps both players entirely aware of the movements of each other. Although all play is conducted through recognized moves, specifics of these moves vary between styles of play. The combinations of these moves and the connections between them (the connections becoming moves themselves) are so numerous that the variation of each game is almost infinite" (Willson 21).

Indeed, many inhabitants of the birthplace of capoeira, Brazil, have experienced the poverty and struggle, love, joy, and despair eminent within the game of life, and necessary to the origination of the dance, certainly having "walked through the valley of the shadow of death," to quote another spiritual teacher. Such "shadow of death" was the African slave trade, or the "Great Tragedy," *Ma'afa*. Beginning in the mid–1500s, and continuing up through and until the mid–1800s, the Portuguese exported nearly four million Africans to Brazil for the purpose of slave labor. While it is certain that African slaves developed capoeira based on cultural traditions brought from Africa and eventually integrated on Brazilian soil, several theories exist as to the origin.

First, some consider the "Bantu" Africans from Angola to be the creators of capoeira. When these Africans saw any opportunity to flee slavery, they took to the Brazilian forests, forming independent communities called "quilombos." These communities were always under attack; the slave owners fought for the return of their "free" labor. Yet, for at least sixty-seven years, these communities (one of which, Palmares, grew to be 20,000 strong) staved off their oppressors and retained their freedom. They are believed to have developed a guerilla warfare fighting technique similar to capoeira. (The legendary teacher of these warriors was a leader named Zumbi, born inside a quilombo in 1655. Though he was later captured and beheaded, he is now considered a national hero, a symbol of freedom.)

One description of such tactics can be found in the 1824 description by the German artist Rugendas: "The Negroes have yet another war-like past-time, which is much more violent—capoeira: two champions throw themselves at each other, trying to strike their heads at the chest of the adversary whom they are trying to knock over. The attack is avoided with leaps to the side and with stationary maneuvers which are equally as skillful" (qtd. in Capoeira 7).

Another theory posits capoeira was actually born when slaves from Salvador, Recife, and Rio de Janiero added music, singing, dance moves, and rituals from African culture to their fighting techniques. But, as this theory entails, it was much more than a dance; it was also a method of survival. If outsiders or spies thought the slaves were only performing a dance, they would not implicate those who were in reality involved in personal combat training. Curt Sachs, in the 1834 book *World History of Dance*, describes witnessing the addition of music and song: "Two dancers and a singer take their places in the center of the circle. One sings praises to the old chiefs and maybe also to his favorite bull, and marks the rhythm with hand claps, while the other two dancers execute acrobatic moves and flips" (qtd. in Capoeira 8).

A third point of view argues that capoeira was brought to Brazil from the African tradition known as N'golo or Danca de Zebra (from the Mucupes in the South of Angola). This dance was an initiation ritual for girls when they were to become women and mimics the fighting tactics of zebras. A chant still used in the roda supports this theory:

Capoeira is an art
That the Black Man invented
Out of the dance of two zebras
N'golo was created
Arriving here in Brazil
It was called capoeira...

Neither theory can be proved historically nor can it be factually documented. In all probability, capoeira developed as a result of the "synthesis of dances, fights and musical instruments from different cultures, from different African regions ... a synthesis created on Brazilian soil, probably in Salvador, the capital of the state of Bahia, under the regime of slavery primarily during the nineteenth century" (Capoeira 4).

Up until the early 1800s, slave owners allowed Africans to practice their culture, as such practice was thought to quell rebellion and uprising. Black rebellions had occurred within Brazil from the early colonial days and up to the last great black insurrection, the Malês in Salvador. Once territorial control was achieved and Brazil's army and police force were established, all races understood "that the possibility of an armed black rebellion that could overthrow the ruling class and seize power no longer existed, and ... the state no longer feared the negroes as an armed group ... the state started to fear the black-skinned man as an individual" ("Roots" 123–4). Brazilian slaves, in turn, noting the impossibility of a military coup or a return to Africa, turned toward culture, for culture "turns itself into a weapon to conquer space and status, to attack and seduce the owners of power" (Muniz qtd. in "Roots" 125).

In 1808, Portuguese king Don João VI, fleeing an invasion by the ruthless French leader Napoleon, traveled with his court of over 2,500 people to Brazil. Because of the "success" of the quilombos, by 1814 João had targeted Capoeiro dancers in order to destroy their sense of unity, self-confidence, and fighting skills. The first criminal code "created a new category of crime, *vadiagem* (vagrancy, bumming around), to control the black 'strange bodies.' It also outlawed capoeira" ("Roots" 134). So began a one hundred plus year persecution of those who participated in the dance, called the capoeiristas.

In Rio de Janeiro, capoeiristas (many urban slaves), poor and starving, formed gangs (*maltas*) as a means of survival. The wrath of the *policia*, by mandate of the ruling monarchy and wealthy landowners, fell upon the capoeiristas. Between 1810 and 1821, nine percent of the arrests constituted participation in capoeira. In fact, "by 1821 *Capoeiras* had become one of the central concerns of the police and every effort was made to punish them. At the same time *Capoeira* had become an important symbol of African culture and slaves practiced it proudly and ostentatiously. They were arrested in the very center of the city for whistling *Capoeira* tunes, wearing their symbolic red caps and ribbons or carrying the musical instruments utilized in their meetings. José Rebolo, a slave of Alexandre Pinheiro, was arrested for wearing a white hat with a yellow and red ribbon attached to it and for carrying a knife. He was sentenced to receive three hundred lashes and spend three months in jail" (Algranti 35). Of note is that in 1810, the penalty for capoeira did not involve corporal punishment. By 1816, flogging, incarceration and forced labor were common punishments. Also, the significance of the colored caps and ribbons is "white is purity, joy, dedication to saints who were not martyrs, and to Holy Mary. Red is blood, blood of the martyred saints, the flames of Pentecost.... The African Holy Ones, the spirits of jeje-nagos, have their colors: Oxalá, the creator of man, is white; Xango, the god of fire and thunder, is red" (Talmon-Chvaicer 89). Or, in Kongolese cosmology, "red symbolizes power, charisma, and leadership; yellow embodies knowledge ... red is connected with the gods while yellow is associated with the dead. The ribbons adorning hats, held in the hands, or tied to staffs, enable Capoeiras to communicate with their gods or with the power linking the gods with the dead for protection or help or to intimidate an enemy" (Talmon-Chvaicer 39).

Due to dwindling profits resulting from Great Britain's piracy and bombardment of slave ships, the slave trade was abolished within Brazil in 1850. As the slave system slowly faded, some ran away, some bought their freedom, and many *quilombos* dispersed, creating complete slum villages within the city of Rio de Janeiro (the current slum Morro do Estado was once a quilombo). Slave owners were strapped for free labor, and "the result of this ongoing tension between the state's demand for order and the slaveowners' demand for labor was 50 more strokes of the lash for every slave brought in for capoeira" (Holloway 652). Finally, in 1888, Brazil became the last country in the world to abolish slavery. Of course, freedom did not end persecution, and, though prosecuted since the time of Don João, the new penal code of 1892 "specifically prohibited practicing in the streets and public squares, the exercise of agility and corporal dexterity known by the term capoeiragem" (Holloway 671). Upon the code's adoption, Rio police chief João Ferraz became known as "the steel goatee" when he began deporting arrested capoeiristas to a prison colony on Fernando de Noronha Island (to break the strength of the gangs).

Nevertheless, due to their physical prowess and defensive abilities, highhanded politicians began hiring capoeiristas "to protect polling places for favorites, disrupt the rallies of rival candidates, and intimidate opposition voters ... and while some hired thugs employed by corrupt politicians may have fought like capoeiras and been of similar ethnic stock and social origin, the more consistent pattern was for agents of the state to maintain constant vigilance against capoeira gang activity, and for those arrested to suffer ruthless repression" (Holloway 648–9).

In the midst of all this drama and tragedy, capoeiristas continued to develop their *malacia*, or cunning. Dancers took on two or three nicknames as a means of escaping police investigation. They practiced in private, or in inventive, yet safe, public situations, such as city parades. One early description says, "They are present at all large gatherings. One sees them especially in the front of parades at popular festivities, engaged in a gymnastic performance or special dance, also called *capoeira*" (Holloway 670). Ironically, evidence suggests that members of the police, national guard, and army soldiers began adopting capoeira and "at the level of the street the social division between the forces of order and the forces of disruption was more like a permeable membrane than a solid barrier" (Holloway 671). In essence, capoeiristas played a game of trickery, which allowed their art form to actually flourish while outlawed! As one scholar states, "The Capoeiristas can thus be mythologized as Robin Hood type figures ... a righteous avenger, a freedom fighter who could take recourse to the supernatural in order to surmount the insurmountable."

These powerful associations actually "saved" capoeira, and players began to be idealized. In the famous *Rio de Janeiro in the Viceroys Period*, Luis Edmundo wrote, "The capoeira player although not having the negro's athletic build, or even the Portuguese noble's stocky and healthy look, is an individual everyone fears and Justice itself respects in a prudent way. He incarnates the spirit of adventure, of street smarts, of fraud. He is calm and bold. In the hour of fighting before thinking about the two-edged 'iron' or the straight razor always hidden in his cloak, he makes use of his splendid skillfulness, confounding and beating the strongest and best-armed competitors. At that moment the frail and light player transforms himself. He throws his hat and his cloak aside, and jumping like a monkey, like a cat, he retreats, attacks, swirls around, agile, cautious, smart, decided. In these unexpected and rapid movements, this creature is a being one cannot touch. An imponderable fluid, a thought, a flash of lightning. He appears and disappears; he shows himself and quickly hides again. His strength resides in this elastic dexterity that astounds everyone. Facing it, the slow European hesitates and, astonished, the African loses his footing" ("Roots" 147–8).

Eventually, the Rio police force arrested a member of the gentry, Juca, who performed capoeira. Many within the Brazilian president's cabinet favored Juca, whose father was well-known and respected. The practice of capoeira was no longer the province of slaves, ex-slaves or gang members; it was an art enjoyed by all classes.

In Salvador (Bahia), gangs were not used for political purposes, as in

Rio, as the "special and subtle link with religion" proved more prominent. Thus, police persecution was directed toward individuals, especially in the 1920s under Police Chief "Pedrito" de Azevedo Gordilhowho. Heroes emerged accordingly, most notably Besouro de Manganga, whose fame spread throughout Brazil, though he was from Maracangalha, near Salvador. Besouro's name meant a stinging beetle (besouro) and the hive of a wasp (manganga). Besouro defied police capture on numerous occasions, and some say his level of *malacia* and *mandinga* allowed him to "change himself into an animal or object — a cat, dog, or banana tree — in order to elude the police" (Willson 28). Folklore says that his death only became possible because of the use of an "enchanted" wooden dagger. A detailed account from the 1960s by Besouro's pupil, Maestre Corbrinha Verde, or little green snake, reads:

> There came a time, after many fights, Besouro got a job as a cowhand for a man named Dr. Zeca. This man had a son by the name of Memeu who was very mean. He had an argument with Besouro. The ranch owner had a friend who was the administrator of Usina Maracangalha, named Baltazar. They sent a letter to Baltazar, delivered by Besouro, ordering the administrator to really put an end to Besouro there. Baltazar received the letter, read it, and told Besouro to wait until the next day for a reply. Besouro passed the night at the house of a woman of life and the next day went to collect the response. When he arrived at the door, he was surrounded by forty men who were to kill him. None of the bullets got him. Then one of the men wounded him with treachery, with a knife. This is how they managed to kill him [qtd. in Willson 29].

Persecution continued until 1930, especially in Salvador, where police would "persecute a capoeirista as if he were a mad dog. One of the punishments for capoeiristas caught fighting was to tie his wrists to two different horses. The two horses were set loose and made to run to the police headquarters" (Bibma qtd. in "Roots" 163). Thankfully, in 1934, under the direction of new statesman Getúlio Vargas, the law forbidding capoeira and the practice of Afro-Brazilian religions was rescinded. Vargas wished to "create support for his policy of social uniformity ... supported by a 'body rhetoric.' His political platform was marked by obligatory physical education in schools and a sports-oriented curriculum" ("Roots" 166).

Along with this change in social status, two figures surfaced as additional "saviors" of capoeira, Mestre Bimba and Mestre Pastinha. In 1937, Bimba opened the first official capoeira dance academy, having learned the dance at the age of twelve while working the shipping docks. As Bimba later stated, "In those times capoeira was practiced by horse-coach drivers, longshoremen, dock workers, and *malandros*. I was a dock worker but I did a bit of everything" (qtd. in "Roots" 173). Bimba created an unofficial school in 1918 at only 18 years old, recruiting students from the upper classes. (He later met and befriended Vargas and other famous politicians and writers who espoused his cause.) Bimba popularized and fought for the respectability of the dance in many ways:

- He performed for the governor of Salvador and the president of Brazil.
- He developed a faster form of capoeira, known as the regional style, emphasizing kicks and leaps (athleticism).
- He mandated clean, white uniforms (still worn by those who practice the art today) and demanded grade proficiency among his students.
- He implemented a course curriculum and a systematic training method which encouraged a strong work ethic.
- He defined a musical ensemble for accompaniment purposes.
- He trained two disciples, from two very distinct backgrounds, who still teach the dance around the globe today: Mestre Deputado, an upper classman, and Mestre Onca Negra, Bimba's adopted son, rescued from the poverty of the streets.

In essence, Bimba used the ploys of the dance, the ability to dodge and dart and become as flexible as a willow, to distract public opinion away from historical "bad-mouthing," and overcome capoeira's history of "thuggery" and violence. One account says: "Bimba's greatest merit was to transform capoeira, from an attack and defense instrument used mainly by undisciplined troublemakers from the most humble classes, into a sport that attracted many followers, due to the technical improvements that he brought, including blows from the *batuque*. He created a true 'learning methodology' for the blacks' way of fighting, transforming it into a real physical education course. It was Bimba who put on the finishing touches, stamping onto capoeira a special feature . He was responsible for the interest that came from other social classes, middle class, and the bourgeoisie" (Moura qtd. in "Roots" 176).

Yet, some believed Bimba distorted authentic capoeira, "whitening it in opposition to its African roots" ("Roots 195). Hence many players began following the traditional style perpetrated by Mestre Pastinha, also known as the Angola style. Pastinha's efforts prevented the more philosophical and religious style of the art form from being lost to Bimba's athletic-based, modernized and popular innovations. Pastinha concentrated on:

- Drama (acrobatics, head butts).
- The importance of talent, rather than social status.
- Personal style, creativity and originality (improvisation).
- History and technique (he wrote the first book on the subject of capoeira).

Chants written by Pastinha reveal the mindset of the Angola dancer:

God is Great.
God is Great, small am I.
What I have, it was God who gave it to me.
In the capoeira roda, big and small am I.
Sorcery from slaves who long for freedom
Its principles have no method.
Its end is inconceivable to the wisest of mestres.

Pastinha's history itself, in fact, is elusive, for "it is said that Pastinha was initiated into capoeira by an African from Angola called Benedito, who had witnessed how Pastinha was constantly beat up by an older boy. But some say he started later" ("Roots" 199).

Similar to the dichotomy of both capoeira and the game of life, Pastinha is known to have described capoeira as "loving, not evil ... it is a habit like any other, a gentle practice that we create inside ourselves" (qtd. in "Roots" 198). Diametrically, it is known that at the age of 16, Pastinha was invited to take care of a gambling house in a boisterous Salvadorian neighborhood. He noted, "Because I was very tender and loving towards those who wished me evil, when I was young I used to carry a small scythe sharpened on both sides ... if there existed a third side I would have sharpened that too, but as the blade had only two edges ... I would fix a ring to the handle of the scythe and in the moment of pain I would fit the blade to the end of the berimbau. I would then proceed to wield it" (qtd. in "Roots" 200).

Today, capoeira is practiced around the world. One Canadian master, Mestre Barrao, instructs over ten thousand students living in the U.S., Russia, Peru, Bermuda, and Barbados! Dance scholars study the history, form, origin, and meaning of capoeira. Capoeiristas dance at the Olympic games, in movies (*The Protector*), before governmental leaders, in military academies, at universities and at elementary schools. Dance academies dot every continent. Dancers are taught that one's greatest competition comes from within, emphasizing the inner "works" so important to the mastery of capoeira: respect, responsibility, safety and security, cleverness (street smarts) and — of highest import — liberty and freedom.

What has been learned from this study of the "slice of life" known as "capoeira"? First and foremost, capoeira is not just kicks, jumps, and other physical movements. It is an artistic study in the opposites found in life: joy and sorrow, victory and defeat, mystery and knowledge, good and evil. To quote the famous playwright Dias Gomes:

Capoeira is a fight for dancers. It is a dance for gladiators. It is a duel between pals. It is a game, a dance, a struggle, a perfect mixture of strength and rhythm, poetry and agility. The only one where music and singing command the movements. The submission of force to rhythm. Of violence to melody. Sublimation of antagonisms. In Capoeira the opponents are not enemies, they are comrades. They don't fight, they pretend to fight. In a very ingenious way they try to give an artistic view of a combat. Above the spirit of competition there is a sense of beauty. The capoeira player is an artist and an athlete, a player and a poet [qtd. in "Roots" 230].

Or, using Mestre Patinha's definition, it is "all that the mouth eats."

Might a Brazilian Mestre of the twenty-first century impart additional understanding? Of course. "Get in the game! Learn about life through Capoeira, and about Capoeira through life. Improvise!"

11

The Orient's Raqs Sharqi (Belly Dance) Faces Trouble

"In life, as in art, the beautiful moves in curves."— Bulwer-Lytton

Just like a snake shedding its skin, humans are born, then die, only to live again through their progeny. Might a dance help explain the mystery of rebirth? Human beings living eons ago apparently thought so, for they created dances featuring pelvic waves mimicking the contractions of a woman's stomach during childbirth (and also, yes, the movement of a snake, an ancient symbol of renewal). "Discoveries in Egypt and India have revealed early representations of full-breasted, pregnant women, painted on stone walls and as terra-cotta statuettes, in positions suggestive of dancing. Archaeologists have dated some of these artefacts to 25,000 B.C." (Dils 128). Additionally, in *World History of the Dance* Curt Sachs described the pelvic dance of the Bafioti (West Africa). Labeling it a "birth mime," Sachs stated, "The purpose of this particular dance is for ancestor worship and the glorification of future generations via the birth process" (Dils 129). Buonaventura notes, "A similar dance has been found in the South Seas, New Guinea, the Solomon Islands, eastern Polynesia, and throughout Africa" (Buonaventura 28). Yet these dances took root in secluded female societies found in Greek, Indian, Syrian, Persian, Turkish, and Egyptian cultures. (The practice took the greatest hold in Egypt, finding its place in wedding celebrations, private and public performances, and, today, in tourist establishments.)

Sachs places the beginning of the dance in the Neolithic era (5500 B.C.), during which period a "Mother Goddess" religious tradition was firmly established. As Shay states, "This dance genre might be best conceptualized as a complex of movement practices that originated in a vast region extending from the Atlantic Ocean in North Africa and the Balkans in the west to the eastern areas of China, Central Asia, and the western portions of the Indian subcontinent in the east" (Shay 14). Ancient literature also makes reference to the female pelvic dance, such as the Roman poet Martial, who described dancers in Cadiz who "swing their lascivious loins in practiced writhings" (Dils 128). Plato also mentions it in the *Symposium,* while Pollux linked all such dances by their "swaying rotation of the hips. In the *Metamorphosis* by Apuleius, a girl stirring a pot at the fire attracts a young man's attention by the rhythmic swaying of her hips and shoulders" (Buonaventura 28).

The dance appears on vases from the Byzantine Empire, and Empress Theodora, prior to marrying into royalty, worked as such a dancer. In Roman society, Telethusa, with her ivory castanets, was also mentioned by Martial, who alluded to her "sophisticated postures," such as

The sophisticated awalim, circa 1860 (Library of Congress).

back bends. As Islam spread across the world beginning in 600 A.D., "dances and dancers were exchanged and both Islam and the *danse du ventre* moved beyond the shores and deserts of Arabia" (Dils 129). Additionally, harems approved by Muhammed allowed women to "go unveiled, share the workload of children, and dance. Behind these walls, the dance had its own life; it was an art form created by women for personal entertainment and an avenue for sexual expression" (Dils 129). In respectable harems, these women were known as *awalim,* who were "highly educated and gifted in all the arts. At weddings their role was to instruct the bride in the art of lovemaking, through the language of song and dance" (Buonaventura 50). One writer of the 1860s noted: "The upper body of the *almeh* dances a solemn minuet, while the rest of her person is worthy to figure in a wild quadrille" (Buonaventura 65).

The Middle Eastern terms for the dance are *raqs* (dance) *sharqi* (Eastern), *raqs baladi* (folk dance), *raqs Arabi*, and *raqs Masri* (dance of Egypt). Nevertheless, the old Spanish term, *la danza serpiente*, describes the "undulating movements which snake up and down the spine and round the hips" (Buonaventura 10). And, upon Napoleon's invasion of Egypt, the French labeled the dance *danse du ventre* (French for "dance of the belly"). The familiar names for the dance in Western society include "belly dancing" and "cabaret," yet proponents of the art form are beginning to use the more respectful name "Oriental dance." (Dox determines: "The use of the terms *danse Orientale* and *Oriental Dance* to refer to belly dance also serves to distinguish belly dancing from forms of professional Western erotic dance and stripping, even as they evoke the odalisques, harem women, concubines, and dancers who Flaubert, Delacroix, Ingres, and other Orientalists depicted as sexual entertainers. At the same time, the term 'Oriental dance' avoids acknowledging belly dancing's associations with stripping or prostitution in countries such as Lebanon or Turkey" [Dox 57].)

The music for Oriental dance is highly improvisational and primarily melodic, because "in Arabic music a single octave may contain anything between eighteen and twenty-two notes, with intervals as fine as a ninth of a tone and rhythms separated by slight pauses" (Buonaventura 181). The music is very percussive; the instruments included the hand drums *bendir* and *duff*. Goblet-shaped drums covered in fish skin produce a deep sound at the hand of musicians expert in embellishing sounds with the use of their palms and fingers, and include the *darabouka* (North Africa) and *tabla* (Egypt). Wooden clappers (*klavos*) are used along with castanets and finger cymbals. At women-only gatherings, different sorts of clapping is used, such as hollowing the hand or slapping the fingers against the palm, as well as finger snapping (*beshkan*). Flutes and lutes are also a major component of Arabic music, such as the *nai* (an instrument evoking the emotional state of yearning) and the *qanoon* (which produces a shimmering, vibrating tone). The unit of dance (movement) is the *taqsim*, in which musicians strive to build the music to higher keys, exploring the musical scale. Buonaventura notes: "*Taqasim* are linked, like pearls on a chain, by rhythmic passages in which the entire band unites, as if to chorus an agreement of what the solo instrument has just been saying" (Buonaventura 187). These links allow the dancer to "display a rich variety of mood and technique, expressing the emotion called forth by each of these instruments in turn" (Buonaventura 197). In folk dance (*baladi*), accordions may also be used. (According to Buonaventura, "A professional dancer finds it difficult to perform with a band she has never met before. They do not know her style and she has to be particularly alert to theirs. If things are not going well, she will use the informal element always present in the dance to pause at the end of a section in the music and make clear to her musicians what she wants. All this is done unobtrusively, without the audience being aware of any negotiations taking place between the performers" (Buonaventura 194).

Because ancient Egyptian drawings depict dancers moving their hips and wearing scarves around their midriffs, most historians believe the dance evolved primarily within Egyptian culture. For centuries after the downfall of the ancient Egyptians, Byzantine, and Roman civilizations, gypsy tribes known as the *ghawazi* or *ghawazee*, preserved raqs sharqi. They lived on the "Street of the Open Hall" in Cairo with other gypsy tribes who made their living from entertaining. Other ghawazee camped along the banks of the Nile and became a major attraction at popular religious festi-

Young Egyptian dancer, circa 1890 (Library of Congress). Note the coin-like jewelry.

vals. Buonaventura describes the independent spirit of the ghawazee: "Like many who live by their wits on the fringes of society, the ghawazee knew several languages and had a secret code of their own, which was not understood by outsiders. The dancers could be found performing in public squares, in cafés and on the steps of hotels. Unlike the awalim, they were not invited to 'respectable' harems. The awalim left Cairo during Napoleon's occupation of the city, refusing to entertain his soldiers. The ghawazee, on the other hand, fraternized with the French. Napoleon's generals, blaming them for creating unrest, recommended that they should be severely punished if they did not keep away from the barracks. According to the French writer Auriant, the women were not deterred by this threat. As a result, 400 of them were seized and decapitated and their headless bodies thrown into the Nile" (Buonaventura 61).

The ghawazee were elaborate dancers, performing the woman's solo

Lithograph circa 1846, from drawings by David Roberts (1796–1864) (Library of Congress).

dance, or baladi, which could involve mime, acrobatics, or even swords. Traveler Leland noted, "They all seem to have the power of moving any part of the body freely, just as certain persons can move their ears; and it is wonderful how they will continue to agitate every muscle in the most violent and rapid manner for hours, quivering from head to foot as if electrified, without being in the least fatigued, and what is incredible, without perspiring" (qtd. in Buonaventura 65). English painter James Augustus St. John wrote: "One of the *ghawazee* took a little glass, filled it with rose water, between her teeth, and held it so without spilling a drop, whilst she executed the most rapid and difficult movements" (qtd. in Buonaventura 65). The dress of the ghawazee was also elaborate, including a chemise, pantaloons, waistcoats, shawls tied around the hips, strips of bright satin wound tightly around the hips, silver and gold jewelry, pearls or gold spangles braided into the hair, and a small velvet cap on the crown of the head. Historian Lane referred to the ghawazee as the finest women in Egypt as far as dress was concerned and noted they "contributed over a tenth of all taxes collected in Cairo when they were still in residence, and, as a result of their banishment to Upper Egypt, the citizens of Cairo were subjected to an increase in taxation" (Buonaventura 68). (In 1866, the ban was lifted and dancers returned to Cairo.)

Another set of dancers were the Ouled Nail, whose dance had an African, ritualistic influence, especially concerned with nature. Buonaventura describes it: "The feet shuffle back and forth, pressing the ground and beating the soil to awaken the earth spirits, movements symbolic of penetration and fertility. Gestures of the hands express a desire to create a link between heaven and earth, the individual and the community, the mortal and the immortal. With elaborate, fluttering hands a dancer indicates her audience, touching her breast in greeting ... while beneath her heavy costume her hips and stomach rhythmically rise and fall" (Buonaventura 90). Ouled Nail costumes were embroidered smocks worn one on top of the other, around which was a *haik*, a type of cloak secured by a *bezima*, a clasp with chains and talismans to ward off evil.

Ouled Nail beauty, 1917 (Library of Congress).

Bracelets were huge, really murderous-looking objects with studs and spikes to ward off thieves. These dancers also wore tiaras inlaid with coral, turquoise, and enamel, from which hung coins or bangles.

Just as the types of dancers varied, so did the dance itself, as can be seen in modern-day stylistic executions: "Professional Moroccan dancers, known as *shikhat* ... perform a gentle lifting and lowering of the pelvis. In Tunisia, dancers execute large, sharp movements of the hip from one side forward, while in Egypt, the dance is largely focused on rolling, articulated movements of the abdomen and vibrations of the hips that can be rapid or slow. In Turkey, the *cifte telli* concentrates on both rapid and slow shoulder and breast shimmies. Iranian dancers utilize the torso, but graceful dancers are evaluated by the bearing of their upper body and the carriage of their arms. Outstanding dancers also manipulate their eyebrows and lips in humorous or sensual ways. In Afghanistan, Uzbekistan, and Tajikistan ... the dancers utilize shoulder movements and shimmies and, like Iranian dancers, emphasize the upper body and graceful, minute movements of the hands and arms" (Shay 15).

Raqs sharqi is certainly a dance by women for women. A famous Egyptian belly dancer of the 20th century, Armen Ohanian, called the dance "our poem of the mystery and pain of motherhood." In Egypt and Saudi Arabia, raqs sharqi is considered "proper" only when performed in a female "space," i.e., for a daughter or female friends and family members in the spirit of sisterhood. A witness to such an event in Saudi Arabia in 1972 noted: "Belly dancing is bounded first of all by spatial constraints. It takes place indoors in the female section of the house. Curtains are drawn, doors are closed, and servants who are allowed to see women unveiled are physically and visually isolated from the dancing area" (Deaver 1978). In a highly-restricted society, women may therefore find a sort of "power and inner self-worth through dancing in private all-female meetings" (Turley 188).

Traditionally, the art form was passed on from mother to daughter before the daughter was married. As previously noted, the dance was associated with female rites of passage, such as childbirth, menstruation, and marriage. (Girls were considered extremely vulnerable as they passed from girlhood into womanhood. Participating in raqs sharqi allowed the girl/woman to release negative energy, "shake-off" evil spirits and remain calm and under control.) A modern-day advocate of the dance, Al-Rawi, says "Only a woman's life experience can lend the dance meaning and true depth." Buonaventura agrees: "Those well past their youth sometimes prove to be the most exciting performers at these private gatherings, for their dance is invested with the grace notes of maturity and fullness" (Buonaventura 178).

Raqs sharqi represented maternity and fertility, the mystery of conception and the suffering and joy women must endure and experience as they bring a new life into the world. In fact, mothers and daughters danced around a woman in childbirth, urging her to join in and enter the trance state of the dance in order to forget her pain. The pelvic movements of the dance itself were thought to help the baby pass through the birth canal. Raqs sharqi is the only performance art in history filled with movements whose aim is to ease the pain of childbirth. (Some modern day birthing clinics utilize this child birthing technique).

The dance also served as a social outlet. It cemented the intense, close-knit nature of communities of women who would gather to dance for relaxation and fun. Everyone danced; there were no spectators in raqs sharqi. Dancers were clad in loose, flowing, silken clothes and performed one at a time. The woman in the spotlight would have a scarf around her waist to accentuate hip movements. As she finished, she passed the scarf along to the next performer.

As noted above, women supported each other's dances by providing musical accompaniment in the form of hand-clapping, singing, drumming, and calling out words of praise, such as, "You are my eyes; You are my light;

or "How sweet you are." They also showed approval with the use of the *zha-gareet*, a trill created by fluttering the tongue from side to side while sounding out a high-pitch note.

Raqs sharqi wasn't just a method of socialization. It was also a way for a woman to affirm her own worth and beauty. Single women danced to impress prospective mothers-in-law. Married women danced to confirm their continuing ability to attract their husbands. Rosina-Fawzia Al-Rawi, author of *Grandmother's Secrets: The Ancient Rituals and Healing Power of Belly Dancing*, comments: "The dance stirs up the strongest energy that can be formed in the body. It strengthens and vitalizes a woman's sexual force" (qtd. in Nopper 26).

Playful hip swings, circles, and spirals speed-up and slow-down according to the rhythm of the music. Dancers roll the muscles of their belly, tracing figure-eight patterns. Circular "pop-and-lock" shimmies of the hips and shoulders add a striking touch as bones seem to pop out of their sockets only to snap right back to their normal position. The feet are bare, to emphasize the physical connection between the dancer and her Mother Earth, and are used to perform flat footed, back-and-forth steps. The dancer's eyes are downcast and frolic from side to side, and she always wears a flirtatious smile on her lips.

Finger cymbals called "zills" are placed on the thumb and forefinger as a form of percussion. Gold "coins" jingle and jangle around the headband and belt of the dancer's costume. (Dancers began sewing coinage into their costumes for safekeeping around 2000 B.C.) Shawls, veils, and scarves accentuate the dancer's flowing movements. Gold bangles are worn up and down the arms to display a woman's status and her husband's continuing appreciation and affection. Turley notes, "The costumes and other forms of adornment selected by dancers are nonverbal communications that express the dancer's needs for social inclusion and personal actualization. Their exotic nature and blatant femininity make them particularly effective means by which women can achieve a connection with other women yet communicate their individuality" (Turley 192). Specific to the raqs sharqi costume is kohl, eye makeup. According to actor Richard Burton, who utilized kohl in his acting career, "Kohl is a black powder, with which most of the Arab and many other women blacken the edges of the eyelids. The most common kind is the smoke-black which is produced by burning a kind of frankincense. An inferior kind is the smoke-black produced by burning the shells of almonds" (qtd. in Karayanni 31).

Of course, the *ghawzee* performed publically, and when Napoleon conquered Egypt in 1798, the French and other Europeans immediately seized upon the entertainment aspects of the dance, forcing many dancers to conform to Western ideals of costume (bra and pant style) and performance (individual performances before groups of men). They called their version of the art "*dance du ventre*" or "belly dance." Persian Shah Nasir ed-Dini, after visiting Paris, insisted that his own dancers revise their costumes. "Dancers had previously worn floor-length flared dresses with wide pantaloons underneath and a slender girdle at the waist, hanging down in front. Their new ballet-inspired outfits, with knee-length skirts and a virtually transparent chemise, were regarded as a shocking innovation" (Buonaventura 49). By 1834, possibly due to this European interference colliding with the moral tenants of Islam, Muhammed Ali exiled Cairo's dancers 500 miles up the Nile to the small village of Esna. As noted by Buonaventura, "The public's attitude towards professional dancers in North Africa and the Middle East has always been ambiguous. A principal reason is that dance is frowned on by Islam, the dominant faith in the Arab world ... the safest solution was to condemn the art in its entirety" (Buonaventura 53). French author Charles Didier noted, "The few dancers remaining in Cairo were so frightened that they did not dare to come out of hiding; not one was willing, at any price, to expose herself to the dangers of arrest. As long as they were under my roof, or in the home of any other European, they were safe, but the police, alerted by the sound of the tars and the dancers' finger cymbals, might be waiting outside for them" (Buonaventura 62).

Dancers became "the principal public expression of sensual joy and beauty," creating a clandestine trade: professional, commercial dancers, who were paid for their talent, but disrespected in society. However, the degree of reputation depended on the customer. Those who performed for the wealthy were sometimes highly regarded, professed faith in Islam, and even owned their own property. Despite Ali's edict, the wealthy hired professional dancers as an emblem of wealth and status.

Europeans and other foreigners were mesmerized by the dance during their travels, seeking out dancers despite the ban. In the 1850s, American journalist G.W. Curtis described a visit to dancer Kutchuk Hanem in Esna:

> The sharp surges of sound swept around the room, dashing in regular measure against her movelessness, until suddenly the whole surface of her frame quivered in measure with the music. Her hands were raised, clapping the castanets, and she slowly turned upon herself, her right leg the pivot, marvelously convulsing all the muscles of her body. When she had completed the circuit of the spot on which she stood, she advanced slowly, all the muscles jerking in time to the music, and in solid, substantial spasms.... It was the very intensity of motion, concentrated and constant.... Suddenly stooping, still muscularly moving, Kutchuk fell upon her knees and writhed, with body, arms and head upon the floor, still in measure — still clanking the castanets, and arose in the same man-

ner ... still she retreated, until the constantly down-slipping shawl seemed only just clinging to her hips [qtd. in Buonaventura 72].

Curtis ended his description with the comment: "It was the lyric of love which words cannot tell. Profound, Oriental, intense, and terrible" (Buonaventura 19).

Maxine du Camp, traveling with Flaubert and Curtis, provided a woman's view of Kutchuk Hanem's dance:

> She is elegant and almost awesome, with her black skin, like bronze in its nuances of green and copper; her crinkly hair, full of gold piasters, is barely covered by a yellow kerchief dotted with blue flowers: her markedly slitted eyes seem like silver globes inset with black diamonds, and they are veiled and languid like those of an amorous cat. Her white, even teeth glitter from behind the thin lips of her mouth; a long necklace of sequins hangs down to her belly, which is circled by a girdle of glass beads that I can see through the diaphanous folds of her clothing.... Between her fingers her noisy castanets tinkled and rang unceasingly. She held out her two long arms, black and glistening, shaking them from shoulder to wrist with an imperceptible quivering, moving them apart with soft and quick motions like those of the wings of a hovering eagle. Sometimes she bent completely over backwards, supporting herself on her hands" [qtd. in Karayanni 102].

The dance was introduced in the United States by a dancer known as "Little Egypt" at the 1893 World Trade Fair, held in Chicago. The *New York Herald Tribune* at the time printed, "She drew more attention than the seventy-two ton telescope or the six-block-long Manufactures and Liberal Arts Building" (qtd. in Buonaventura 98). Maira notes: "The scandal surrounding the exotic Dancing Girls boosted the profits of the exposition, underscoring that transnational cultural tourism and commodification have been part of belly dancing spectacles ever since their introduction to the United States" (Maira 322). By the 1920s, variations of Oriental dancing "entered the private sphere of Western salons as a form of exotic artistry and self-expression, a vision reinforced by stage performers such as Ruth St. Denis and Maud Allan" (Dox 53). Between 1920 and 1950, Hollywood sensationalized "belly dancing," depicting it as an isolated, exotic performance used by Arab women to lure men. Meanwhile, back in Cairo, the capital of Egypt, clubs were set up for *awaalim*, working artists who danced only for women or for street weddings. Both in Egypt and the United States, the 1950s were considered the "golden age" of belly dancing, a time when Hollywood frequently featured belly dancers in popular movies, creating starlets who became millionaires as a result of film royalties. Unfortunately, these films "reinforced the negative attitudes toward solo improvised dance by depicting professional dancers as fallen women who inhabit male-centered night clubs and improperly display their bodies by performing sexually suggestive movement in revealing costumes" ("Dance" 75). Maira reiterates: "Belly dancing was reinvented as a highly sexualized, nightclub performance that was then

"The Elite Dancing Girl of Cairo, Egypt," circa 1897 (Library of Congress).

exported back to Cairo and other Arab cities to be performed as 'local' culture for tourists. This 'hybrid dance style' is still mutating into new forms and continues to be shaped by encounters between imperial fantasy and global markets and local capitalisms and cultural economies" (Maira 322).

Only entrepreneurs and male consumers were pleased with this recreation of the dance. The famous Egyptian dancer Arman Ohanian angrily defied the Western influence, writing: "In Cairo one evening I saw, with sick, incredulous eyes, one of our most sacred dances degraded into a horrible bestiality. It was our poem of the mystery and pain of motherhood. In olden Asia, which has kept the dance in its early purity, it represents maternity, the mysterious conception of life, the suffering and joy with which a new soul is brought into the world.... But the spirit of the West has touched this holy dance and it had become the *hoochie koochie*, the *danse du ventre*, the belly dance. I heard the lean Europeans chuckling, I even saw lascivious smiles upon the lips of Asiatics, and I fled" (qtd. in Buonaventura 113).

In the 1960s and '70s, the traditional precepts of the dance were revived, and "Raks el Sharki, with its association with fertility and child birth, allowed women to explore the erotic/sensual side of themselves by participating in a form that was legitimate and safe because of its association with childbirth" (Sellers-Young 150). "Dancers such as Daniella Gioseffi ... connected belly dance to childbirth rituals, female sisterhood, sensuality, and New Age spirituality and performed for the National Organization of Women" (Maira 323). As a result, the 21st century Western woman embraces the dance as a means of exercise, cultural exploration, and self-expression. In fact, dancer Anne Maclean believes the dance may now be more Western than Oriental: "Oriental dance may have originated as a performing art 'over there,' but the dance has taken on a life of its own in the United States where I now live. I'm sure the same could be said of Canada, Australia, Europe, Brazil, and other places where this dance has taken root" (Dox 66).

In the "Western" world, women belly dance in same-sex dance troupes as a way to celebrate their bodies (lean or plump), express their beauty, and become physically fit. "Belly dancing becomes an escape from the restrictive fashion codes of American mainstream culture because it allows for a fuller, more curvaceous body type than other forms of Western dance," dancer Dondi Dahlin writes. "Most of us have spent years in bliss that we found a dance where we don't have to have boob jobs and tummy tucks to perform and shine in public venues. We can be women and it has been honored in this dance" (Karayanni 170). Dancer April remarked, "Ballet is about restricting your body, almost having an eating disorder, but belly dance is just the opposite." Troupes such as Heavy Hips Tribal Belly Dance emphasize that it is a way for women of any age and size to "reclaim their varied bodies as powerful, creative, sensual" (Maira 333). It is truly ironic that in a post 9/11 world, "American women find liberation through a Middle Eastern dance ... while Arab/Muslim female sexuality is potentially liberated through the preservation of belly dancing in the West" (Maira 340).

The reverse holds true in Egypt and the Middle East, where the dance is embroiled in a money-versus-morality conflict. "Women in the Arab world become dancers because performing is a job that enables them to earn a good living" (Buonaventura 158). Although Egypt earns 250 million dollars each year in tax revenue from the earnings of both Egyptian and foreign dancers who perform in hotels and clubs, many Islamic clerics and political leaders want to ban the dance. Recently ousted president Mubarak blamed civil unrest in the 1990s on "bellydancers and drummers from the slums" ("Dance 78). A special "morals" police force frequents hotels to make sure Egyptian dancers are not sitting at men's tables or wearing provocative costumes. "There is strong pressure, sometimes accompanied by threats of violence, to prevent belly dancing in both public and social contexts such as weddings. Video dealers in the bazaar in Cairo report that they avoid certain dance videos in their stores because of threats" (Shay 16–7). Shay also notes, "Not only do government officials and organs such as the Taliban in Afghanistan, until their defeat in October 2001, and the Islamic Republic of Iran mount attacks against dance as a public performance activity, but they also often launch assaults against dance as a private social activity that happens behind closed doors. This is most frequently done through the use of zealous vigilantes.

Consequently, these attacks constitute an assault against the rights of individuals to freely perform dancing and express their joy, in fact, to freely use their bodies. In Egypt, Iran, and previously in Afghanistan, official and quasi-official goon squads, known as the *pasdaran* and *basij* would regularly patrol the streets listening for the sounds of dance music, native or western, not hesitating to break into people's homes to arrest and physically assault people whom they would find dancing" ("Dance" 68). Islamic "brotherhoods" disturb weddings, break instruments, and chase women from the stage.

The dance cannot be shown on television. On January 1, 2004, foreign belly dancers were forced out of Egypt ("It is not an industry where we need foreigners," said Ministry of Labor Nawal El-Naggar), but the ban lasted only a year, probably because of the government's loss of tax revenue. As Buonaventura states, "That this ruling did not apply to singers and musicians suggests that it was yet one more instance of pressure being applied to dancers in a culture that has a long history of trying to control, if not eradicate, their presence in public life" (Buonaventura 160).

Clerics continue to attack experienced Egyptian dancers (even proclaiming that dancers cannot take part in religious rites, such as Ramadan or the Hajj Pilgrimage), and the number of belly dancers within the country shrinks day by day. In the 1950s, Egypt supported five thousand dancers, but this number was less than four hundred in 2007. Yet one conservative columnist wrote in a Cairo newspaper in 2011, "There are belly dancers everywhere. Why on earth is that? Are we introducing a new type of art which could be called the navel-shaking civilization? Let us get tough about all this nonsense and clean up our arts" (Antar 2). In April 2011, Egypt experienced a political revolution, and perhaps will again embrace their dying art, to reflect the words of Dina, one of Egypt's few remaining native-born belly dancers: "Egypt will be back to what it used to be" (qtd. in Nordland 1).

Belly dancing is also being attacked in other Middle Eastern countries, for "in the Middle East, performance of the dance as a professional practice is held in strong disrepute, contrasting with public and elite attitudes in Islamic Java where dance is an esteemed classical art form. This disrepute stems not from prudishness, but rather from Islamic mores that dictate that women must not appear uncovered in front of males who do not stand in proper kinship relation to them. Female public dancers who appear in male (public) space strongly contravene these mores and reinforce the widely held notion that professional dancers are prostitutes. This is a stated reason from Afghanistan to Morocco when attacks are made on dancers" (Shay 16). One Iranian dancer explains why women should not receive money for dance, pursuant to her culture's mores: "In Persia one dances for a good cause — what you call in America a 'benefit.' It would not be appropriate for me to dance for money, to entertain strangers, to make a career. Professional entertainers in my country are applauded but they do not belong to the upper classes" (qtd. in Shay 30). Finally, Islamic fundamentalists believe all music, and especially dance, are sinful and unlawful.

After the fall of Saddam Hussein's regime in 2003, Iraqi belly dancers were murdered for having participated in an "impure profession." On the Gaza strip adjoining Egypt and Israel, the Palestinian cultural minister has banned belly dancing in an effort to "clean up" society. Qatar has banned the dance outright, as has Iran, Pakistan, Turkey, and Afghanistan (rescinded in the later country after the fall of the Taliban in 2002). Additionally, in Turkey and Iran dancers are marked as prostitutes. Morocco, a New York dancer, states, "It's totally OK for Arab women to display themselves in spontaneous, improvised *raks sharki* in socially acceptable and family settings. But put on a costume in front of strange men for money? Absolutely not!" (qtd. in Dox 56). Notwithstanding the bans, due to the religious tradition of the region, many Middle Eastern women choose not to dance in public as "an affirmative gesture that reinforces emotional and psychological autonomy, offers privacy, preserves family honor, demonstrates resistance to sexual permissiveness, and organizes social hierarchies" (Dow 61).

Egyptians dancers are concerned. Could a five-thousand-year-old tradition become only a part of history instead of a living art? To quote one dancer, "We are not even able to open a formal institute to teach in Egypt. So how will our heritage survive?" Liza Laziza, Iranian–born, states, "Egypt has been the central nervous system of the dance for a long time now. It's not as great as it used to be and that's because of the climate of the times, socially, economically, religiously" (Brabant 1). In order to continue, even private women dance gatherings in Middle Eastern countries "depend on religious and political developments in the face of which women hold limited power" (Buonaventura 210).

Perhaps Egyptian raqs sharqi dancers will find ways to give the dance "a new skin" by continuing to reach out to the international community, where today "it continues as part of the performance life of many communities and has developed into a worldwide phenomenon with performers, teachers, and students in such diverse countries as Germany, Australia, and Japan. *Arabesque, Habibi, Middle Eastern Dancer,* three of the primary periodicals for the belly dance population, have subscribers on almost every continent" (Sellers-Young 144). Additionally, international conferences held in North America support academic papers, film screenings, dance shows, presentations, and dance workshops.

Perhaps the dance will again offer an "escape both into oneself and beyond one's time and place as the spiritual and carnal merge" (Deagon qtd.

in Dox 54), and a chance to "reveal one's self to one's self, celebrate women's bodies and childbirth, transcend political and social systems, and serve as an alternative to the skinny bodies promoted in Western advertising and fashion" (Dox 55). Dance, despite zealous clerics and Islamic extremists, always manages to return (consider the Egyptian revolution of 2011), and with it "the right for human beings to possess the legitimate use of their own bodies" ("Dance" 81).

Perhaps young ladies across the globe will now join a belly dancing troupe or class. While supporting the dance performances of worldwide sisters, these young women certainly won't regret getting in tip-top shape, bonding with other gals, learning to love the shape of their body (a distinct and unique figure all its own), and recouping "notions of ancient spiritualities, woman-centered environments, access to hidden knowledge, and the universality of women's experiences" (Dox 66), "moving in the old spirit of a dance whose flame neither commercialism, religious disapproval nor changing times have managed to extinguish" (Buonaventura 24).

PART III. REVELRY

12

Bringing in the May

"Unite and unite and let us all unite,
For summer is a'come unto day,
And whither we are going we will all unite,
In the merry morning of May."— Padstow May Day Night Song

Ever since ancient times, the first of May has been considered a time of magic. In fact, the month itself is named after the Greek goddess Maia, a mountain nymph who was the mother of Hermes, the god of magic. The Romans held a five-day celebration at the first of May known as Floralia, to honor their goddess of flowers, Flora. During this holiday, a procession of singers and dancers carried the flower-bedecked statute of Flora past a sacred blossom tree.

The Druids, or priests of the Celts (the ancient people of the British Isles), described the first of May as the time of the "burgeoning springtime sun," and celebrated the day with a festival called Beltane, or the day of new fire. At this celebration, on May Day eve, the winter hearth fires were extinguished and the new fire of spring lit. The Celts believed dancing and singing around the fire insured a bountiful planting season. They also jumped or walked over the coals as a means of good luck and drove their cattle between two "lucky" bonfires to ward off evil spirits.

The Gothic tradition (German tribes, the Goths, who supposedly contributed to the downfall of Rome) also celebrated the first of May, considered a day of thanksgiving to the sun in return for a high season of fishing and hunting, and bountiful flowers, fruit, and grain. Considered a boundary-line sort of day, the line between winter and summer, celebrations included a "war" between winter and spring, and "the mock-battle always fought booty; the spring sure to obtain the victory, which they celebrated by carrying triumphantly green branches with many flowers, proclaiming and singing the song of joy, of which the burden was in these or equivalent terms: We have brought the summer home" ("The May Pole" 355).

Europeans most likely borrowed all these ideas for celebration, plus a few of their own, for the tradition known as May Day pole dancing (with associated festivities). The first historical evidence of the tradition dates back to 1240, at which time English bishops wrote to their priests complaining of the priests' participation in games known as "bringing in the May." Our first literary record of the celebration of May Day appears in Chaucer's 1346 poem "Court of Love": "Now win who may, ye lusty folk of youth, This garland fresh, of flowers red and white, purple and blue, and colors full uncouth, And I shall crown him king of all delight!" (Chaucer also mentioned not only the day of celebration, but the May Pole as described below in his poem "Chaunce of the Dice," referencing the May Pole erected each year at Cornhill in London by the Church of St. Andrew.) Also, a reference to a May Day celebration is found in a record of payments by the village of King's Lynn to minstrels and a player (1375), and in 1437, Bower, in *Scotichronicon*, "speaks of the rabble as making merry with plays of Robin Hood" (Baskervill 44).

Basically, in the English tradition, on May 1 villagers visited the woods to find the tallest tree in the forest, whether pine, elm, birch, or ash, an event known, per the priests' description of 1240, as "bringing in the May." In fact, villages vied with one another to determine who might find the tallest tree, many times erecting the May Pole in a market square or a church yard, where it might stand for decades. In 1603, John Stow indicated the "bringin'-in" activity allowed villagers an opportunity to reconnect with nature, writing, "In the month of May, namely, on May Day in the morning, every man, except impediment, would walk into the sweet meadows and green woods, there to rejoice their spirits with the beauty and savour of sweet flowers, and with the harmony of birds, praising God in their kind" (Thompson 18). But historian Ronald Hutton believes the May Pole "simply represented a focal point for the rejoicing of the returning strength of vegetation" (Thompson 18).

Villagers stripped all the branches except for the top leaves, which remained as a symbol of spring, or new life. They gathered blossoming flowers to drape around the tree's trunk, garlands of flowers twining down the shaft. Ironically, Puritan Philip Stubbes wrote an engaging description of such an event in 1583:

Against May Day ... all the young men and maids, old men and wives, run gadding overnight to the woods, groves, hills and mountains, where they spend all the nigh in pleasant pastimes; and in the morning, they return, bringing with them birch and branches of trees, to deck their assemblies withal.... But the chiefest jewel they bring from thence is their May–pole, which they bring home with great veneration, as thus. They have twenty or forty yoke of oxen, every ox

"May Day in Merrie ol' England," *Harper's Weekly* engraving, 1874.

having a sweet nose-gay of flowers placed on the tip of his horns, and these oxen draw home this May–pole, which is covered all over with flowers and herbs, bound round about with strings, from the top to the bottom, and sometime painted with variable colors, with two or three hundred men, women and children following it with great devotion [Rowe 21].

On the trip home, villagers played flutes and blew horns. For the remainder of the day, everyone made merry: playing pipes, singing songs, and performing circle dancing, hands joined, around the May Pole. They would sing:

> *Good morning, missus and mister,*
> *I wish you a happy day.*
> *Please to smell my garland.*
> *Because it's the first of May.*

Associated festivities included:

1. Processions of Robin Hood and his entourage — Little John, Friar Tuck, and Maid Marian — and impersonations of St. George and the Dragon.
2. The garlanding of girls and young women.
3. Mock battles between Summer and Winter.
4. Dancing in the streets by folk in less desirable jobs, such as chimney-sweeps, milkmaids, and bunters (rag-pickers). Chimney-sweeps are mentioned in the "Romance of Kyng Alisaunder" (13th century)

holding high revel on May Day. The dancers have their faces blacked ... and they are dressed in red, blue, and yellow. They dance around the bush. The leader is a clown who wears a tall hat with a flapping crown and a fantastical dress. There is also a man with a fool's cap, and black figures fastened in his white pinafore, the representation of a grid-iron. Two boys complete the group, one wearing a girl's hat adorned with flowers. They hold out ladles and spoons and strike the bystanders with bladders fastened to a stick.... At Cambridge the children went about swinging a doll in a hoop of flowers singing: The first of May is garland day and chimney sweepers' dancing day; Curl your locks as I do mine, One before and one behind [Lincoln 1].

5. The milkmaids started a tradition of parading through the streets with a pyramid of silver cups and plates on their hand, to both amuse the crowd and to obtain tips. Fiddlers, of course, followed the dancing procession.
6. Festival participants ventured out before sunrise on May Day to collect dew in the belief it could remove blemishes and freckles and heal rheumatism and consumption. (Hence, the Mother Goose nursery rhyme which remains a mainstay of children's literature: The fair maid, who, the first of May, goes to the fields at break of day, and washes in dew from the hawthorne tree, will ever after handsome be.) The most famous "dew-seekers" were Henry VIII and Catherine of Aragon who rode out of Greenwich Palace on May Day, 1515, to gather Maydew and feast in the woods of Shooter's Hill.
7. Children fastened flowers to hoops or sticks fashioned in the shape of a cross and paraded their creation throughout the village and/or around the boundaries of the fields; and
8. Girls dressed May dolls with ribbons and flowers, sometimes placing them in a small chair and carrying them about, with a smaller doll in the lap of the larger doll, as a representation of the Virgin and her child; and
9. "This holiday gathering of garlands was widely known in Europe from the middle ages as associated with the choice made by girls between rival lovers in the games, and with the selection of festival queens" (Baskervill 44).

The very early American colonies enjoyed the dance and its festivities as well. Nathaniel Hawthorne wrote in his *Twice Told Tales:*

Never had the May–pole been so gaily decked as at sunset on midsummer eve. The venerated emblem was a lofty pine tree bedecked with brilliant hues and ribbons, golden flowers of the wilderness. The wreath of roses on the lowest green bough was later to be hung over the heads of the lord and lady of the May as a symbol of their flowery union, who at this merry making were to become partners for the dance of life. Voteries of the May–pole cried the flower-decked priest,' all day long have the woods echoed to your mirth. Be this your happiest, up with your nimble spirits, ye morris dancers, green men and shy maidens, bears and wolves and horned gentlemen! Come, a chorus now rich with the old mirth of merry England, and the wild glee of this fresh forest, and then a dance to show the youthful pair what life is made of, and how airily they should go through it" [Lincoln 9].

Alas, a political movement known as the Puritan revival eventually led to the banning of the dance in both countries (1627 in America and 1644 in Britain). Christian Puritans were an elite and socially respectable group in British society by 1620, with corresponding political clout, and successful colonists in the New World. In the Puritan worldview, God is vengeful

"Fiddler, Chimney Sweep, Jack-in-the Green and Queen of the May," 18th century print (courtesy Si Garb).

and humorless, a far cry from the joy associated with May Pole dancing. For this religious group, the dance was a "heathenish vanity of superstition and wickedness."

Puritans began demeaning the English May Day celebration in the late 1500s (by means of Puritan sermons held throughout the countryside) in an attempt to weaken the traditional Anglican church and its associated political structure, supported by the royals. As the traditional church embraced gaiety and festivity, to include the May Day festivities and dancing, the Puritan leaders attacked the Anglican social structure by lumping May Poles, May Day dancing, and the like into one "heathenish vanity." Basically, these sermons did not speak to lawful or unlawful, but to wicked or not wicked! One example of such a sermon, circa 1585, reads:

> Whereas a heathenish and ungodly custom hath been used before time in many parts of this land about this time of year to have Church ales, May Games, morris dances, and other vain pastimes upon the Sabbath Day, and other days appointed for common prayer, which they have pretended to be for the relief of their Churches, but indeed hath been only a means to feed the minds of the people and specially of the youth with vain sight which is a strange persuasion

among Christians, that they cannot by any other means of contribution repair their churches but must first do sacrifice to the Devil with Drunkenness and Dancing and other ungodly wants" [Forrest 4]

Around 1615, Puritan preachers caused a ruckus near Shakepeare's Stratford, as they "did violently, furiously, riotously, and in warlike manner march up to the green, and did then and there in most furious and outrageous manner ... assault the said Maypole, and with hatchets, saws, or otherwise, cut down or saw the same into several pieces. And not content with this, the Puritan preacher appropriated the wood to his own use" (Hotson 205). Basically, the Puritans felt Charles I and his court were betraying the precepts of the Protestant Reformation, and/or the ability of Puritanism to reach a pinnacle of religiosity.

Adding insult to injury, the relationship of Charles I with a Parliament besot with Puritan members became tense, as he ruled without consult from 1629 to 1640, placing the highest rate of taxation on the rich (primarily Puritan merchants and storekeepers). In 1640, however, he was forced to call Parliament due to a Scottish rebellion (Charles attempted to force Anglicanism on Protestant Scots). This Parliament lasted 20 years and became known as the "Long Parliament."

Amidst all this tension, between Anglicans and Protestants, Royalists and Puritans, a civil war ensued (1642). The Parliamentary faction (Roundheads) included mainly middle class citizens, and gained the support of the Puritans, while the Royals and land owners, opposed to extreme Protestantism (and therefore Puritanism), were known as "Cavaliers." The Parliamentary faction eventually won the war (1649), a commonwealth was established in which Puritan military leader Oliver Cromwell became "Lord Protector," and Charles I was beheaded (Swisher 103–6).

In accordance with their longstanding attack against the dance, the Puritan Long Parliament of 1644 outlawed May Pole celebrations. The law stated: "All and singular May Poles that are or shall be erected shall be taken down and removed by the constables, borshoders, tithing men, petty constables, and church wardens of the parishes, when the same be; and that no May-pole shall be hereafter set up, erected, or suffered to be within this kingdom of England or dominion of Wales" (Kingsley 434). This ban remained in effect for seventeen years, until 1661, at which time Oliver Cromwell died, his son proved an ineffective leader, and the only solution was to restore the monarchy (with the understanding that Parliament would remain a representative body).

King Charles II, son to Charles I, took the throne of England and repealed many Puritanical laws, one of the first being the edict against May Poles. On May 1, 1661, a 134-foot May Pole, a gift of the Duke of York, was cut, floated down the Thames and erected in the London Strand with the use of seamen's "cables, pullies, and other tacklings." Trumpeters, drums, and flying flags accompanied the procession into the square, and "little children did much rejoice, and ancient people did clap their hands, saying, golden days began to appear" (McDermott 12). The lane sporting the celebrants and their famous May Pole was renamed "May-Pole Alley." Per King Charles' II edict, the pole remained on the strand for over fifty years. Due to deterioration from the weather, the pole was finally lowered in 1717. Part of the wood taken from the pole was sent to the famous astronomer and scientist Sir Issac Newton, who fashioned a stand for a 124-foot Royal Society telescope from the lumber!

Unhappily, in the early 1700s, the Puritans once again exerted pressure for the removal of the custom. Also, the Napoleonic Wars created widespread social disruption across Europe. And, due to the increase of manufacturing, a significant migration to major cities ensued. Apathy with regard to the May Pole dances waxed, but beginning in the 1770s, people beset by urban problems (sanitation, economic and crop failures) "sought comfort in an idyll of the past. They looked longingly back to Meeire England, a dream-time bathed in mellow hues ... untroubled by economic and class strife" (Thompson 24).

By the 1850s, England again embraced May Day festivities. Literature lauded its triumphant return. Robert Herrick's poem "Corinna's Going a-Maying," read:

> Rise and put on your foliage, and be seen To come forth, like the spring-time, fresh and green, And sweet as Flora. Take no care For jewels for your gown or hair: Fear not ; the leaves will strew gems in abundance upon you : Besides, the childhood of the day has kept, Against you come, some orient pearls unwept ; Come and receive them while the light hangs on the dew-locks of the night : And Titan on the eastern hill Retires himself, or else stands still Till you come forth. Wash, dress, be brief in praying :Few beads are best when once we go a-Maying [Herrick 82].

As a result, traditions associated with modern day May Pole dancing evolved during the Victorian period. A combination of dance steps, known as figures, were introduced, and long, colorful ribbons were placed at the top of the pole. The use of May Pole ribbons, and associated dances, which formed elaborate plaits, first captured England's attention in 1836 at a drama (*Richard Plantagenet*, by J.R. Haines) held at the Victoria Theatre in London. One set in the second act included "a handsomely-decorated May–pole, center, with an elegant light on the top, and glittering streamers of different colors appended" (Thompson 29). By the 1850s the ribbon-dance had left the theatre to become a highlight in public festivities, the dances themselves spread by master teachers. Written instructions did not appear until 1884.

To complete these plaits, each May Pole dancer held a colored ribbon, boys dancing to the right, girls to the left. The dancers then, at carefully chosen moments, turned and danced back to their spot. Consequently, the ribbons interlaced to form different patterns, depending on the movement of the dancers. Patterns included "Barber's Pole," "Single Plait," "Spider's Web," "May-Pole-Ka," and the "Three-in-Hand."

King Charles II (1630–1685), restorer of revelry (Library of Congress).

For example, in the "May-Pole-Ka" (performed to, you guessed it, the polka), the dancers take their places around the May Pole in groups of three. Dancer #1 stands on the left; #2 in the center; and #3 on the right. Then, the dancers plait their ribbons as follows:

• Dancer #3 passes across in front of #2 and behind Dancer #1.
• #2 passes in front of #1 and behind #3.
• #1 passes in front of #3 and behind #2.
• The dancers repeat the steps until the ribbons are braided, eight braids in all.

In modern day Britain, May Pole dancing remains an annual time-honored custom. In fact, the first Monday of May is considered a bank holiday, in which the entire country does not work or go to school. May Pole dancing, the Victorian style with plaited ribbon, is performed at various festivals throughout the United Kingdom, including the dance for children at Charlton-on-Otmoor (near Oxford University), dances at the Rochester "Sweeps" and Padstow "Obby Oss" Festivals.

Returning to a discussion of the history of May Pole dancing in America, on May 1, 1627, in a community known as Merry Mount near Boston's south shore, an easy-going Anglican "rebel" named Thomas Morton raised a May Pole eighty feet high, complete with a pair of buck horns nailed to the top! Morton's purpose in raising the pole in his community, which he had named Mare Mount (mountain by the sea), and which the Puritans changed to Merrie Mount due to Morton's celebrations of English traditions such as May

A Victorian May Day, circa 1913 (Library of Congress).

Pole dancing, was to create a beacon for travelers at sea and to honor Maja, "the Lady of Learning." Morton realized his celebrations were not enjoyed by all. He wrote: "This harmless mirth made by young men was much distasted of the precise Seperatists ... troubling their brains more than reason would require about things that are indifferent: and from that time sought occasion against my honest Host of Ma-reMount to overthrow his undertakings, and to destroy his plantation" (Morton 133).

Indeed, Puritan leaders Myles Standish, William Bradford, and John Endicott were watching. Bradford noted the villagers were "drinking and dancing about it (may-pole) many days together ... prancing and frisking together like so many fairies and worse practices. As if they had anew revived and celebrated the feasts of the Roman goddess Flora, or the beastly practices of the mad Bacchanalians" (Thompson 40). Forthwith, Standish captured Morton, labeled the "Lord of Misrule," abandoning him on an uninhabited island for several months before he was sent to England for trial on trumped-up charges (violating a proclamation of the late King James against the sale of arms to Indians). In an effort to rebuke and warn the remaining dancers, or "profanes," Endicott cut down the pole and burned Morton's home (Stern 48–9). May Pole dancing became somewhat obsolete in America ... for a time.

Perhaps the colonists remembered the injustice perpetrated against Morton, for they began raising May Poles as Liberty poles, around which regiments seemed to have danced war dances. In 1778, one Dr. James Thacher noted: "Last evening [April 30] May Poles were erected in every Regt in the camp

May Day in Central Park, circa 1910 (Library of Congress).

and at the revelle I was awoke by three cheers.... The day was spent in mirth and jollity the soldiers parading marching with fife and drum and huzzaing as they passed the poles ... one serjeant dressed in an Indian habit representing King Tamany ... in the evening the officers of the aforementioned Regt assembled and had a song and dance in honour of King Tamany" (Thompson 43–44). (Tamany was a Delaware Indian chief who lived in the 1600s and who came to represent peace, Philadelphia, and patriotism.)

The earliest record of a May Pole dance and celebration in peace time is an 1833 May Day Fair held in Boston, in which a 15-foot pole was erected and from which hung, four feet from the top, "a circle of evergreens, clustered with festoons of roses, and suspended by beautiful garlands" (Thompson 46). And Hollins College in Roanoke, Virginia, began the tradition of holding May Day celebrations at women's colleges. The headmaster at Hollins wrote in 1838 about "a delightful party here on the 1st day of May, which day is generally celebrated with great rejoicings in nearly all female schools" (Thompson 46).

May Day dancing also grew in popularity at women's colleges due to a widely disseminated article and engraving published in *Harper's Weekly* in 1874 which touted the day. Also, physicians of the period believed women who were "over-educated" became physically ill, "taking blood to the brain and away from the generative organs" (Thompson 51). Thankfully, women's colleges did not close due to these arguments, but rather increased physical education programming, due in part to the support of Elizabeth Burchenal, the founding leader of the International Folk Dance Movement. Burchenal encouraged college students to participate in the dance and taught May Pole dances within the New York City public school system. Indeed, one newspaper account from Indiana University dated April 16, 1908, described engagement in the dance during that period: "The gymnasium will assume its most festive appearance to greet the merry may-Day frolickers. The scene will be one of unusual beauty, when on that day, twenty-four co-eds, clad in white, join in winding the may-pole with cream and crimson streamers [the school colors]. The graceful, yet stately movements of the dancers will recall the days of 'Ye Merrie England.'" (Thompson 67).

Beginning around 1900, in New York and other large urban school systems, students danced around the May Pole as a form of physical education. One educator leading this revival was Luther Gulick, who published The Heartful Art of Dancing in 1911. Community settlement workers and politicians also encouraged youth to participate in May Pole dancing as a means of escaping the rigors of urban life. In fact, it is believed that when New York City celebrated its 50th May Day festival in 1957, every May Pole was painted gold, and more than 12,000 children enjoyed the festivities (Thompson 89).

In America plaiting ribbons as part of the May Pole dance also evolved into two types: the closed plait, in which the ribbons are tightly wound round the pole (such as the single plait created by dancers performing a grand left-and-right); and the open plait, in which a conical tent is formed outward from the pole (such as the Gypsy's Tent, formed when half of the dancers loop their ribbon around stationery partners) (Thompson 132). Many books were published in America describing the dance formations, most notably Elizabeth Burchenal's *Folk-Dances and Singing Games* (1909) and Jennette Carpenter Lincoln's *The Festival Book: May-Day Pastime and the May-Pole* (1913).

May Day festivals were also held in children's playgrounds up through and until the beginning of World War I and II, thanks to the work of Elizabeth Burchenal and her widely distributed pamphlet "May Day Celebrations." In 1909, for example, 12,000 children danced at the May Day Festival held in Schenley Park near Pittsburgh (witnessed by 25,000 spectators). At a May Day Festival in Parkersburg, Virginia (1926), 5,000 children danced before an audience of 10,000. And a festival entitled "May Day as Play Day" in 1936 was the 16th anniversary of the May Day celebrations held in Palo Alto, California (Thompson 87–9).

As a result of these traditions, American educational institutions which continue to faithfully perform May Pole dancing each spring include Bryn Mawr College in Pennsylvania, Bluffton University in Ohio, and the Packer Collegiate Institute in Brooklyn, New York. (In fact, approximately 80 colleges throughout our country continue to celebrate the day and the dance.) In the quaint community of Glen Rock, Pennsylvania, the dance is highlighted at the annual May Day Fairie Festival.

Unfortunately, in America the dance never became a national celebration, probably due to puritanical belief systems. But, as noted above, the tradition is still alive across the country, not only because of the educational and public park influences, but also due to literary influence. Great early American writer Nathaniel Hawthorne inserted Thomas Morton's story into the plot of his short story "The Maypole of Merry Mount" (1837), based entirely upon the historical incident. In this story, Morton shouts, "Never did the woods ring to such a merry peal as we of the May Pole shall send up!" And, on Washington Irving's visit to England in the early 17th century, he wrote in his *Sketch Book*:

> I shall never forget the delight I felt on first seeing a May–pole.... My fancy adorned it with wreaths of flowers, and peopled the green bank with all the dancing revelry of May–day. The mere sight of the May–pole gave a glow to my feelings, and spread a charm over the country for the rest of the day [Irving 417].

Whether traveling to one of these fine festivals to participate in May Pole dancing in person, delving into the imaginative world of literature, or only stepping out the back door and into the woods to search for wildflowers, as in the days of Merrie 'ol England, and in the spirit of Morton, Hawthorne, and Irving, be sure to put a skip in your step, a flower in your hair, and a song in your heart each and every merrie morning of May!

13

All's Well That Ends Well: The English Morris Dance

"The hobby horse doth hither prance,
Maid Marian and the Morris Dance."— ol' English phrase

An English folk dance called the Morris became intimately associated with and performed on May Day, though it is also performed throughout the year at various festivals such as Whitsuntide (Pentecost). "That sounds like someone's last name instead of a dance," most would say. Not the case. Though the name appears common and ordinary, the dance itself is steeped in mystery, and its steps and theatrical nature is far from ordinary.

Scholars debate the origin of the dance even today and recent findings (see Heaney) have determined the Morris was already established in England by at least 1448, as reference to a set of payments made by the Worshipful Co. of Goldsmiths to "Moryssh dancers" for their annual feast (May 19, 1448) became a part of the London Wardens' Accounts and Court Minutes. Nevertheless, the spelling of the dance in this particular reference seems to indicate a Flemish, or Dutch, term.

Scholar Rodney Gallop, on the other hand, believes the dance derives from a ceremonial combat between Christians and Moors which is the basis of the play *Auto de Floripes*, performed once a year on August 5, pilgrimage day to the shrine of Our Lady of the Snows near Barcelos, Portugal. The subject of the play is the historical warfare between Charlemagne and the Moors.

The ceremony within the play is almost identical to what we know of the early Morris dancers:

At each end is a sort of draped sentry-box crowned the one with the Christian and the other with the Turkish standard. In the centre, on the frontier as it were, stands a drummer who marks with a drum-beat or prolonged roll the most important events of the play. The Christians wear blue coats, white trousers and yachting-caps and carry muskets. The Turks, who are armed with swords, wear rich crimson robes, and cylindrical headgear recalling that of many ritual dancers. The frequent battles are more akin to dances than to a realistic representation of fighting, and the play concludes with a hymn and a sort of "Three Meet" danced by the principal characters ... King Ismar carries a jester's bauble, and this combined with his comic role suggests that he derives from an earlier Fool similar to that accompanying many Morris teams [Gallop 125].

Gallop, while in Portugal, also witnessed a dance which simulated two armies, Mouriscos and Bugios (buffoons), at the end of which the King of the Mouriscos is captured and then rescued with the help of a dragon. As we shall see in later discussion, Morris dancers form in lines of three, dance with swords and sticks, and are accompanied, at the outskirts of the line, by buffoons and dragons.

Eighteenth-century scholar Francis Peck believed the dance travelled from Spain or Portugal slowly up through France and the Low Countries, and into England in the fifteenth-century (when our records of the dance appear). Peck noted, "The genuine Moorish or Morisco dance was, no doubt, very different from the European Morris, but there is scarcely an instance in which a fashion or amusement that has been borrowed from a distant region has not in its progress through other countries undergone such alterations as have much obscured its origins" (Forrest 8).

Still others believe the dance originated in the pagan rituals of the British Isles. James George Frazer equated Morris dancing with the traditions of Plough Monday, an ancient festival held on the Monday after Twelfth Night (January) in which farm workers "ploughed" the streets, dancing and entertaining as they solicited money during the lean winter season. The plough dance included a fool complete with animal skins and a tail, dancers with swords who were dressed in "strange" attire, and an old crone. Frazer wrote, "It is worth observing that in some places the dancers of Plough Monday, who attended the plough in its peregrinations through the streets and fields, are described as Morris–dancers. If the description is correct, it implies that they had bells attached to their costume ... for the chief characteristic of the Morris dance is that the performers wear bells fastened to their legs which jingle at every step. We may suppose that if the men who ran and capered beside the plough on Plough Monday really wore bells, the original intention of this appendage to their costume was either to dispel the demons who might hinder the growth of the corn, or to waken the spirits of vegetation from their long winter sleep" (qtd. in Forrest 9).

One of the dances' revivalists, Cecil Sharp (who shall be discussed hereinbelow), described the dance as "no more than survivals of different aspects of the same primitive rite" (qtd. in Forrest 9). Puritans also believed the dance stemmed from paganism. One minister, in 1736, wrote, "Morris dances, so called, are nothing else but relics of Paganism" (Forrest 4). And for a period in the history of the Spanish Peninsula, the word "Moorish" designated "anything non–Christian or specifically pagan" (Gallop 128).

Other early references from the 1400s suggest that Morris dancing was, initially, the province of the elite, as silver cups sporting engraved Morris dancers were mentioned in wills (1458, 1510) and on gold salts (1547 inventory made when Edward VI succeeded his father, Henry VIII, and on a 1606 inventory of James I and VI's valuables).

Early public performances include the Morris dance as part of a procession through the streets of London at the St. Peter's Festival of June 28, 1477. Around this period, reference is made to one other performance in London and a third in Cornwall, 340 miles away. Early accounts of the performance (1511) indicate a troupe of two ladies, six men, and a fool, the men sporting "fashionable jackets of green and white stain with pendant sleeves" (Forrest 73) as well as black gowns serving as an initial "disguise." The dance itself was identified by "high leaping, fighting, mimed action, individual rather than concerted or figured action, dancing in a circle around the room, rhythmic stepping, beating time with implements, and the use of dancing bells" (Forrest 74). Morris dance leaps were described in early accounts as "vigorous," and an early description of the step pattern (by dance master Jehan Tabourot in 1540) revealed a rhythmic alteration of heel motions (tap left heel, tap right heel, tap both heels) which created a pulsing, repetitive ringing of the leg bells in a five, rest, five, rest, four, four, five, rest sort of pattern.

King Henry VIII allowed the Morris dance to be performed on Twelfth Night (or what some people call "Old Christmas") in 1510, when "there was a pageant like a mountain, out of which came a Lady in Cloth of Gold, and the children of honor called the henchmen, which were freshly disguised, and danced a Morice before the Kyng" (Lowe 62). King James I, in his *Book of Sports*, suggested several recreational activities suitable for a Sunday afternoon: "the continuation of May games, Whitsun ales and Morris dances, and the setting up of May Poles."

At some point during this period, the date still undetermined, a carved window panel appeared in Lancaster Castle depicting the characters, events, costumes, and steps involved in early Morris dancing:

(1) The Maid Marian — a grotesque figure of a man dressed as a woman and holding a ladle for contributions;

(2) The taborer, with his pipe and drum;

(3) A nude girl dancer (or a curly-headed boy impersonating a girl);

(4, 5, and 6) Morris men in short coats (which might be of white fustian, spangled), the middle one with bells at his knees;
(7) the fool, with cap, bells, and bauble or bladder [Gilchrist 86].

Following the interests of their Kings, from the early to late 1500s the primary venue for the Morris dance became urban street festivals, such as May Day (first reference 1552), Whitsuntide, Christmas revels, and midsummer guild processions. In fact, the dance became a regular item in the great Christmas Lords of Misrule processions, which were the "English equivalent of Carnival" (Lowe 67). The dancers in these festivals were paid well, acquired agents, and obviously carried a high social status.

Shakespeare mentioned Morris dancing in three of his plays in the late 1500s:

- A passage in *Henry VI* reads: "In Ireland have I seen this stubborn Cade, Oppose himself against a troop of kerns, and fought so long till that his thighs with darts, were almost like a sharp-quill'd porpentine; and in the end being rescu'd, I have seen him caper upright like a wild Morisco, shaking the bloody darts as he his bells" (Shakespeare 360–1).
- A line in *Much Ado About Nothing* states: "For O, for O, the hobby-horse is forgot!" (Shakespeare 156).
- A simile in *All's Well That Ends Well* is: "As fit as a morris for Mayday" (Shakepeare 24).

Perhaps Shakespeare made reference to the Morris in his works because he so enjoyed all the characters which accompanied the dancers: the fool, hobby horse, dragon, and a man-woman, referred to as Moll or Maid Marian, Betty or Bessy. And one of the actors who performed in his plays, William Kempe (who, in fact, was the first to play the part of Lancelot, Touchstone, and Dogberry), is said to have Morris danced from London to Norwich, about a three-hour drive in today's terms! Kempe chronicled his adventure in a book, *Kempe's Nine Day's Wonder*.

The association of Morris dancing with the May Pole eventually led to a migration of dancers to rural areas, where dancers were part of certain guilds, especially grocers and shoemakers, and, as recorded in Leicester in 1603, tailors, bakers, saddlers, shoemakers, smiths, and glovers (Forrest 137). One description of a May Day Morris dance from 1661 reads, "After that came a Morice Dance finally decked, with purple scarfs, in their half-shirts, with a taber and pipe the ancient music, and danced round the Maypole, after that danced the rounds of their Liberty" (Forrest 133). Thankfully, this progression from court to city to country helped to insure the perpetuation of the dance form, as will be discussed below.

The Morris dance, like life itself, has evolved throughout the centuries, and just as the origin of the dance is enigmatic and uncertain, the dance is complex and varied, steps and patterns of evolution oftentimes dependent upon locale and region. Shakespeare no doubt enjoyed the dance immensely, referring to it in his plays because it parodies, or is comparable to, the pageantry of color, costume, and sound that is the theater. A court record from Henry VIII described it this way: "The Morris dancers wear a friar's coat of russet and pants of red cloth, or a Moor's coat of buckram, or four coats of white spangle and green satin coats and coats of cotton and six pair of garters with bells." Com-

Morris dancers with a May Pole, from *Chambers' Book of Days* (1869). Note Friar Tuck, Maid Marion, the Hobby Horse, and the Jester.

mon dress throughout history, and into the present day, included a tall-hat with plaited ribbons of red, green, and white; frilled, puffy, and pleated shirts were worn, with free-moving, blue ribbons tied from the wrist and elbow. Tan three-quarter length breeches were held by suspenders, from which attached rosettes of red, white, and blue ribbons freely flowed. Heavy boots supported the dancer's feet through all the jumping required for the dance, and wool socks were pulled level with the breeches. Bells were tied around the calf of each leg. In some villages, dancers blackened their faces "so that one shan't know you, sir" (a form of disguise). In many ancient dance rituals, performers did blacken their faces, for if the gods recognized the artist, bad luck might befall the dancer. As a dance was a type of sacrifice, the individual was in essence casting his or her wishes aside for the well-being of the whole. Other scholars have indicated the dancers were imitating the "look" of the proposed originators of the Morris, the Spanish Moors.

Traditional instruments used for the dance were pipe and tabour, a small drum which usually accompanies a fife (as per the Lancaster Castle window panel) or the bagpipe. Modern instruments include the fiddle or concertina.

Traditional tunes for the Morris dance have included "Constant Billy," "Blue-eyed Stranger," "Country Gardens," "Trunkles," and "Rig O'Marlow."

To describe the patterns and steps involved in Morris dancing, reference is made to folk collector Cecil Sharp's *The Morris Book*, Sharp having collected dances in the rural areas of England at a time when the dance was fading into obscurity (the early 1900s). Sharp described the Morris as "a manifestation of vigor rather than of grace ... it is, in spirit, the organized, traditional expression of virility, sound health and animal spirits ... not

Will Kempe Morris dancing from Norwich to London, 1600.

at all of sinuous grace or dreaminess" (Sharp 38). The dance revolves around the sound of the dancer's bells, in Sharp's opinion, because "the bells are there that they may ring their music — and a fine wholesome music it is, too: to ring, they must be well shaken; to be shaken, the leg they are strapped to must be kicked and stamped. Get that principle into your head, and that practice into your legs, and you make the first long stride towards acquisition of the art of Morris dancing" (Sharp 39). Sharp also described the bells as costume: "A common form consists of a square or oblong piece of leather, slit to within about an inch of top and bottom so as to form four to seven vertical strips, upon each of which four to six latten bells are stitched. A braid or ribbon tie, which passes round the leg, is attached at top and bottom" (Brissenden 3–4).

The second most important aspect of Morris dancing is the jump, the "vigor" so important to the execution of the dance. The jump is usually as high as a man's foot. When lifted the foot is never drawn back, but always forward, many times as a kick (to make the bells ring). As the right foot (always the leading foot) lifts, the rear foot hops or jumps. In a high step, or caper, the dancer raises the foot as high as the knee of the supporting leg. Right and left foot step and jump patterns vary by musical notations, such as 4/1 (R L R L), 4/2 (R R L L R R L L), 4/3 (R L R R L R L L) or 4/4 (R R R R L L L L).

Commonly, dancers stand in two parallel columns of three each, either facing out (a column) or each other (a front). The dancer standing at the left front column is the leader and dance caller, who will call modes of performance, such as "Corners," "Chain," "Back-to-Back," and to end the dance "All in." Columns will stand approximately arms-length apart, and in the case of stick or handkerchief dancers, props used in many forms of the Morris, near enough to clap hands or tap sticks together (again, dependent upon region), proceeding with steps and jumps in evolutions, such as down-and-back, up-and-back ("S"-shaped patterns which form a figure eight with circles progressing within the circles of the figure eight); cross-over (passing right-shoulder to right-shoulder, turning about and crossing back over with the same shoulders); back-to-back (passing right-shoulder to right-shoulder and backwards to position, then left-shoulder to left-shoulder and backwards to position); go-and-come (a crossover without the turn–about); and the ring (formation of a circle). A hard-and-fast rule associated with each evolution is "every dancer whose turn it is to execute any movement whatsoever, must jump on the last half-bar before that movement begins" (Sharp 53). When making these jumps (including capers), the hands will many times be thrust above the head, arms rigid, then swung backwards, forwards, back again, and back to position. Other times, especially with the handkerchief dance, the hands are waved in a double circle over the head, lowered straight in line with the body, and then, upon the jump, straight above the head with rigid arms.

As alluded to above, three kinds of Morris dance exist: stick, handkerchief, and corner dances. As described in a 1906 edition of *The Musical Times*, "In the stick dances each member of the side hold a staff some eighteen inches long in the right hand; these staves are clashed together or thumped upon the floor...; In the handkerchief dances, waving of white cloths all together-at the sides, above the heads, or sometimes bunching them in the hands and striking hands across with the opposite dancer — is peculiar. In the corner dances the handkerchiefs are waved rhythmically also, but as already told the feature of these is the change and re-change of places and the caperings" (Macilwaine 804).

Apparently, cakes or short breads have been impaled upon the sticks at points (and in specific regions) throughout history, including at Ducklington and Ascot-under-Wychwood in Oxfordshire and Sherborne near Gloucestershire. Even today, at Bampton, England, a cake is placed upon the stick and carried before the dancers as they proceed to a performance. Sharp believed the practice indicated the survival of a pagan sacrificial ceremony, and literary critic and Shakespearian scholar E.K. Chambers confirms this belief in his writing: "at every agricultural festival ... animal sacrifice may be assumed as an element, and the fertilization spirit was sacrificed at the village festivals in its vegetable as well as in its animal form" (Brissenden 3–4).

Chambers, speaking about all sword dances, commented: "The use of the swords in the dance was not martial at all; their object was not to suggest a fight, but a mock or symbolic sacrifice" (Smith 309). Others believe the practice may serve as an expression of the Eucharist. No matter what symbol of sacrifice, death or resurrection is used today, in all probability swords evolved into sticks and sticks into handkerchiefs as a means of creating a more fluid, flexible movement of the arms and hands to create a symbolic gesture.

As to the intriguing peripheral characters associated with the Morris dance, perhaps the most intriguing is the hobby horse, a man covered with pasteboard fashioned to form the head and hind parts of a horse, a long cloth placed between head and hind, the framework itself slung over the dancer's shoulders as a means to imitate horse and rider. The hobby horse is thought to be a symbol of fertility and death and resurrection, i.e., the death of the year in winter and its rebirth in spring, as well as the cycle of life, death negated by birth. To symbolize this cycle of fertility, during the dance, the hobby-horse, will die, "sinking to the ground, his skirts fluttering to stillness around him" (Brissenden 9). He is revived, as townsfolk in Padstow claim, "by two or three girls creeping under his skirts.... Certainly one of the horse's activities is to chase women, and it was considered lucky to be caught by him" (Brissenden 9). Luck, in this instance, refers to the ability to have children.

Maid Marian is dressed in bright colors, and she and the fool could "walk where they would in a Morris dance" (Lowe 73). The "maid," ironically was quite a bawdy character, chased by Robin Hood, Friar Tuck (of course, in the dress of a monk), the fool (sometimes referred to as Squire), and the hobby-horse. Appearing as a fertility bringing figure, Marian completed a circular "hey" (or figure eight) through the male characters (many times "she" was actually a male dancer dressed as a woman, a figure of "ribald humor" in Elizabethan times). The Maiden carried a ladle, which she exchanged for a ring, apple, or flower offered by one of her "suitors."

The fool's role is not only that of appealing to the crowd with his bright clothing, attentions given to Maid Marian, and improvised dancing (in Oxfordshire, he is usually one of the best dancers), but also that of keeping the crowd back from the actual Morris dancers with the use of "a short stick with a calf's tail at one end and a bladder attached to a string at the other ... belabouring the wenches with the bladder and the men and boys with the tail" (Brissenden 11).

A major work of art which portrays these characters is the Betley window, dated to approximately 1621, depicting Morris dancers, a hobby-horse, a pipe and taborer, a May Pole, a friar, and Maid Marian. The fool is dressed as a jester, the Morris dancers with bells and ribbons, Maid Marian with a high steeple headdress, long, flowing dress, tight bodice, and in her hand she holds out an apple. Even the Friar appears to be dancing!

It's hard to believe that anyone would object to such a creative, symbolic dance, aptly described by Washington Irving in his *Sketch Book*: "A band of country lads, without coats, their shirt-sleeves fancifully tied with ribbons, their hats decorated with greens, and clubs in their hands, was seen advancing up the avenue, followed by a large number of villagers and peasantry. They stopped before the hall-door, where the music struck up a peculiar air, and the lads performed a curious and intricate dance, advancing, retreating, and striking their clubs together, keeping exact time to the music" (Irving 100). But that's exactly what happened when the Puritans, the hard-working, yet guilt-ridden religious and political group mentioned in the chapter on May Pole dancing, also attacked Morris dancing. In 1633, William Prynne published an all-out attack in response to James VI and I's *Book of Sports*: "After the end of Divine Service, our good people be not disturbed or discouraged from any lawful recreation ... such as morris dancing" (Forrest 201). Prynne wrote, "The gate of Heaven is too strait, the way to bliss too narrow, for whole rounds, whole troupes of Dancers to march in together: Men never went as yet by multitudes, much less by Morris–dancing troupes to Heaven" (Forrest 203). Many priests before Prynne actually helped to establish the eventual proscription of Morris dancing. The first actual ban by the church occurred in 1571 when Edmund Grindal, newly appointed archdiocese of York, established an injunction: "The minister and churchwardens shall not suffer any disguised persons or others in Christmas or at May Game or any minstrels morice dancers ... to come into any church or chappell or churchyard and there dance" (Forrest 192). Churches continued to ban Morris dancing across the countryside during the reign of Elizabeth I, James VI and I, and Charles I.

Of course, when Oliver Cromwell, the Puritan military leader who helped the "Roundheads" win the Civil War fought in England in the early 1600s, appointed himself Lord Protector (after beheading Charles I), he associated Morris dancing with the Royal Crown. The Puritan "Long Parliament" banned the dance and all the festivals which sponsored it, such as the Whitsun Ales. Following suit, "ecclesiastical commissions forbade their (Morris dancers) appearance in the church or churchyard, and secular authorities suppressed them on the grounds that concourses of people in the streets spread the danger of plague" (Lowe 76). The tradition moved underground. Only people in very rural areas kept the art of Morris dancing alive.

Nevertheless, when Charles II took the British throne back from the Puritans in 1660, he demanded the return of "Merrie ol' England." Charles insisted that the Whitsun Ales Festival and its primary dance, the Morris, be celebrated on his birthday. Morris dancing was revived because of happy-go-lucky King Charles, though by that time, due to Cromwell's ban and earlier prosecutions beginning in the Elizabethan era, the dance had fragmented into at least three traditions:

> The Cotswald Morris, which emphasizes the handkerchiefs or sticks, plus particular attention to traditional steps and patterns.
> The Northwest Morris, a dance which seems more military and serious in style. The dancers also use clogs.
> Border Morris, dancers blacken their faces and dances in "rag clothes," or ribbons streaming down the length of their body.

The performance of the Morris dance had been crippled by the actions of the church and the Puritan Long Parliament, taking over a century to recover. Unfortunately, at the height of the dance's revived popularity (the 1800s), the Industrial Revolution struck England. As one historian described it, "Young people left the farm to work in urban factories; railroads brought 'progress' to the villages—and the 'old-fashioned' Morris became irrelevant and unpopular." In fact, by 1899, the "Headington dancers and those of Bampton-in-the-Bush, who still celebrate their annual Whit-Monday festival, were the only surviving traditional Morris teams" (Karpeles 139).

The dance might have died completely if not for the work of a musicologist from America named Cecil Sharp. In 1906, Sharp visited a friend in England, William Kimber, who asked the Headington Quarry Morris Dancers to perform for his visitors. Sharp was immediately entranced. He and Kimber spent over ten years chronicling the dance, and Sharp even wrote a book to preserve all the steps, The Morris Book. Altogether, Sharp collected about a hundred Morris dances, representing eighteen different Morris traditions. As one folklorist from the English Folk Dance Society indicates, "Sharp perceived immediately that these songs and dances which had lingered on in the memories of old people were something more than a relic of the past-the mere shell of beliefs that have been outgrown and forgotten. He saw that they contained the germs of life, and that as a living expression of those unchanging human emotions which we share with our ancestors they belonged as much to this generation as to the past" (Karpeles 139).

It should be noted that the Morris dancers consulted by Sharp were unemployed laborers earning extra money by performing for the gentry. This fact confirms the earlier discussion as to how the dance migrated within all social classes throughout the centuries, first embraced by royalty (1420–1550) and then by the upper class social order (priests, officials, public figures, artists, etc., 1550–1660), to select villages and open country venues and thereafter (with the exception of the brief period during which Charles II encour-

Morris dancing with sticks and traditional colors, Wells Cathedral, Wells, England, 2006.

aged dance performances) to private homes and laborers (1701–1906 revival). As Sharp indicated, there is "nothing more characteristic of merrie England than the Morris. It figured at all the chief village festivals and ales. Every village had its Morris dancers. Is it not worth reviving?" (Judge 137).

Another person who worked with Sharp to revive the tradition was a dressmaker named Mary Neal. She led a dressmaker's club in London called the Esperance Club. The young women in this club were the first to perform the Morris in London after the Industrial Revolution, doing so in 1910. The ladies also sponsored an instructional summer school at Stratford-on-Avon.

By 1934, six Morris teams, or *sides*, performed in London. More and more teams were formed, until the folk revival of the 1970s and '80s encouraged people from all over the world to join Morris dance sides. The Cotswald Morris in still performed around Whitsun (Pentecost) every year. Today, in America alone, over two hundred Morris dancing sides exist, one of which is the American Traveling Morrice. This side is made up of dancers and musicians from all across the nation, as well as one or two "odds and sods" from England. Since 1976 these dancers have performed in Massachusetts, Maine, New York, Vermont, Connecticut, Rhode Island, and Pennsylvania.

It is obvious that people still love the spirit behind the Morris tradition — the dancing away of evil, the return of good luck. The English people in particular are delighted the dance has survived, because, as one website states, "It evokes a merry England far removed from troubled urban reality ... an icon of fun." The title of the play in which Shakespeare introduced Morris dancing to the world tells the story: *All's Well That Ends Well*!

14

Feet on Fire: Irish Dance
at the Crossroads

*"In every field a fiddle and the lasses footing it till they are all of a'
foam."*—Richard Head, Irish traveler, 1674

Ireland, 1674. The Celts are history, yet the civilization's cultural nuances
are preserved in customs such as dance. As early as 1510, inhabitants (by then
a mixed race of Celtic, Norman, Norwegian, English, and German heritage)
refer to *damhsa* (dance), one writing for posterity: "Why do you not dance
with your feet?" (*Cidh na dena damhsa frit cosaibhz*). Queen Elizabeth, visiting
her "second empire" during the mid- to late 1500s, revels in the Irish, those
who, according to her representative, Fynes Moryson, "delight in dancing."
The Irish are indeed "very much addicted (on holidays after the bagpipe,
Irish or Jewish harp) to dance after their country fashions ... Master, Mrs.,
servants" (Dineley qtd. in Brennan 18). Dancing is of such high import that
even class barriers are broken, and "dancing is very general among the poor
people. Almost universal in every cabin ... besides the Irish jig which they
can dance with a most luxuriant expression, minuets and country dances are
taught and I even heard some talk of cotillions coming in" (Young qtd. in
Brennan 20). Similarly, when King James II visits in 1689, "all along the road
the country came to meet his majesty ... orations of welcome being made
unto him at the entrance of each considerable town and young rural maidens
weaving dances before him as he travelled" (Dineley qtd. in Whelan 11), for
the Anglo-Irish have "assimilated part of the rich cultural heritage of Gaelic
Ireland and even take pride in it" (Lydon 293). Ireland is steeped in circle
dancing, jigs, minutes, hornpipe, and country dance, performed during harvest gatherings, religious ceremonies, fairs, weddings, wakes, patterns (the
celebration of a local saint's day), and pilgrimages.

The fact that an Anglo-Irish assimilation and island-wide dancing culture exists at all (in seventeenth-century Ireland) is quite amazing, considering the dark period endured by Ireland's inhabitants during the late twelfth century. The Statues of Kilkenny of 1366, enacted by Parliament in an attempt to suppress Irish culture (including the love of dance mentioned in a 1300 song "Ich Am of Irlaunde," or "Come and Dance with Me in Ireland"), were indeed Draconian, reading:

> Whereas at the conquest of the land of Ireland and for a long time afterwards the English of that land used the English tongue, manner of riding and dress, and were governed and ruled ... by English law...; now many English of that land, forsaking the English speech, outward appearance, manner of riding, laws and customs, live and conduct themselves according to the customs, appearance and tongue of the Irish enemies, and have also entered into many marriages and alliances between themselves and those Irish enemies; through which that land, its liege people, and the English tongue, the allegiance owed to our lord the king, and the English laws there are subordinated and diminished, and the Irish *enemies* are exalted and raised up, contrary to right.

Heavy penalties were imposed upon all those who practiced Irish customs, as the English believed their world was under "cultural as well as military siege" and thus "subjected contacts of all sorts, from marriage and the fostering of children to the movements of minstrels, to official monitoring" (Frame 100).

Dance, targeted during this period, declines, continuing only in private. Over the next 150 years, dance waxes and wanes. (In 1540, the Lord Deputy of Ireland noted a round dance, and from the mid–1500s, the Irish performed the *Rince Fada* [or long dance], the *Hey* [a figure eight], jigs, the Trenchmore, and sword dances. And, according to Brennan, "during this period there were repeated attempts by the English to suppress Irish culture, including a ban on piping and the arrest of pipers" [Brennan 15].) In 1569, one of Queen Elizabeth's courtiers in Ireland mentions witnessing "the dancing of an Irish jig by a number of beautiful Irish girls in magnificent dresses" (Brennan 16). Obviously determined to preserve their cultural and national pride, the Irish continue their dance in private, secret locations, the practice of which, at least by 1674 and Richard Head's visit to Ireland, is intact.

Alas, in 1688 King James' throne is usurped and he is exiled to France. William and Mary and a Protestant Parliament pass the "Penal Laws," what Edmund Burke describes as "a machine of wise and elaborate contrivance, as well fitted for the oppression, impoverishment and degradation of a people, and the debasement in them of human nature itself, as ever proceeded from the perverted ingenuity of man" (Savage 16). Known as the Protestant Ascendancy (1695), these laws strive to curtail and control the cultural, legal, and economic activities of Irish Catholics. The ordination of Catholic clergy is banned, children cannot be educated in Catholic schools, and again laws are set in place to suppress native Irish language and customs. The laws themselves last for over a century (1829), yet are overlooked somewhat as the decades turn, due to the difficulties associated with enforcement. (Unfortunately, however, dance scholars may never understand the impact of the Statutes of Kilkenny and the Penal Laws upon Irish dance. Both, more than likely, were the direct cause of the extinction of numerous dances which Ireland might have included in their repertoire to the present day if not for such draconian legislation.)

By 1775, writers were again describing the extent of Irish dancing. Rev. Dr. Campbell relates: "The Irish girls are passionately fond of dancing, and they certainly dance well, for last night I was at a ball and I never enjoyed one more in my life. There is a sweet affability and sparkling vivacity in these girls which is very captivating ... they moved as if dancing had been the business of their lives" (qtd. in Brennan 20). In 1805, John Carr notes, "A Sunday with the peasantry in Ireland was not unlike the same day in France. After the hours of devotion a spirit of gaiety shines upon every hour, the bagpipe is here, and every foot is in motion. The cabin on this day is deserted, and families in order to meet together and enjoy the luxury of a social chat, even in rain or snow, will walk three or four miles to a given spot" (qtd. in Brennan 23). And, in 1812, English visitor John Gamble remarks, "The fields were swarming with people, men, women and children, running, wrestling, throwing long bullets and dancing" (qtd. in Brennan 23). Dance, again, is victorious: "A very just indication of the spirit and character of the people; so much so, that it would be extremely difficult to find any test so significant of the Irish heart, and its varied impulses, as the dance" [Carleton 69].

As the above vignette imparts, and as the historical record indicates, dancing in Ireland suffered multiple oppressive setbacks from 1300 to 1800. Thereafter, the art exploded throughout the countryside, growing exponentially, in large part due to the influence of the "dancing master who appeared on the social scene in Ireland in the second half of the eighteenth century. He was the person who shaped the future of Irish dance by introducing refinement and discipline in the group dances and cultivating and developing the footwork of the solo dances. With the coming of the dancing master, Irish dancing reached the height of its perfection in the solo or step dances" (Whelan 11). The dance master was employed by both well-to-do families and by farmers and rural villagers to teach children to dance. He was paid, according to archived contracts, around "six and 20 shillings" by the upper class and approximately 6d a quarter by the peasantry.

A social highlight, the arrival of an itinerate dance master (always accompanied by a piper or fiddler) promised not only classes by day (usually between October and March) but also group dances by night, "after the hours of labor ... in return for this, they would get up a little underhand collection for him, amounting probably to a couple of shillings or half-a-crown" (Carleton 70). Well-admired and "of the people," yet homeless, dancing masters stayed in village homes or inns (rivalries sometimes ensued for the honor of "putting-up" the dance master), his presence quite the spectacle. Flynn notes, "He had a tall hat known as the Caroline, a long-tailed coat and white knee breeches, white stockings and turn pumps. He carried a cane with a silver head and silk tassel — indicating that he was a cut above the normal wandering musicians. He regarded himself as a well-mannered and dignified gentleman, and he attempted to instill these attributes into his pupils" (Flynn 21). Comically, the *Irish Penny Journal*, reporting in 1840, noted "the finest stocking, the lightest shoe, and the most symmetrical leg, uniformly denoted the most accomplished teacher" (Carleton 60). And the master was not only highly regarded for his dancing and teaching abilities, the organization of community dances, and high etiquette (and sometimes matchmaking, fiddling, or fencing skills), "but also for his ability to compose steps; the art of composing new steps was a skill carefully guarded by the dancing master. Even up to the present day, the status of dancing teachers is often judged by their ability to compose new steps of an acceptably high standard" (Whelan 12), as masters should be able to "dance on eggs without breaking them and hold a pan of water on the head without spilling a drop" (Wulff 7).

Queen Elizabeth I, lover of Irish dance.

Dance masters were also territorial, serving a 10–20 mile radius. When masters met at fairs and festivals, or when a dispute rose as to which master served a particular parish, they might "dance to the death," reaching a determination as to who would serve the territory. "It seems that each dancer 'called the tune,' that is, nominated a particular melody, and if his rival could not 'follow the music,' or perform steps which fitted the particular tune, he lost the challenge" (Brennan 50).

The first two steps taught to young students, helping pupils learn to balance on either foot, were the rising step of the jig and the side step of the reel (names derived from the words "jigeánnai" and "rileánna," borrowings from the English, "giga" meaning an old dance and "rulla" meaning to whirl). The jingle "Rise upon sugar, sit upon straw" (rise being hop and sit being stationary) exemplifies one traditional method of instruction: Dance masters fixed a wisp of hay to the right foot of the student and straw to the left foot, for, while facing his class the dance master provided a mirror image, which can be confusing for a beginning student learning new steps, such as the heel and toe, pushing step, cover the buckle, upset and curl, spring and flourish, shuffle, grind, skipping, drumming, the butterfly step, and the double and single batter. Nonetheless, masters could create, name, and teach their own steps as well. They were not static, and "it is fair to say that, at any period, he would have taught the main solo dances based on the hornpipe, jig, and reel and the group dances which were in demand locally, depending on the fashion of the time. The universally popular group dances which were the mainstay of the traditional repertoire — the two-hand, three-hand, four-hand and eight-hand jigs and reels— were passed on by the dancing masters. Where there was a dance craze, for example the quadrilles in the nineteenth century, the dancing masters were not slow to respond and indeed were only too willing to graft on the new arrivals to the local repertoire" (Brennan 51–2). Thus, both solo and figure dances, whether traditional or fashionable, Irish or foreign, were collected, created, shared, and preserved by dance masters, "who lived by their trade of disseminating the currently popular dance trends" (Brennan 52).

The goal of dance masters was to instill a sense of graceful action and control within the movements of individual dancers. "The body would remain rigid and the dancer would only move from the hips downwards, with the arms flat by the side. The only thing by way of an arm movement that was practiced was a threatening gesture with a clenched fist, seen in the jig danced to what was known as a Tune of Occupation" (Flynn 24). One of the last remaining dance masters, Joe O'Donovan, says some dance masters would go as far as to weigh down their male students' hands with stones if they showed a propensity toward arm movements (Brennan 57).

A picture of a typical lesson is painted by Patrick Kennedy's account from the early 1800s: "The fiddler playing his best known air, and the pupil standing as far as the clear space allowed from the master, danced forward till they nearly met, the scholar making use of steps recently learned. He then returned to his place with backward steps, still facing the teacher, and repeated the operation a couple of times" (Brennan 53). Steps, of course, were taught from simplest to most difficult, for example: "A dancing master in County Cavan in the late 1880s began his lessons with the side step of the reel. Then came the single roll down, the double roll down, the winding step, and the pupils finished with the hardest step, which he called the salmon's leap" (Brennan 54). Gender balancing depended on the county or region, for as P.W. Joyce noted in 1855, "In Cork the women endeavor to emulate men in all the various and difficult movements, with few exceptions; while in Limerick, this for a woman, is considered unbecoming" (qtd. in Brennan 56). To keep weaker students from becoming disheartened, the masters might also organize round dances in which all pupils employed two basic reel or jig steps. Or, to allow a particularly adept student to shine, "half doors were taken off hinges or tables cleared to provide an exceptionally gifted solo dancer with a platform" (Flynn 22).

The dancing master tradition survived into the early twentieth century (and a few older masters are still alive and teaching), especially in Counties Kerry and Clare. They were replaced by dancing schools operated by either male or female teachers. The influence of the dance masters is beyond measure, as the tradition was largely oral or kinesthetic rather than written. We do know, however, that "we owe them the very existence of Irish solo and figure dances. Through their enthusiasm and dedication in good times and bad, they laid a great foundation for Irish dancing as we know it today" (Whelan 14). As they say in Ireland, "Ní bheidh a leithéidí arís ann," or "Their likes will never be seen again" (Brennan 61).

A sample of the dances preserved by the Irish dance masters and enjoyed today on a global scale include solo and figure dances (the complex solo dances are today performed mainly in competition or exhibition, while figure dances, composed of basic steps, lend themselves to social dances, or *céilí*).

Solo Dances

Reel: Originally brought to Scotland by the Celts, this dance arrived in Ireland around 1800, subsequently transformed into a true Irish form. In 4/4 time and danced in soft shoes (with the exception of the treble reel), dancers perform side steps and chaining figures while performing complex leaps.

Jig: Long associated with Ireland, performed in 6/8 time, the emphasis of the jig is the step, not the figure. Jig refers to a vigorous up-and-down movement, and as P.W. Joyce remarked, "No description can give an idea of the quickness, the dexterity and gracefulness with which these movements are performed by a variety and minute complication, scarcely a note of music is allowed to pass without its corresponding stroke — there are movements of the human body that require so much skill, dexterity and muscular action all combined" (Flynn 91). The single jig is light and sound —free, danced in soft shoes, and the heavy jig emphasizes sound and rhythm with the dancer's use of hard shoes.

Hornpipe: Originating in Elizabethan times, the hornpipe evolved in Ireland, "slower than the other solo measures, allowing great complexity of steps" (Brennan 66–7).

Solo dances may be performed in varying styles and are based upon local tradition. In the *Munster* style, a dancer "is poised on the ball of the foot with the heel being raised about two inches from the floor ... the heel does not touch the floor except in the execution of certain movements ... the feet should be slightly pointed outwards, though not exaggeratedly so" (Brennan 65). Accomplished dancers in this style can perform reels, jigs, and hornpipes.

In Ulster, two dancers face each other, inviting one another to the *Northern* style of the dance ("Will you face me?"). Steps are distinguished with "the use of a constant heel-toe balancing movement by the foot not engaged in performing the distinctive features of a particular step. It is what could be described as a persistent drumming action which lends both balance and a subtle percussive intricacy to the dance" (Brennan 69). The steps are conducive to the reel. The Northern style does not contemplate competition, primarily performed at local social functions. Brennan notes, "Unfortunately, there are very few dancers left who can perform in this style" (Brennan 70).

In Connemara, yet another style has been preserved, thankfully, the *sean-nós*. Again danced primarily in reels, the Connemara dancer performs a flat-footed dance in which "the dancer uses the heel and the ball of the foot in a rapid rhythmical movement (*timeáil*) which has prompted some commentators to posit a link between this style and Spanish *flamenco*. The dancer in this style occasionally raises the arms to shoulder height or even higher. Swaying movements of the body to left and right may also be used" (Brennan 71). The sean-nós dancer also kicks the floor with the toes to the rear of the starting position, stamps with either foot, and brushes the floor forward in a shuffling motion, brushing it again upon the return. As in the Northern style, sean-nós dancers are rare.

Social Dances

Moneen Jig: From the Irish *móinín*, translated as village green, in which the figure advances down the middle, up again, set to your partner, change sides, set again, dance to your partner, recede, dance up again, recede again, turn half around with one hand, back with the other, set again, turn with both hands, bow to the piper.

The Sweets of May: A eight-hand jig which "originated in County Armagh and dating from the nineteenth century, is believed to have been inspired by the dancing of the fairies on May Eve. An old dancing master ... passed by a fairy rath and saw 'the wee people' perform this dance. When the dancers reached the clapping movement (ringing the bells), all the bell-shaped flowers (buttercups, bluebells) shook on their stems, ringing in unison with the tune" (Flynn 34–5).

Waves of Tory: Referring to an island off the coast of Donegal where the sea is rough, this long dance which imitates the motion of the waves, structured for a number of couples, is similar to the Appalachian Virginia Reel: A row of men stand opposite a row of women. The rows advance and retire twice. Each set holds right hands and dances in a circle, followed by a circle holding left hands. Each row marches up the center. "The lead couple hold hands and raise their arms to form a bridge and the second couple go under the bridge of the lead couple. The third couple make a bridge and the lead couple pass as waves under a bridge formed by the second couple. Then all couples alternatively form bridges or waves and proceed with this formation until each set returns to its original place" (Flynn 36).

Stack of Barley or Seven Steps: A couple dance involving a side step to the left, then to the right; repeating the foregoing; then, finally, a dance around.

Irish Highland: A dance for three, two women and a man, man in the middle. Dancers move forward together, backwards to place, and the women turn under the man's arms in a series of patterns.

What makes the group dances distinctly Irish are the "dance rhythms of the reel, jig, polka, and hornpipe as played in Ireland, as well as the characteristic stepping patterns of the traditional dance style ... what it lacks in scientific objectivity it more than makes up for in patriotic fervor" (Brennan 102). For as a nineteenth-century dance master J.J. Sheehan wrote:

> Let foreigners brag and crow
> That dancing's their devotion
> 'Tis little the craychurs know
> Of the poetry of motion;
> Their polkas and quadrilles
> Are nothin' else but prancin'
> An' Irish jigs and reels
> The King and Queen of dancin' [qtd. in Brennan 102].

As mentioned, during the late eighteenth and early nineteenth century, Irish dance, as imparted formally by the dance masters and informally by family, friends, and neighbors, was, for the most part, allowed to flourish, and was "perceived to be integral to the way of life of the people and played a facilitating role within the rural mutual aid system" (Foley 41). Performed at cross-roads dances (in the afternoons or evenings at the junction of two roads), at house dances, kitchen *cuairds* (from the Irish *cuiart,* to visit), or in barns (universally popular due to the loft and wooden floors) were the Moinin jig, reels, country dances, and in the late nineteenth century, the Barn dance, the highland Schottiche (setish), the varsovienne (Shoe the Donkey), the quadrilles, solo dances such as the jig, reel, and hornpipe, and the waltz ("Reinventing" 22).

Dancing was a lifestyle. According to fiddler and storyteller Junior Crehan, "The country house was the center of all social activity in those days. It was not only a place of entertainment, it was also a school where the traditions of music making, storytelling, and dancing were passed on from one generation to the next" (qtd. in Ó hAllmhuráin 17). In the summertime, the most popular venue was the crossroads "on the green field on a bright night," a dancing deck, or portable floor of wooden boards nailed together providing an acoustical platform for those who could "dance on a sixpence." Dancer Jeanie Peak noted, "Those were good times. There was a corner there just where we lived and that's where we danced ... out to the corner to dance. My mother and father were dancers themselves. The people all knew each other ... It was no badness, it was clear pure fun you know" (Wulff 12).

Group dances were interspersed with singing and solo dances, and, at the end of the night dancers would "face each other" in friendly rivalries to "tire each other down." Excellent dancers were highly regarded and spoken of as "very sweet on the feet," "as loose as a hare," "can dance on a plate," or "You'd go to the butt of the wind to see him dancing." Money was sometimes thrown at their feet (and/or to the musicians as well). At Neddie's Cross in County Meath, crowds of up to 500 would gather, and many times famous dancers were invited for step-dance exhibitions. Raffles were held to help struggling community members, "a lamb, a goat or a pair of shoes were donated as prizes, and everyone attending the Sunday crossroads dance subscribed according to their means—a shilling, a sixpenny piece or a penny or two" (Brennan 117). In fact, "during the lean years of the Economic War (1933–38), when cattle prices collapsed and Ireland's small farmers struggled desperately to survive, country house dances were often used to collect funds for destitute families. Referred to as 'raffles' or 'benefits' in Clare, house dances were also used to raise money for *soirées,* wren dances, American wakes, and on rare occasions to collect funds for local priests home on holidays from the foreign missions" (Ó hAllmhuráin 10).

In Kerry, the long dances would extend on both sides of the road for a hundred yards! Cooperative harvesting within a coor (group of neighbors who joined together to harvest one another's crops) always ended in a dance. One grocer even joined the fun, organizing a coor to pluck his chickens, culminating in a ball at which "the drink and feathers flew."

The early musicians for dancers were pipers (many musicians in Ireland, traditionally, were blind, as they could not help with the crops, instead sharing a form of enjoyment with their community). When pipes were outlawed by the English in 1601, the Irish improvised and made whistles from corn cobs, these innovations gradually evolving into the popular traverse flute. Harpists also traveled the country. According to English Jesuit William Good (16th century), "The Irish love music mightily, and of all the instruments are particularly taken with the harp, which being strung with brass wire and beaten with a crooked nail, is very melodious" (qtd. in Johnston 43). The most famed harper was Carolan, known for the *Carolan Concerto*. Yet, legislation eventually prevented these early musicians from playing in public, and other instruments became preeminent. (The Irish harp was saved from extinction during World War II by the Cork School of Music, the Royal Irish Academy of Music, and nuns and lay teachers.)

Dating back to the 13th century, the tin whistle (*feadán*) is conducive to what flutists know as cuts, or the frequent use of upper and lower auxiliary notes, similar to the auxiliary percussion created by an accomplished dancer. "To perform cuts correctly, the fingers must remain very close to the finger-holes and feel no tension — they must press lightly in order to facilitate rapid configurations of successive cuts" (Johnston 38). As Johnston notes, "Irish flute playing is instantly recognizable. The music of a given society comprises a discreet configuration of sounds unique to that society, by virtue of that society's distinctive sociocultural history" (Johnston 39). Certainly dance, the cultural heart of Ireland, definitively shaped its music, and music its dance.

The fiddle also "stood-in" for pipes and harps, an instrument easily built and cared for, and Irish fiddlers possess "an unsurpassed technique of rolls, slurs, glissandi, and other embellishment idiomatic to Irish instrumental music, and possess an unrivalled knowledge of the style and repertoire necessary to accompany all forms of Irish folk dance. For variety, Irish fiddlers may double-stop (play on two strings at once), and may also change the tuning of the open strings, letting a peg down and returning a string" (Johnston 51). In essence, the fiddler became the dance masters' sidekick, for according to poet Hugh F. Blunt:

> Will you listen to the laugh of it,
> Gushing from the fiddle;
> More's the fun in half of it
> Than e'ev an Irish riddle.

Sure, it's not a fiddler's bow
That's making sport so merry;
It's just the fairies laughing so–
I heard them oft in Kerry.
Will you listen to the step of it,
Faith, that tune's a daisy;
Just the leap of it
Would make the feet unaisy [qtd. in Johnston 50].

Other instruments used at dances included the handheld harmony instruments the *melodeon*, forerunner of the accordion, with a range of twenty notes, "its piercing tone and rhythmic capabilities ideal for dance accompaniment" (Johnston 54). The accordion has a second row of keys and became popular in the 1920s, replacing traditional instruments for a time. The concertina, also used traditionally, is

The earliest musician for dancers: the piper (photograph by the author).

part of a céilí band, which can include the flute, fiddle, pipes, accordion, concertina, whistle, banjo, harp, guitar, piano, and *bodhrán* (that which deafens) drum. The bodhrán, consisting of a wooden hoop frame and goatskin covering and played with an 8" stick, is used to accompany reels, jigs, hornpipes, and some polkas. Jigs (songs) and tunes played by these bands are mostly native in origin, or adapted from English or Scottish tunes, and include *The Fairy Reel, Garden of Daisies, Hurry the Jug, Stack of Barley,* and *Bonaparte's Retreat*. As this discussion makes clear, over the centuries "the Irish people have seen...musical instruments undergo novel introduction, popular indigenous adoption, emergence as nationalistic symbols, banning by decree, decline in popular favor, rediscovery, renaissance, and adaptation to new musical roles and social function" (Johnston 58).

Not only has Irish dance been targeted and banned by those outside, but also from those within Ireland, most notably dance commissions and the clergy. Beginning in the 1920s, Irish dance and its customs was, in the words of a west Clare resident, "closed against the country people." As Brennan notes, "Its demise was not gradual and natural. On the contrary, it was brutally

Top: On the Festival of Hallow Eve, 1833, by Daniel Maclise (1811–1870). "On the occasion of the artist's visit to Blarney, Ireland in 1832, and his attendance at a Halloween barn dance." The caption in the exhibit catalogue read: "There was Peggy dancing with Dan, while Maureen the lead was melting." *Bottom:* Irish countryside, 1890, Enniskerry, County Wicklow...at the crossroads (Library of Congress).

The Four-Hand Reel, 1905, an Irish social dance labeled "foreign" by the Gaelic League (Library of Congress).

and prematurely ended" (Brennan 119). First, in 1893 the Gaelic League, "founded primarily to promote the Irish language" and whose impetus came from London no less, wished to attach a "social dimension" to their activities. While working in London, two prominent members of the League, Fionan Mac Coluim and J.G. O'Keefe, held the first ever céilí, limited to the only dances then known by the League, the jig, quadrille, and waltz. A trip to Ireland from London to discover other dances landed members of the League only in County Kerry, where "collection was always very random." The main concern was to develop a new canon of "Irish" social dance, not to carry out surveys. Thus, Irish people, dancers, and musicians were in fact never consulted regarding the creation of such a canon. A noted music collector and champion dancer, Frank Roche, explains, "It was unfortunate that in the general scheme to recreate an Irish Ireland the work of preserving or reviving our old national dances should have fallen largely to the lot of those who were but poorly equipped for the task. For the most part they were lacking in insight, and a due appreciation of the pure old style, and had, as it appears, but a slender knowledge of the old repertoire" (qtd. in Brennan 43).

The results: (1) The Munster style was regarded as "superior"; (2) Certain dances were labeled as "alien" and thus unsuitable for the nationalist trend. These included the Highland Schottische, the Sweets of May, the barn dance, and four- and eight-hand reels, "despite the fact that they were part and parcel of the repertoire of the ordinary people of rural Ireland amongst whom traditional dance was strongest" ("Reinventing" 23); (3) Attacks were made on the Northern style, one commentator saying, "It is a series of 'batter'— more batters indeed than the best Irish dancer would be called on to execute and the pity is that those whose wonderfully intelligent feet mistake the 'clog' for the real article should not have the opportunity of practicing the *real Irish hornpipe*" ("Reinventing" 23); (4) The Connemara sean-nós style was totally rejected; (5) All dance teachers were required to register with the League, "ironically excluding the older layer of dancing masters who had attended school before Irish was on the curriculum. Thus, contact with the older tradition was further weakened" ("Reinventing" 24); (6) Registered dance teachers were forbidden to participate or assist in any dancing other than what the *League* considered Irish (which is, as discussed above, an inaccurate portrayal). This regulation became known as "the Ban." As Whelan states, teachers were denied "the freedom of creative expression and not allowed to have an interest in other forms of dance" (Whelan 44); (7) Dancers were not allowed to enter competitions unless all items worn were manufactured in Ireland; (8) Country house and barn dances, as well as crossroads dancing, locations favored by the people of Ireland, were frowned upon and replaced by formal céilís, held in local halls and schools; and (9) The emphasis of dance became a competition. Hence, "the agenda and rulings of this hierarchical cultural and political organization served to centralize, homogenize, institutionalize, and standardize Irish step dance. In so doing, the League declared itself the mainstream, or center-zone, in Irish step-dance practice, while at the same time assisting ... in the gradual demise of both the transmission and performance of Irish step-dance practices in the margins, placing them on the *periphery*" (Foley 36).

The traditional style was set aside for a modern style steeped in gimmicks: elaborately embroidered, stiff costumes; the use of wigs by very young girls; rapid movements back and forth and diagonally instead of "on a sixpence;" a rigid rather than erect body posture; rigid arms rather than loose, by the side arms held with hands face forward; absurd "kick" heights rather than the old-style "knee never raised above hip height"; and the slowing of music to accommodate "trepling" feet patterns, rather than "the sound pattern of the dance closely following the rhythm of the music" ("Reinventing 24) as in olden times. As noted set dancer Martin Byrnes observes, "Dance teachers added new pieces for competitions. The audience and outside adjudicators would be highly impressed with the gimmicks but they didn't know it was not traditional. Competitions destroyed it and are still destroying it" (qtd. in Brennan 159). And, as Brennan notes, "The idea that any dance could be seen as unsuitable because of its 'foreign origins' would have been simply incomprehensible to the dancing masters, who lived by their trade of disseminating the currently popular dance trends" (Brennan 52). Alas, "social group set dances were almost completely wiped out in the first seventy years of the twentieth century as they were considered foreign by the Gaelic League" (Whelan 28), as were the Northern and sean-nós dance styles.

In close companionship with the Gaelic League, the clergy, who influenced legislation in the early twentieth century, unfortunately insured the complete demise of the country and crossroads dances. The church's "crusade" against Irish dance carried quite a history:

1670: Women dancers are the cause of many evils because it is they who bear arms in the devil's army. The devil compels them to gather on holidays for dancing, a thing which leads to bad thoughts and evil actions.

1790: Condemnation of the "promiscuous assembly" of both sexes on Sundays for the purpose of dancing.

1800s: "Father" Casey in County Kerry found a piper playing for dancers and kicked, cuffed, and beat him unmercifully, breaking his pipes so that he could not earn a living. Locals had to gather a collection for the piper.

1912: A commentator writes, "The heart and spirit gave way in a sort of terrorism before the priest. In his day of dominance, he did much to make Irish local life a dreary desert. He waged war on the favorite cross-roads dances — with exceptions here and there — and on other gatherings where young men and women congregated in the company of their older relations and friends" (qtd. in Brennan 123).

1924: Dr. O'Doherty, Bishop of Galway, admonishes fathers to lay the lash upon their girls if they dance. Plus, the Lenten pastorals show a preoccupation with dance: "The Irish bishops in their Lenten pastorals refer to the existence of many abuses. Chief among these may be mentioned women's fashions, immodest dress, indecent dancing, theatrical performances and cinema exhibitions, evil literature, drink, strikes, and lock-outs" (qtd. in Smyth 51).

The bishops' cry for legislation which controlled personal behavior led to the Irish government forming the "Carrigan Committee" to investigate the "indecent dancing." Skewed by the influence of the church, the committee found "dance halls" to be a "chief cause for the present looseness of morals" (Smyth 52). Department of Justice civil servants, thankfully, thought otherwise: "The committee might equally have concerned itself with housing, education, unemployment, or any other matter which might have had an indirect effect on prostitution and immorality. Their suggestions amount almost to a suppression of public dancing" (qtd. in Smyth 53). Bishops only stepped up their campaign, organizing a demonstration in 1934 attended by over 3,000, at which Cardinal McRory read the following: "All-night dances are objectionable on many grounds and in country districts and small towns are a fruitful source of scandal and ruin, spiritual and temporal" (qtd. in Smyth 54). (It should be noted that the Gaelic League was in favor of preventive legislation as well, passing a resolution for a boycott of jazz music. By the early 1940s, as a result, jazz was banned from the airwaves.)

Finally succumbing to clerical pressure, the Fianna Fáil government passed the Public Dance Halls Act of 1935, in which "all public dancing would require a license, which can only be obtained by persons of good character from a district justice" (Ó hAllmhuráin 11). Priests began working in tandem with the *gardaí* to enforce the act. The Department of Justice was swamped with letters from music and dance enthusiasts "complaining about harassment of dancers by the gardaí and clergy. On March 10, 1935, James Maher of Killaloe, County Clare, wrote to the department claiming that "there will exist no means by which our youth can get a knowledge or desire for Irish dance and music and in a short period, Irish dance will be forgotten and Irish music non-existent" (qtd. in Ó hAllmhuráin 12).

As stated earlier, the economy of Ireland in 1935 was faltering. Unemployed families were holding house dances to raise a few shillings to feed their family. The need for a license, of course, was a low priority for those struggling to feed their family. In December 1935, "a small farmer in Shanaway, outside Ennis, was summoned for holding a private dance in his house for his neighbors who helped him with his crops," as was a widow in Cooraclare who "ran dances for neighbors who helped her with her farm" (Brennan 130). As Smyth notes, "The lack of concern on the part of the hierarchy for the plight of the poor is explicable in the context of a clerical near-monopoly-of welfare services, such as they were, through the network of charitable organizations. These organizations were not only inadequate but also punitive and repressive" (Smyth 52).

Priests even threatened local justices, prompting one such justice to write, "It was a very insidious thing for the Parish Priest to write to me and say that if I granted any more licenses, I would hear more about it. I hope I will get no more letters of that description from that quarter, or from any other quarter either" (qtd. in Ó hAllmhuráin 14). Parishes began building their own halls, allowing only the restricted dances of the Gaelic League to be performed, and charging admission for "church related social and economic projects," becoming "an untapped source of taxation for the government" (Ó hAllmhuráin 16). In fact it was 25 percent of the ticket price.

Despite the threat of prosecution, the shame of being "read-out" from the Sunday altar, and the chance of having one's names printed in the paper, dancers tried to continue their art in the spirit of genuine "crack," evidenced by the following story: "A local mass server had given the wine and the water to Canon Tom and had gone back to his place down at the step of the altar and he was going off to sleep again when Canon Tom turned around. Our friend at the end of the night and a half-an-hour in bed was still hearing 'The Sally Gardens' and 'The Bucks of Oranmore,' you name it. I suppose he wasn't in such a great liturgical state. Anyhow, when Canon Tom turned around and said 'Let us pray brethren' the lad woke up and said: 'Is it a reel or a jig, Canon?' Clearly, he was in the right department, but in the wrong house" (Fr. Fitzpatrick qtd. in Ó hAllmhuráin 15).

Nevertheless, the family-based dance tradition was essentially lost to public, church-sponsored dance halls employing céilí bands rather than traditional fiddlers. The tradition of respect for the dancer and music maker, community support networking, and rhythmical subtlety from both musician and dancer gave way to formality, nation-building, convent-trained pianists and rasping accordians, all of which would "serve to rupture even further the cultural contours of the kitchen *cuaird,* the traveling dance master, and the country house dance" (Ó hAllmhuráin 18). West Clare fiddler and storyteller Junior Crehan aptly summarizes the sad story:

> Country people found it hard to adjust and, to them, the dance halls were not natural places of enjoyment; they were not places for traditional music, story-telling, and dancing. They were unsuitable for passing on traditional arts. The Dance Hall Act closed our schools of tradition and left us a poorer people. As a musician, I played at many house dances and there was nothing there but inno-cent fun, with fathers, mothers, brothers, and sisters. It was there that we learned the music and the sets. It was there that we learned the step dance and where we met our wives [qtd. in Ó hAllmhuráin 18].

In the 1940s, emigration increased, as Ireland's youth foresaw nothing but continuing poverty. The government and the church had a "falling pop-ulation" from which to collect dance hall dues! Crehan continued: "The coun-tryside was once more going through that terrible silence which it had suffered after the Famine, the silence of departing people and a dying of music and song. These were indeed the Black Forties" (Crehan 4). The League and the church continued their control over dancing, and in 1970 the League (now the Irish Dancing Commission) formed and began administering the World Championship in Irish Dancing competition. The League strove to convince parents, teachers, students, and the nation as a whole that competition (local, national, and international competitions) should be the goal of Irish dancing, not revelry, personal development, or community-building, as in times past.

Without doubt a saving grace, *Riverdance* exploded onto the international scene in 1994, a theatrical presentation eventually viewed by over *1 billion* people across the globe! The show explored the truth of Irish dancing: "A fusion of many influences, both from within Ireland and beyond" (Wulff 25). It helped the nation to recover from years of cultural abuse which had rendered Irish dancing "a stoic movement encased in too much embroidered velvet" (Brabazon 12). One lyric from *Riverdance* within the song "Heartland" verifies: "We circle the world with our wandering airs, gathering here and there, leaving behind our share" (qtd. in Brabazon 10).

It is of note that the traditional costume for ladies was a peasant dress and shawl and for men pants (or kilt), waistcoat, and cloak. The shawl and kilt were symbols of rebellion associated with multiple periods of repression — such garments helped dissenters to endure all sorts of weather as they hid from authorities. Favorite colors were, of course, bright green and white, and red was avoided due to its association with England. Many times women danced without shoes to display their lightness of feet. (Yet, beginning in 1924, they wore soft shoe pumps for light dances and jig shoes, with plain leather uppers and leather soles sporting built-up toe pieces for greater sound, for heavy dances. Men traditionally wore homemade rawhide shoes or brogues, but today wear shoes with soft leather uppers and thin soles for light dances and the same kind of jig shoes as the ladies.) Nevertheless, the strict sense of competition instituted by the Gaelic League led to the creation of elaborate costumes, especially for the female dancer, who wore a black velvet "peasant" dress with heavy Celtic embroidery, applique, lace collars, and Vilene, a thick firm material similar to cardboard which made the dresses "stand on the floor by themselves." The dresses can weigh up to eight pounds and cost $1,000 or more. As Brennan notes, "The heavily embroidered and occasionally lurid color schemes of the modern dance schools have no basis in historic Irish dress and serve simply to identify and advertise the school concerned ... then you have the embroidered tiaras, plaited hair bands, satin pants, dress covers, half-covers, smocks, aprons, magic wand curlers, caps and Kangol berets to go over the hair curlers, Tara brooches, poodle socks, banana clip hair pieces, headbands, crowns, scrunchies, and finally, wigs. The main item of the boys' stage and competition dress, the kilt, sometimes teamed with an embroidered cummerbund and velvet waistcoat, is the source of much painful mockery of young male dancers and is often cited as the main reason why so many boys abandon the dance" (Brennan 151–7).

Thankfully, *Riverdance* awoke a sleeping giant, the rich heritage of Irish traditional dance, "conjuring up the image of Irish bodies on the move, conquering the world ... moving away from the problematic state of post colonialism" (Wulff 56). Celebrating connections between peoples who have withstood and surmounted repression, oppression, and famine, the show is "a full-length Irish dance show where scenes of Irish dancing and music alternate with the crossover of flamenco, Russian folk ballet, African American tap dance, gospel and an Irish choir. Beginning by recalling the origin of humanity, the show proceeds by praising Ireland, its lands and legends, moves on to depict the distress of emigration and the excitement of urban life in the New World. This is mixed with a crossover journey around the globe. The show ends with a happy homecoming to Ireland" (Wulff 55). The show creates a sense of *recovery* of identity: the return of the strong masculine contribution to Irish dance; the increased use of arms to inscribe space; and the return of free-flowing, dance appropriate costuming; as well as a *rediscovery* of identity. Due to the diaspora, Irish dancing circles the globe; tap, Northern, and sean-nós steps can be assimilated into the Munster style for purposes of performance; and the queen of England can safely attend a theatrical performance (May 2011), creating a climate in which "the British are made to feel marginally marginal through Irish music and dance" (Brabazon 14).

Though it seems as if *Riverdance* exploded onto the "scene" overnight after the oppressive and lackadaisical years between 1935 and 1993, in reality Irish traditional dance reared its head again beginning in the '70s, thanks to the remaining dance masters, rural survivalists, elderly dancers, and, of course, rebels who preserved suppressed and oppressed traditions. First, "the recent upsurge in Irish dancing should be seen in relation to the remarkable expansion nationally and globally of Irish traditional music, which has been going on since the '70s" (Wulff 25). Second, the Connemara Civil Rights Movement, founded in the late '60s, insisted that sean-nós be recognized by the annual gathering of the Gaelic League, leading to a first-ever competition during the national gathering in 1977. (Today, Connemara dancers exhibit and compete each September, *ar nós coileach ag taispeáint don chearc go bhfuil sé beo*—like a cock showing the hen what life he has in him, at the annual *Pléaráca Chonamara*.) Third, a more mature group revived the social dances, such as the Sweets of May and the Waves of Tory, virtually wiped out in the first seventy years of the twentieth century as a result of the Gaelic League's shunning.

Fourth (ironically), a priest incorporated Irish dance into the dance/theatre company he founded at Tralee County, Kerry, in 1974, *Siamsa Tire* (meaning "coming together for entertainment"). Father Pat Ahern, himself taught by a dance master in his youth (and also a fiddler), began the company in honor of fond childhood memories of crossroad dancing: "The picture of a lone musician, an accordionist usually, because the accordions were loud enough to carry over the noise, sitting on a fence, under a bush maybe. On a summer evening after all the work was done and people just relaxed for an evening. It was a unique, unusual kind of experience" (Wulff 11). "I had come into contact with the dancing master. He came to teach us at the school. They would have disappeared at the turn of the century, but some were still around here. He came for 6–8 weeks at a time" ("Memories" 55). Father Ahern's choreography was a crossover texture between traditional and modern, and he also welcomed such traditions as ballet and ethnic dance (for example, flamenco), as did the producers of *Riverdance*.

One of the Irish legends set to dance by Father Ahern and his company was "The Children of Lir" in which Lir, lord of the sea, who wears a gold crown and long red robe, takes a second wife, Aife, who dresses in green and black. Aife is insanely jealous of Lir's four children, and sets herself to a course of destruction. Despite her attempts, the children cannot be murdered. Calling on extraordinary supernatural powers, Aife conjures only one enchantment, turning the children, two male, two female into swans. When she takes the children to a lake to throw them in, under the pretense of a family outing, the children pass the toll of a church bell and are released from the spell.

Oisin Kelly's *Children of Lir*, a statue in the Garden of Remembrance, Dublin, Ireland ... Lir's children are in flight.

Perhaps the history of Irish dance mirrors this legend, having overcome the negligence and abuse of red-robed Lir (Britain) and the shiftiness of black-and-green laden Air (Irish church and state). The bell has rung (Father Ahern); Irish dance glides into high form (*Riverdance*). Her children are in flight!

15

Sacred, Yet Profane:
The Afro-Brazilian
Batuque and Samba

"Long Live Ze Pereira
Who no one harms
Long Live ... in these days of Carnival..."— samba song

On October 1, 2009, Muslim Hezbollah clerics "torpedoed" and banned a performance by goodwill Brazilian *samba* dancers and musicians within the Lebanese village of Tyre, although only a month before citizens and tourists of Zahle and Joanieh had enjoyed just such a performance. Apparently, the clerics used intimidating and terrorizing pressure tactics to persuade local city council members to abandon the performance permit. A newspaper noted, "The ongoing war of suppression and terrorism that Hezbollah is waging and forcing on Lebanon is escalating. This war confirms without any shred of a doubt that the current serious ongoing conflict in Lebanon is between two educational systems and cultures: the first is the Iranian mullah's evil teaching of jihad, death, suicide, fanaticism, oppression, terrorism, rejection of the other, awkwardness and isolation; and the second one is the historical Lebanese education and culture of peace, human rights, civil society, openness, multiculturalism, democracy and freedom. In the event that the Lebanese yield with no heroic resistance to Hezbollah's derailed mullah's logic that torpedoed the Brazilian samba band, Lebanon is definitely very soon going to lose its identity, history, and civilization, as well as its freedoms, creativeness, education and the deeply rooted mosaic society of different cultures, religions and ethics" (Bejjani 1). Perhaps the drum call of the *batuque*, samba's forerunner, should sound the call to all *sambistas* (samba dancers), for samba and its dance of origin (batuque) have been fighting such a battle since 1796, winning the heart of a country (Brazil) as it stepped out, and onto, the front lines!

The origin of batuque is West African, having traveled from Angola and the Congo to Portugal as early as the 16th century, as a result of the slave trade. In Portugal, it was performed as either a solo or couple dance inside a surrounding circle of spectators (ironically, samba may be performed in either of these styles today). At that time, the dance featured handclapping, percussive instruments, shuffling feet, and wiggling hips. Emperor Manual I banned the Portuguese batuque because of its "wild" expressive movements (in Spain, however, the dance continued, and was used in the 18th century as a "flirtation piece featuring finger snaps"). Ultimately, however, the batuque was adopted by the country of Brazil, as Portuguese colonists transferred thousands of Afro-Portuguese slaves and/or African captives to Brazil to work in the country's multitudinous plantations. In Brazil, according to W.G. Raffé, the batuque was sometimes performed as a game, similar to capoeira, but in most instances was a seductive, improvisational dance in which the soloist or the couple within the circle, after having performed a dance of (hopefully) great prowess, would indicate who was to replace them by performing the *umbigada*, the most unique aspect of the batuque. (A dancer performing the umbigada touches his or her belly button against the navel of another, inviting the other to take over the dance.) Upon arriving in Brazil, European components of Catholicism (batuque ceremonies are usually prefaced by a Catholic prayer, and a spirit named João da Mata, or John of the Forest, i.e., John the Baptist, is present) and Amazon indigenous practices were also incorporated within the batuque, creating a new pantheon and "ceasing to be an alien religion associated with things African, but rather a Brazilian religion" ("Fun-Loving" 108). Today, batuque is another name for candomblé, the Afro-Brazilian religion in which rhythm is used to "call forth the Gods."

Batuque, in essence, became a trance dance, in which "possession takes place, as in other Afro-American religions, to the beating of drums, the shaking of gourds, and the singing of songs and invocations at a public ceremony in the open pavilion of the *terreiro*, and its forms again vary widely in accord both with the possessing spirit and the person possessed" (Torrance 115). According to the religious intent of the dance, the *encantados*, or "enchanted ones" wish to possess the dancer for a variety of fun-loving reasons: (1) to dance and sing; (2) to smoke cigars; and (3) to drink alcohol. The relationship between possessor and possessed is a reciprocal one, and "in return for being able to dance, sing, and perhaps drink, the deity does many favors for his devotee, such as looking out for his economic well-being, prescribing remedies for his sick relatives and friends, and predicting the future. If the encantado proves to be popular enough, it is sometimes possible for the dancer to engage in relatively lucrative curing practices" (Leacock 345). And: "Not only do the *encantados* possess their followers during ceremonies, but they also look out for their welfare and are always available for consultation in time of crisis" ("Fun-Loving" 96). (The most popular drink used during possession, never partaken *before* ritual possession, is Brazilian white rum, *cachaca*. The common length of a possession is one hour, though some encantados remain for days.) Two types of encantados may possess the dancer: a noble, or *senhor*, "conceived of as being basically serious and dignified, they bear their great power with quiet aplomb" ("Fun-Loving" 100), and the *caboclos*, those who "descend and possess the cult members because they enjoy a good time" (Leacock 95), "expressed by a variety of behaviors, including a marked predilection to sing, dance, smoke cigars, drink rum, joke with one another and with members of the audience, wear odd costumes, and in general behave in a gay, light-hearted manner. They are in some ways the antithesis of the *senhores*, but they do share with the latter the same supernatural power which can be used to assist those humans who are willing to be possessed by them and do their bidding" ("Fun-Loving" 100). While many belief systems would chastise these practices, one dancer, Clara, proves that the caboclos do in fact have the best interest of the possessed in mind, as "for many years, in spite of a propensity to drink too much in her secular life, she was able to control her consumption of liquor because her *encantado*, Japetequara (who does not drink) 'looked after her.' This supervision took the form of possession whenever Clara was about to drink too much, or punishment after she had drunk to excess" (Leacock 351). And, as Leacock notes, "most dancers in a trance state seem to act much the same whether they drink or not, and alcohol is not in any sense necessary either for high spirits which are manifested or the atmosphere of friendliness which prevails. The ties that bind in *batuque* would seem to include shared beliefs about the *encantados* and shared experiences in which possession is the central activity. Since alcohol is not used to induce possession, is not drunk as a part of a communal rite, and is not even consumed by all those present, its integrating effects would seem to be relatively slight" (Leacock 351).

Alternately, when possessed by a *senhor*, the dancer is "serious, dignified, even pompous. Movements are deliberate, facial expressions suggest pride and often condescension; pronouncements are couched in absolute terms and in careful language. Major deities do not stay very long, rarely over half an hour, and they often spend part of their time being consulted by people with problems who have attended the ceremony specifically in the hopes of being able to talk to this particular deity" ("Fun-Loving" 102).

The stages of the dance include: (1) assembly (sometimes more than 200 people gather for a dance); (2) the sounding of drums; (3) a song inducing an encantado to possess dancers (according to Leacock, "Three songs are sung for each *encantado*, and if no one is possessed, another *encantado* is called" ["Fun-Loving" 101];) (4) the dance steps. The first part of the ceremony is dedicated to the senhores, and the second half to the caboclos.

The dance locations were known as a *terreiro*, a gentle slope in which the women were placed on the higher level, creating a *descerem as damas*, or dance interaction (lines were 10–12 meters apart).

The drums, of course, were of high import in creating the trance state, and included:

The tambu: a long, cylindrical, single-headed drum with a deep tuning, painted blue and made of a hollow piece of wood over which a membrane was nailed with small wooden nails to create tension.

The quinjengue: Also painted blue, the quinjengue was a smaller, goblet-shaped, single-head drum with a long, tooth like supporting leg. Of a higher tune, a cowhide membrane covered the drum.

The matraca or mitraca: Cut from the wood pau de goiabera for elasticity, the matraca consisted of two 35 centimeter percussion sticks connected with a string or strap of cloth, used to strike a pattern on the tambu.

The guaia or chocaio: the double-cone rattle.

Song verses were either of a competitive nature, the *carreiras* (accompanied by the rattle), or *modinhas*, with varying themes surrounding the dance and music proper. The dance steps were similar in nature to today's samba or Charleston (both thought to have originated from batuque) and included the *visagens* (caricature), *pião parado* (pawn standing), *granché, cortesia, vênia,* and *cã-cã* (Kubik 116).

The dance itself was described extensively by travelers both to Brazil and Africa. Joachim Monteiro, a Portuguese visitor who spent years in Angola, wrote in 1875 of dancers "swaying the body about with only a slight movement of the feet, head, and arms, but at the same time the muscles of the shoulders, back, and hams are violently twirled and convulsed ... passing one another backwards and forward, then retreat facing one another, and suddenly advancing, bring their stomachs together with a whack. They then retire, and another couple instantly takes their place" (Fryer 181). Descriptions from Brazil include Martius (1817) and Freyreiss (1820s), quoted below, respectively:

The baduca is performed by one single male and one single female dancer, dancing alternately towards and away from each other, snapping their fingers with the most wanton movements and licentious gesticulation. The main attraction this dance holds for Brazilians is to be found in rotations and artful twists of the pelvis.... Despite its obscene character, this dance is nevertheless widespread throughout Brazil and is everywhere the property of the lower class of people, who refuse to be deprived of it even though it is banned by the church. It appears to be of Ethiopian origin and to have been transplanted to Brazil by Negro slaves, where, like many of their other customs, it has taken root [qtd. in Fryer 98].

The dancers form a circle ... the dancer standing in the middle moves his lower abdomen against a person in the circle, usually of the opposite sex. At first the music is slow, as are the dancer's movements; however, both accelerate, and, as the music reaches its emotional peak, the dancer quickly presses his or her lower abdomen against somebody in the circle who then assumes his or her role, and so the dance goes on, often lasting whole nights. No more lascivious dance can be imagined..., and consequently it has no lack of opponents [Fryer 101].

In Bahia, participants were more likely to dance in a circle, whereas in São Paulo, dancers formed rows which alternately advanced and withdrew. Ironically, the custom also took root, gradually, amongst whites, growing in popularity amongst all classes, most likely due to the intoxicating nature of the music and dancing (the Bantu word *batukue* means "they who have become excited"). Rugendas wrote:

Soon there began the batuques, those lewd dances which the inhabitants of Brazil have borrowed from the Africans. They were danced only by men to begin with. Nearly all were whites; they would not have wanted to fetch water or wood like their Negroes, but they did not think they were demeaning themselves by copying the ridiculous and uncouth contortions of the latter. The Brazilians show a good deal of indulgence to their slaves, with whom they mingle so often, who have perhaps contributed to teaching them the system of agriculture they practice and the way to extract gold from streams, and who moreover were their dancing masters [Fryer 101].

As noted in these descriptions, the Catholic Church, and many European citizens, were shocked and frightened by the batuque. In 1802, a professor from Salvador noted the "barbarous *batuque* throughout the city streets to the beat of horrible atabaques, indecently dancing to pagan songs and speaking various languages" (Fryer 96). Bahia's newspaper, *Correio Mercantil,* reported: "Horrifying scenes are witnessed in this city on Sundays and Holy Days, and especially during the eight days of coronation celebrations. Let us speak clearly: in view of the tumultuous and numerous African *batuques* to be seen all around every day by the peaceful resident, making him hurry in terror to reach his house, who would not justify, to a certain degree, the sudden terror that takes over a whole population" (qtd. in Reis 209). A district police officer, Antonio Luiz Affonso de Carvalho, defined batuques as "the most barbarian and immoral dances, with non-rhythmic and loud voices ... the most complete orgy, a stage for drunkenness, fights and crimes" (qtd. in Reis 212).

Also, many citizens and leaders were afraid of slave uprisings, thought to be enticed by the dances attracting crowds in the hundreds and thousands. Others believed the batuque was a method of controlling aggression. Thus, the debate began: should officials be rigid and prohibit the dance, or would the batuque prove to be "the safest and most efficient way to avoid the disorders caused by black slaves" (Count of Arcos qtd. in Reis 207). Arcos believed "revelry helped relieve the slaves' souls from oppression, made them forget their miserable lives for a few hours, and, more importantly, promoted ethnic division among them" (qtd. in Reis 207). A fellow official, medical doctor and liberal politician João de Oliveira, equated the batuque to any other type of music or dance and felt "there was no way to enter the human heart and say 'I hereby extinguish this source of passion.... The law should reconcile civil liberty with social rights" (qtd. in Reis 213).

The Count of Ponte, nevertheless, agreed with the sentiments of Luís Vilhena, a Portuguese Greek language teacher, who wrote:

> It does not seem to me to be sound politics to tolerate that in the streets and its environs crowds of blacks of both sexes should make their barbarous *batuques* to the sound of so many horrendous tambours, dancing impudently, and singing gentile songs, speaking diverse languages, and with much noise and such horrendous and cacophonous shouts that cause fear and strangeness ... due to the consequences which can emerge from this situation, given the ... number of slaves that there are in Bahia, a fearful corporation which deserves much attention" [qtd. in Reis 206].

As Reis notes, the fears of officials such as Ponte were well-founded: "African slaves continued to arrive by the thousands every year, even after the prohibition of the slave trade in 1831. At least 170,200 were imported to Bahia between 1820 and 1850, the majority illegally. Slaves formed 40 percent of Salvador's 65,000 strong population in 1835. Approximately 60 percent of these slaves had been born in Africa, and hence including the African freed men and women, 34 percent of the population came from the continent.... All of this took place in an era shaken by slave revolts, of which the most serious was probably the 1835 uprising of predominately Muslim and Nagô people" (Reis 208).

These fears were expressed in legislation:

- 1779: The Inquisition sought to eradicate the batuque in Pernambuco, associating the dance with pagan rituals.
- 1796: The military commander of Goiana sought to end the batuques on plantations.
- 1814: The Masters of Lisbon ordered the Count of Arcos to put a stop to "batuque de Negros" to enforce a ban of Negroes gathering in groups

of more than four or visiting the city without the owner's permission, the punishment therefore to be 150 lashes.

- 1833: The Rio de Janeiro magistrate demanded a ban on drumming in the city, as they "drew slaves from outlying plantations." Slaves were arrested for dancing to drums.
- 1836: Itamaracá from Peruambuco prohibited batuques at any hour.
- 1845: Batuque and African royal ceremonies were banned in Santa Catarina (in the town of Desterro).
- 1846: The *batuque com algazarra* (with clamour), supposedly disturbing the neighborhood, was forbidden in Diamantina and Minas Gerais. Dancers were thrown in jail.
- 1849: The Rio de Janeiro police broke up a group of more than 200 dancing to the beat of drums.
- 1853: Batuque dancers in Minas Gerais could not dance at night, and had to pay 2 milréis to participate in the dance during the day.

By 1855, a serious slave uprising had not occurred in twenty years, perhaps because batuque did in fact attract participants from all races—white, black, and mulatto. Hence, "the *batuque* and later the samba would not lose the marks of their African moulds" (Reis 213), and would allow all classes to "lay their formalism aside and give themselves to the interest and delight which it incites" (Lindley qtd. in Welsh-Asante 85).

As the bans and ordinances abated in the late nineteenth century, two other dance streams mixed with the choreographical matrix of the batuque, the *lundu* and the *maxixe*, to create the dance of modern Brazil, the samba. The *lundu*, a popular transracial dance, common to all levels of society in the nineteenth century, was "danced by a *mulata*, whose gliding movements are strongly African, and a white partner whose snapping fingers and arm gestures, one hand on the hip and one on his forehead, are unmistakably those of Iberian *fandango*" (Chasteen 35). A *mulata* refers to a woman of mixed racial descent in common terms, who metaphorically "represents the concrete and symbolic synthesis of sexual intercourse between a white master and his black female slave" who also embodies "sensuality, voluptuosity, and dexterity in dancing the samba" (Pravaz 48).

Maxixe was a sort of forbidden dance, belonging to the streets, for it constituted white, middle-class or elite males dancing with women of darker complexion. Maxixe, like the lundu, was a couple dance, involving "very close contact between the bodies of the dancers, who sometimes pressed their foreheads together, their legs interlaced as in *lambada*, with full body contact at all points in between" (Chasteen 39), characterized by seductive movements of the hips, legs and torso. Street pageants (congos) and *festas* also contributed

The lundu, forerunner to the samba, as depicted (circa 1835) by Johann Moritz Rugendas (1802–1858).

to the rise of samba, a black reaction to the white influence found within the lundu and maxixe, and a means of return to authenticity.

At the turn of the twentieth century, Brazil's identity was intertwined with the samba, a dance whose story and meaning speaks to racial contact, conflict, resistance, and integration, whose sambistas truly "speak with the feet" of the "fragmentation of a holy black body ... and the healing of spiritual and political wounds" (Browing 32). Taylor notes: "*Sambistas* 'live the samba,' both as a major source of communal organization and as a vital art form. They are born in a world where the *samba* itself was born, a world defined by and organized around the sentiments and institutions associated with the dance" (Taylor 305). A fictional construct from the turn of the century explains: "In *samba* are absorbed the hatreds of color. The *samba* is— if you will permit me the expression — a kind of pot into which enter, separately, dark coffee and pale milk, and out of which is poured, homogeneous and harmonic, the hybrid *café-com-leite:* coffee with milk" (qtd. in Browning 17). It is a dance of hopelessness and hope, suffering, love and hatred which emanated from the atrocity of slavery, as well as the dance of the deity *de cabolo*, she who manifests herself to those who dance the rhythms, the "enchanted one" who heals by means of pleasure. It is a dance of all and for all, a dance of loss, a dance of triumph.

Indeed, the derivation of the word confirms the samba's diverse origins. *Semba* is the Afro-Brazilian term for umbigada, or meeting of the bellies, and Kimbundun and Ngangelan (Angola) for "belly bounce." In Kimbundu, samba means to be very excited, to be boiling over! For the Kusambans of Angola, it is a jump for joy, to skip or gamble. For the Bangi of the Congo, *somba* is to dance the divination dance. In the northeast of Guinea, samba is a rhythm. *Sánba* in Portuguese is to pray or a prayer. For the Kikongo, *sá amba* is an initiation group in which a person becomes competent for political, social, and religious functions, and, by extension, the hierarchy of deities.

The forms of samba also speak to varying influences, distinct to regional contributions: "In Rio de Janeiro, *samba* presents the gliding step; *tambor de crioula* from Maranhao; *tambor* from Paaui; *bambelo* from Rio Grande do Norte; *samba de roda*, Bahia; *jongo*, from the states of Rio de Janeiro and São Paulo; *samba* and *partido alto*, from the city of Rio de Janeiro; *samba lenco*, São Paulo; *caxambu* from the states of Rio de Janeiro and Minas Gerais. In the samba schools of Rio de Janeiro can be found the creative force of this kind of popular music in a permanent state; it is from those centers that *samba* radiates, influencing the whole country" (Leacock 406).

Browning refers to samba as the dance of "the body articulate," in which "the feet keep up a rapid patter, while the hips beat out a heavy staccato and the shoulders roll a slow drawl" (Browning 2). The dance ignores the "closed, smooth, and impenetrable surface of the body, and retains only its sensuous and instinctual characteristics ... *samba* is movement performed by the body as an end in itself" (Slutskaya 856). The organizational principles of the body movement are: repetition, contrast (a greater emphasis placed on certain movements), and chain reaction (the linear "rolling-out" of the movements). The body's purpose is to project and represent, an abstract going inward only to "discover outward-bound patterns of meaning, granting to the human being the feeling of being able to fully inhabit the world, understand it, and constantly orientate itself within it" (Slutskaya 857). Every dancer does not necessarily know what they are doing, thus "in *samba* one has no choice but to think with the body" (Slutskaya 859).

The dance is on a three count — right-left-right/left-right-left, layered over 2/4 time, the strong beat suspended, the weak accentuated. This accentuated count might read: and A 1 and 2 and 3, 4 and A 1 and 2 and 3, 4 with a ball-heel configuration of b-h b b b-h b b. Hips move with the feet; when stepping on the right foot, they switch left-right, when on the left foot, right-left, for as Guillermoprielo notes, "the magic of samba lies in the illusion that somebody is moving like crazy from the waist down while an entirely different person is observing the proceedings from the waist up" (Guillermoprielo 37). This is a possible metaphorical allusion to the more controlled movements of white European dance and the tempestuous Afro-Brazilian dances from which the samba emerged.

Rhythmically, "samba, the dance, cannot exist without the suppression of a strong beat" (Browing 9–10), encapsulating the political and social history of its origins. Its rhythm, as in batuque, is, again, born upon the sounds of percussion: batuque drums, the *agogo* (a clapperless double bell), and the *cuíca* (also known as the puita or pwita), a friction drum capable of emitting animal-like sounds ranging from a squeak to a roar.

This dance genre, formed by the black inhabitants of the hills (*morros*) on which the shanty-towns (*favelas*) of Rio de Janeiro stood, was the poor Afro-Brazilians "family, our Sunday stroll, our movies, our theatre. It was all we really knew of happiness there on the *morros*" (qtd. in Fryer 156). Bahia played a significant role in the development of samba as well, for "in the late 1800s, many inhabitants from Bahia migrated to Rio de Janeiro as a consequence of the Canudos War, the decline of plantations in Bahia state and the abolition of slavery in 1888. They worked at the docks, as street vendors, and as domestic servants. Bahians brought with them African-Brazilian percussion jams and dances, and settled in the local *favelas*" (Pravaz 54). Bahian women, in particular, figured prominently in the development of the samba, "selling sweets during the day and sponsoring *candomblé* sessions and *samba* parties at night. They were respectfully known as 'aunts,' they had 'samba in the foot,' they had survived, and they kept the culture going. They were root" (Guillermoprielo 52). (The baianas, as the "aunts" came to be known, wore long, ruffled white dresses with white collars and accompanying headdresses. They are still honored today in all samba schools parades with a contingency of dancers.)

One particular Baiana of note is Aunt Tia Ciata, who advanced the creation of the dance, holding religious and informal music-making gatherings with famous samba composers, such as Pixinguinha, Donga, João da Baiana, Heitor dos Prazeres, and Sinho. Guillermoprielo describes these sessions: "In Aunt Ciata's spacious residence on the outskirts of the Old City there may have been formal dances in the parlor, but there were African drum sessions in the backyard, and when the party got hot, there was samba. Her house soon became a meeting ground for sambistas from the hills and professional musicians, and for those who had made the transition from one to the other. Sinhô, the earliest master of the samba form, was a regular. So was Donga, one of the first samba composers to tour in Europe. The samba chronicler

Traditional dress of the Baianas (courtesy André Koehne).

Cold-Feet Turkey never missed a session. It could be argued that it was from Aunt Ciata's house that samba itself made the final leap to respectability" (Guillermoprielo 26). Supposedly, it was in Tia's home that the first samba composition was written in 1916 by Donga and Cold-Feet Turkey, "Pelo (on the) Telephone." The song alluded to corrupt officials; similar to the batuque, police attempted to suppress the sambas performed on the streets or at Carnaval. The lyrics, a dig at police corruption, warned of police raids:

> The chief of police rang me up
> Just to let me know
> That there's a good roulette game
> In Carioca Plaza.

Afro-Brazilians used Catholic religious festivals as a means of freely performing their dances, despite bans, ordinances and regulations. As Englishman James Wetherell wrote in 1856, "Upwards of 20,000 blacks would be assembled and scattered over the hill, upon which the church is situated: hundreds would be dancing ... prohibited for some years, but immense crowds, dressed in the height of negro fashion, go there during the three Sundays in January when the feast takes place" (qtd. in Reis 211). Wetherell's pas-

Entrudo games during Carnaval, circa 1822.

sage is describing "Carnaval," the origins of which date back to the Greek festival of Dionysus (the god of wine), Bacchanalia, and the Roman Saturnalia, in which slaves and their masters exchanged clothes and engaged in revelry. The Roman Catholic Church modified these pagan celebrations with a festival leading up to Ash Wednesday, calling the *festa* Carnaval, a last gasp of earthly pleasure before the commemoration of Lent, a six week sacrificial period prior to Easter. The Brazilian forerunner of Carnaval is the *entrudo*, introduced by the Portuguese King João VI in 1723, subsequent to his exile to Brazil, escaping the wrath of Napoleon. Participants in the entrudo soaked each other with buckets of water, throwing mud and food into the streets as well. Breaking all norms, "hard-core *entrudo* players employed syringes the size of small fire-extinguishers to suck none-too-sweet-smelling water from the gutter and recycle it with deadly aim. Like other carnival activities, *entrudo* refused to recognize limits, so anyone passing in the street was considered fair game — the more pompous, the better" (Chasteen 36). By the early 1800s, the Emperor joined in the celebration with masks, luxurious costumes, and music figuring into the street festivities. Groups of masked and costumed performers became known as *cordões* or *ranchos*. By the 1840s, dance was introduced into the *festa*, specifically the polka and waltz. Masked balls imitated the Parisian Carnaval. A decade later, horse drawn street parades, complete with floats, followed, resulting in the dawn of the modern-day Carnaval. The "wicked" maxixe also became a part of Carnaval, "a fever that no one of the masculine sex escapes" (Chasteen 39). Samba was not introduced into the Carnaval until 1917, but by the mid-30s was practically a Carnaval institution. The most famous Brazilian Carnaval takes place in Rio de Janeiro, although the Bahia Carnaval is quite elaborate as well. Due to the international status of the Rio Carnaval, in 1984 world famous architect Oscar Neimeyer created the *Sambadrome* to host the Rio Carnaval and the over 40,000 samba dancers who participate in the *festa* each year. Today, samba is referred to as the "alive" part of Carnaval.

Turn-of-the-century intellectuals scorned the *mestico*, or person of mixed race, who had become the scapegoat of the international image of Brazilian "backwardness." Of course, the mesticos of the morros played a large part in samba gatherings. Sambistas were also considered "low-lifes," chased by police in public gatherings and driven off the streets. According to the "old-guard" sambistas, the police treated dancers like criminals, subjecting them to beatings and arrests. Donga remembers "how the police used to make a point of persecuting what they called the jungle follies and how police would raid *sambistas'* homes in order to confiscate their guitars" (qtd. in Guillermoprielo 27). Jota Efegê chronicled this contentious period: "In those vanished times of 1920 until almost 1930, *samba* was considered illegitimate. It was looked on as the stuff of lowlife rascals, the carol of vagabonds. And the police, in their chief function of watching over the maintenance of public order, persecuted *samba* without rest" (qtd. in Vianna 11). Anthropologist Peter Fry affirms: that "originally, when *samba* was produced and consumed by the people of the *favelas*, it was severely repressed by the police and forced to conceal itself in *candomblé*, which was then considered slightly more acceptable" (Vianna 12). Ruben Oliven writes, "*Samba*, another legitimate symbol of Brazilian culture, was at first produced and consumed in the *favelas* of Rio de Janeiro and violently repressed by the police" (Vianna 12).

How then did samba gain respectability in just over a decade, becoming the highlight of Carnaval and the prevailing image of Brazilian identity? First, Zé Pereiras, an immigrant shoemaker, formed groups (which became known simply as Ze Pereiras) of drummers who marched on the fringes of Carnaval, wearing feathered, Amazonian-type costumes, while *Cucumbys* danced the maxixe. According to a 1902 chronicle: "All carnival revellers now left home with a spring in their step, ready to dance ... feet begin to tap and the passengers start to bounce uncontrollably in their seats as they approach the reveling. Suddenly, a Zé Pereira passes close by, and leaping down to follow it, off go the passengers" (Chasteen 42). A street dance competition was even initiated in 1906 by the *Gazeta de Notícias*, and, suddenly, "Rio's turn-of-the-century street dancers felt themselves the centre of something distinctively and attractively Brazilian" (Chasteen 43).

Second, due to the ever-increasing popularity of the *lunda* and maxixe street dancing held during Carnaval, the movements and music of the sambistas (who also began following along the fringes accompanied by capoeiristas who parted the waters, so to speak) subsequent to the genre's 1917 breakthrough (the recording of Donga's On the Telephone), also gradually gained acceptance amongst all classes, though first known as ragamuffin bands. (The mixed-race dancers of both the batuque and samba have always been "familiar with the *festa* pattern, not to mention Carnaval, and are thus predisposed to accept a mixture of ritual and hedonism as a normal part of religious behavior" ["Fun-Loving" 106]). Third, *escolas de samba* (samba schools) were eventually opened within the favelas, the first, started by Ismael Silva in 1927, known as Deixa Falar (Let Them Speak). (Deixa Falar first entered the parade in 1929, led by a bugler and horse brigade of the military police.) These schools worked tirelessly throughout the year to develop parade themes associated with samba and other associated Brazilian motifs (the mayor of Rio subsidized the schools in 1933, and the schools were officially featured on the Carnaval program by 1935). Fourth, "the rise of *samba* was part of a larger nationalizing and modernizing project undertaken during the Vargas era" (Welsh-Asante 92). Vargas, who took power during the 1930 Brazilian revolution, was in fact idealized by the Deixa Falar in a 1932 parade sponsored by the *Jornal do Brasil*, entitled "Spring and the October Revolution." Understandably, Vargas fervently supported samba and Carnaval, and "in 1937 the authoritarian national government of Vargas's New State decreed that the samba schools must dramatize historical, didactic, or patriotic themes. The sambistas of Rio accepted the regulations, and the model of Rio Carnival was then extended to the rest of Brazil" (Vianna 90). Vargas's minister, Oswaldo Aranha, announced, "I'm one of those who have always believed in our true national music. I don't believe in foreign influence on our melodies. We are a new people. And new peoples generally triumph over the older ones. Brazil, with its new music, its own music, is going to triumph" (qtd. in Vianna 91). Obviously, as Vianna notes, "the invention of *samba* as a national music involved many different social groups. The *favela* dwellers and sambistas of Rio de Janeiro played a leading, but not exclusive, role. Among those involved were blacks and whites (and, of course, *mesticos*), as well as a few gypsies— also a Frenchman here or there. Cariocas (Rio citizens) and Bahianos, intellectuals and politicians, erudite poets, classical composers, folklorists, millionaires, even a U.S. ambassador — all had something to do with the crystallization of the genre and its elevation to the rank of national symbol" (Vianna 112).

Samba continues to serve as an agent of national unification, "a kind of art which contains the echo of the African laugh, drum sounds and dances, always present with the Brazilians" (Welsh-Asante 92). "Whoever wants to and likes it can participate.... The *samba* today is highly thought of as a sport; even the elite participate" (Taylor 309). Now popular across the globe as well, millions of international visitors arrive in the Sambadrome each year to enjoy samba Carnaval parades. Couple dancers compete in ballroom samba events worldwide.

For Latin-Americans, samba now represents the struggle for social and racial equality. (Fighting the money-making nature of samba schools in today's economy, Black-African groups in the 1980s initiated the "pagoda" samba movement to not only provide alternatives to gang life, but also to once again find the heart of samba, the dance of harmony.) Finally, the ever-energetic samba continues to evolve into new musical and dance forms, for example *samba-reggae*. Perhaps the power of samba is obvious: It keeps leading us "back to Eden, back to our primordial African roots, back to dancing (as a human family) to the 'World Beat'" (Jaeck 49). Perhaps, samba will, once again, provide the courage needed for heroic resistance as the age-old fight against evil returns in the form of fundamentalist terrorism (such as the Lebanese ban mentioned at the opening of this chapter), a resistance "called-down" by the rhythms of the batuque, the samba — a resistance whose purpose is to insure not only the perpetuation of Brazilian identity, history, and culture, but also the perpetuation of humankind's mosaic of cultures, religions, and ethnicities, the prolongation of civil society, human rights, harmony, freedom ... peace. Heed the call.

16

It Takes Two to Tango!

"...sad, severe tango...
Dance of love and death..." — Ricardo Güiraldes

Even before tango reached the pinnacle of its popularity (the Golden Age, 1935–55) within the dance's city and country of origin, Buenos Aires, Argentina, the world had already embraced, then rejected the seductive, mysterious, and complex art form, compliments of the city of Paris, known for finding, sharing, and catapulting the most excellent art, philosophy, and thought from around the world. In 1910, the City of Lights played its global role once more, when Mistinguett, one of France's greatest music-hall stars, introduced "le tango" during a demonstration with Professor Bottallo, director of the Academy of Dance and Deportment. By 1913, "tangomania" "had reached even the most fashionable salons, causing shockwaves in French society.... The tango was everywhere that summer, taken up by almost everyone — beau monde, demi-monde, bourgeoisie, and petite-bourgeoisie.... There were tea-tangos, held between four in the afternoon and seven, where the public, for an entry fee of up to five francs including tea and sandwiches, could dance to their heart's content. There were also champagne-tangos, surprise-tangos, charity tangos, dinner-tangos, and of course tangos in nightclubs, spreading like wildfire to cater to the dance craze.... There were tangos on ice at the Palais de Glace on the rond-point des Champs Elysées.... There was even a 'Tango Train' which plied its way between Paris and Deauville during the summer season" (Collier 76). The tango inspired the Paris fashion industry, and women began wearing smaller hats, raised waistlines, loose sleeves, slit dresses, and even a tango color ranging from yellow to reddish-orange. The dance was used to sell everything from perfume to corsets, and its popularity soon spread throughout Europe, America, and Russia.

The flip-side of the coin, eradication, rather than embracement, also turned up. Germany's Kaiser dismissed his officers if they performed the tango or fraternized with anyone who did. Members of the Royal Opera House ballet were warned against participating in any charity events in which tango was performed. Austro-Hungarian officers could not dance the tango, nor anyone in Bavaria, whose King described the dance as "absurd." The Vatican found it "offensive to the purity of every right-minded person." Cardinal Cavallari of Venice wrote, "It is everything that can be imagined. It is revolting and disgusting. Only those persons who have lost all moral sense can endure it. It is the shame of our days. Whoever persists in it commits a sin" (qtd. in Knowles 124). "Tango madness" took hold. In America, the Baptist church in New York City called the tango "a craze, a form of nervous degeracy ... a civilized 'snake dance' ... in which parents throw their children to the crocodiles" (Knowles 125). Evangelist Bob Jones declared, "New Yorkers are tangoing themselves on the brink of hell ... the only difference between Manhattan and hell is that Manhattan is surrounded by water" (qtd. in Knowles 126). Cleveland, Ohio, banned the dancing of the tango outright. (Teacher Ana Anderson sued the city, demonstrating the art with a pupil at the trial. Judge Vickery ruled: "Every beautiful thing may be vulgarized. But because some dancing is vulgar, we could not bar all dancing" [qtd. in Knowles 126].) Several universities barred the dance, notably Notre Dame and Yale. Even the American Medical Association declared tango could aggravate the kidneys, cause insomnia, strain the heart, or activate arthritis! Some experts agreed it was a "strain on the brain." Fortunately, common sense prevailed in, of all places, Sheboygan, Wisconsin, whose paper, the *Sheboygan Press,* noted: "We have the word of a well known physical culturist that the tango is the very best sort of tonic for good health. For the tango, danced properly, according to this authority, brings almost every muscle into play ... it is a great rejuvenator" (qtd. in Knowles 132).

How is this dance, which caused such an uproar at the turn of the twentieth century, defined? Tango: "An investigation of the nature of human relationships, of the meaning of intimacy, and of what it is to be human and a social creature in a world that is often lonely and isolating" (Denniston 187–8). The most likely derivation: "From the word 'Tangonette'—a special variety of castanet used in dancing—when translated actually means 'I touch,' being the first person singular of the Spanish verb 'tangir,' meaning 'to touch' and doubtless chosen as a title for the dance owing to the somewhat close proximity of the partners.... This gives further proof, if further proof were needed, of the undoubted Spanish origin of the dance" (qtd. in Knowles 105). The reality: "The tango is man and woman in search of each other. It is the search for an embrace, a way to be together, when the man feels that he is a male and the woman feels that she is a female, without machismo ... the dance is the coupling of two people defenseless against the world and powerless to change things" (Copes qtd. in Collier 169). The history: "A cohesion of opposites which has so characterized Argentina's story: rich and poor, immigrant and native, white and black, men and women, the powerful and the powerless, the many pieces that should not fit together but will not come apart" (Savigliano qtd. in Nielsen 17).

Buenos Aires, Argentina, in the 1880s was indicative of the explicitly diametrical nature of a society undergoing rapid economical and technological change: the building of cultural centers, gardens, architectural wonders, restaurants, gardens, pitted against "the illnesses of development," in this instance "too many men, too much fast and unstable money-making, and prostitution" (Savigliano 86). The culture of the cattlemen *(gauchos)* of the *pampa* (plains) was dying, as wealthy landowners were opening vast tracts of land to ranching and agriculture. Technology (steamships, railways, telegraphs) allowed beef and commodities to be shipped to Europe in enormous quantities. Buenos Aires became the economic and cultural "*centre*" of this exchange, seeking workers by the millions. Millions of immigrants from Europe flooded the city, primarily workers from Spain (1/3) and Italy (1/2). The population of the city rose from 180,000 in 1869 to 1,500,000 in 1914, becoming known as the "Paris of South America" (Collier 23). Outlying residential areas, *barrios*, constituted stratified social areas, some affluent, some the dwellings of those who worked in the slaughterhouses or who lived from the municipal trash dump, these districts known as the *arrabals*. (Of note: "Soldiers from the nearby barracks, sailors enjoying shore-leave, enterprising immigrant artisans, factory hands, slaughterhouse workers, herdsman, simple vagrants—these and many other people of relatively modest means made up much of the human world of the ephemeral Buenos Aires *arrabal*" [Collier 38].

The ethnic composition of the arrabals included Afro-Argentines, creoles (French, Spanish, and Portuguese colonizer descendants), the Spanish, Italians, Indians, and Spanish/Indian natives (gauchos). Men overwhelmingly outnumbered women. Thus began the endless conflict between "the many pieces that should not fit together but will not come apart" (Nielsen 17): oppressors and oppressed; men and women; rich and poor; white and colored; immigrant, assimilated, and native. From this forced merger, this competitive, urban spirit, this sense of uncertainty and intense loneliness, grew the tango, Argentina's "mirror of the multitude's soul" (Castro 279).

A mix of dances seems to have created the tango. First, the African *candombe* (a dance signified by jerky, semi-athletic contortions and *cortes*, or cuts, abrupt suggestive pauses) played a part, mocked by European immigrants. The movements associated with this parody of *candombe*, as performed by the *compadritos* (urban gauchos), developed the dance form, the *milonga,* in which "cortes and quebradas were incorporated into dances in which the partners danced together, not, as in the African-Argentina 'tango' apart" (Collier 46). *Compadritos* "reproduced their exaggerated parody of the black dance in the primitive dance-halls, saloons, and brothels ... to make, in effect, a new form of dance" ("Popular Roots" 97). Added into the "melting pot" was the rhythm and melody of the Spanish-Cuban *habanera*. Musical accompaniment included guitars, clarinetist, and violinists as well as the introduction of the *bandoneon,* the German-made squeezebox, the fundamental instrument of a particular style of music which came to be known as tango, itself. (Today, the bandoneon is rarely heard in any other type of music, and the 'archetypal tango sextet' consists of two bandoneons, two violins, a piano, and a double-bass. The bandoneon has 38 buttons for the right hand and 33 for the left. Each note can create two notes, dependent upon inflation and deflation.) As Nielsen notes, "Neither the music nor the dance came first; they evolved together, as musicians experimented with melodies and rhythms in response to the dancers, and like-wise, the dancers innovated to fit the music" (Nielsen 17). This mixture of culture, movement, and experimentation served to create the Argentine "Tango," whose corresponding music, melody, and rhythm evolved only to complement the all-important dance steps of a dynamic couple.

The agreement to dance is entered by use of the *cabezeo,* an intimate contact of the eyes followed by a small gesture of the head. Upon receiving the nod, the man walks to the woman's side and leads her to the dance floor (also returning her to the appropriate table at the end of the dance). The dancers' stance is heart-to-heart, perhaps the most intimate, personal, and emotionally challenging position of any dance, torso moved forward to project the center of each body closer. The knees are slightly bent, the hips and shoulders horizontal at all times. All of the weight is on one leg at a time. As each dancer steps backwards or forwards, the heart, or breastbone, "still has the sense of moving forwards. The heart is constantly searching for the heart of the partner, constantly trying to find a place within the partner's heart" (Denniston 111). Tango dancers begin by just standing still, absorbing the music and the presence of the other, establishing a shared space, a relationship (more important than any forward motion), contemplating a way to "attack" or "escape" life, together. Tango is one of few dances initiated in the leg instead of the hips, creating a springboard for action and reaction.

Little, if any, pressure is placed on the follower's back during the hold; the leader's hand is not pressing against the follower's back. Rather, the leader's right arm circles underneath the follower's left arm, insuring a position in which the leader's heart is in contact with the follower, rather than the leader's hand; rendering the follower the center of the leader's world. A wise leader knows how to "submit" to the follower, correspondingly obtaining the power to carry the follower wherever he wishes. The aim of both the follower and leader is "the giving of pleasure to the other person, with the understanding that giving pleasure to the other person was the wisest road to pleasure for oneself." Necessarily, the couple does not make eye contact, in order to keep the focus of attention on the heart and to allow the leader to be alert to the situation on the dance floor, for the follower's safety must be his priority at all times.

The bandoneon, the instrument for tango (courtesy Pavel Krok).

Steps are forward, back, and to the side, with frequent turns, accomplished by pivoting. The shoulders stay parallel and in front of each other throughout the turn, keeping the hearts in constant contact and alignment. Patterns include the turning walk (forwards, side, back, side, forwards); the forwards ocho (a circle trace, first clockwise, then counterclockwise); the cross (in which the follower is moving forwards, although with a backward step); the backwards ocho (a circle trace performed backwards, first clockwise, then counterclockwise); the sacada (the leader places his leg between the followers, causing a momentum which allows the follower's free leg to swing); the back sacada (the leader places his leg between the followers and steps back); boleos (the leader reverses the follower's back step, creating a momentum in which the follower's step slides or lifts — the faster the change of direction, the higher the foot flies — the softer the follower's leg, the sharper the movement); forward boleo (during a boleo, the leader reverses the turn, winding the follower's free leg around the supporting leg); and ganchos (any movement in which one dancer hooks a leg around a leg of the other dancer). Basically, the goal of the tango's step is to create "an emotional connection, to create a framework that gives the maximum possible choreographic freedom" (Denniston 105). Once accomplishing this goal, dancers use an infinite number of foot and leg rotations to change direction and/or even perform steps different from one's partner, resulting in a spellbinding display of improvised footwork. "Unlike more mechanical dances that are choreographed along well-defined patterns, the tango is biological and organic in design, and limitless in its conception as a dance" (Nielsen 20).

Also contributing to the spellbinding nature of the aesthetic is the immaculate dress of the dancers; men dress in fashionable suits of black or gray with the occasional white scarf or trimming, patent-leather shoes shined to perfection. If a man did not dress so in the Golden Age, it was looked upon as a "*Una falta de respeto a la mujer!*" (a vehement insult to the woman). Women wear flexible high-heeled shoes, strapped high on the ankle for support, and Hollywood-inspired, free-flowing, many times backless, colorful gowns.

Argentine tango dancers El Cachafáz and Carmen Calderon in an undated photograph.

Why did a couple's step dance "outplay" Argentine folkdances to become the quintessential symbol of national identity, especially since its early development may have occurred in brothels? As mentioned earlier, men outnumbered women, and combating loneliness enveloped the populace, specifically the white immigrant "slaves" imported from Europe and the Spanish/Native *compadritos*. Savigliano believes "class, ethnic, and race conflicts were clearly displayed in a gendered code that dramatized complex social conflicts in sexual terms ... Argentina's incorporation into global capitalism, with its promise of class mobility and erasure of racial conflicts, helped render tango a potent, quasi-universal expression of gender and sexual struggle — an issue of passion" (Savigliano 84) for "women were precious and rare creatures, heavily outnumbered by the men in any *milonga* (tango dance arena)" (Denniston 27).

Basically, the tango represented (and represents) the public display of male/female courtship, whether the courtship was *rufianesque*, in which women were the *object* of domination by men (such as is found in a brothel environment) or of the *romantic* style, portrayed in the tango steps of the Golden Age, a style which "assumed both males and females had the freedom to choose their partners, to love, and to experience passion," a style "nurtured by the aspiration of reaching unity with another human being, and the fear of living out one's days alone" (Nielsen 26). Tango, therefore, is the synthesis of true-to-life relationship possibilities, for both forms of relating with the opposite sex may exist in any location (for example, a brothel) or institution (i.e., marriage) in which males and females share intimacy, passion, or love. The dance, at first glance, may portray an encounter between the powerful, dominating male, and the subversive, submissive female, nevertheless, a closer inspection of the dance steps themselves (as provided above), the differing styles, the music, and tango lyrics reveal otherwise, as "what a man in the Golden Age of tango was searching for was a woman who waited — a woman whose presence he could feel, and who did not move unless he moved her" (Denniston 27). The social parallel was an environment in which the poor and downtrodden were subjected to oppression (the arrabales) versus one in which political, cultural, and aesthetic modes of personal and/or social growth governed (evidenced in Buenos Aires "Centre"). The intensity of this double-entendre theme (psychological and sociological) necessarily catapulted human interest in the art form.

How did the message of the newly-developed art spread worldwide even before the pinnacle of popularity crystallized in Argentina? First, "tango in Argentina was a phenomenon of the urban working class. In the homes of the wealthy, it was quite unknown. In their homes, yes, — but the teenage sons of the rich are not always in their parents' home. And somehow, quite a few of the young men who found their way into the most elegant salons in Paris had acquired the skill of dancing the Tango well enough to delight their Parisian hostesses" (Denniston 81). Second, "throughout the nineteenth and early twentieth centuries, Argentine high society traditionally sent its sons to Europe to take the grand tour and do those things young men must do when they come of age" (Baim qtd. in Knowles 111). Third, poet Ricardo Güiraldes was, more than any other individual, responsible for promoting the tango in Paris, writing a poem entitled "Tango" in 1911 and, the following year, per-forming the dance in front of astonished guests at a Paris salon. Fourth, enter-tainment agents discovered tango while visiting Buenos Aires and booked Argentine orchestras and dancers to perform in the clubs and cabarets of Paris.

Back home in Argentina, several factors contributed to the evolution and dispersion of the newborn dance. Performances were held at theatres during carnival. Organ grinders played the early forms of the music throughout the streets of Buenos Aires. Higher class nightclubs such as Hansen's, EL Tambo, and El Velódromo adopted the dance style, and musicians and lyricists began publishing works created specifically for the dances.

Tango lyrics, today the subject of scholarly studies, reflected the urban history of Buenos Aires, "love, the world of men and women, satire, the life of a prostitute, the philosophies of life, and social protest" (Castro 282), reflective and dependent upon the social history of the times: 1910s—the melancholy of an individual lost in a city of docks, harbors, and events, the poignancy of true love, the underworld of *machismo*, the resentment over competition for jobs and women; 1920s—working-class consciousness; 1930s—economic turmoil; 1940s—nostalgia associated with the growth of the city and the tango, a form of nationalism spearheaded by General Juan Perón. In fact, a unique vocabulary formed, the *lunfardo*, or Italian slang, the province of tango lyrics, and, as the dance was evolving, the criminal element within the city. "Although the origins of the language are as obscure as are those of the tango, collections of tango lyrics show that as the song form developed, *lunfardo* words were commonly used" (Castro 283). Though a battle ensued over the use of lunfardo within the civilized element of song lyrics, the language prevailed, for, once again, popular sectors, indeed humanity across the globe, could relate to the triumph and tragedy of life and death portrayed in the lyrical poetry. A sampling of tango lyrics follows: (1. "Giuseppe the Shoemaker," by Guilermo del Ciancio; 2. "From My Barrio," by Robert Emilio Goyeneche; and 3. "Junk Shop," by Discépolo):

> *Clickety clack*
> *Don Giuseppe is back*
> *Working the whole day long again*
> *Without rest [1930]*
> *And surrounded by the lights of every colour*
> *And all the fun of the cabaret,*
> *I sell caresses, and I sell love,*
> *In order to forget the one who left me [1924]*
> *The world has always been a mess and always will be, I know that,*
> *It was in 506 and will be in 2000 as well.*
> *It has always had thieves, schemers, suckers,*
> *Happy and bitter people, genuine objects and fakes,*
> *But the twentieth century's a real showcase of mischief,*
> *And nobody can deny it... [1935]*

Note: Three of Discépolo's songs were banned by the government.

Local celebrities emerged on the scene as well, such as dancer Ovidio Bianquet, known as El Cachafaz (Barefaced Cheek), taken as the all-time master of tango, one who could dance the steps of origin as well as the "softer" steps of ballroom dancing. He died, in fact, at a dance-salon in Mar del Plata, having just finished one dance, preparing to begin another. The son of a single mother from Buenos Aires, Carlos Gardel burst into the public eye with his beautiful baritone voice in 1917, recording "Mi Noche Triste" (My Sorrowful Night), meeting Charlie Chaplin, and starring in seven films, including *Tango Bar*. Touring for Paramount and RCA Victor, he carried the tango to Puerto Rico, Caracas, Maracaibo, Barranquilla, Cartagena, Medellin, and Bogotá before dying prematurely in a plane crash. The fiftieth anniversary of his death (1985) and the centenary of his birth (1990) were celebrated throughout Latin America. Gardel, so they say, "sings better every day." (The metaphor of Gardel's life, since he actually fought his way up from the lower classes, and was referred to as *el Morocho del Abasto*, or "guy of a dark complexion from the Abasto," is that social mobility was possible and Argentina herself could rise to new heights.)

Women singers entered the arena, most notably Azucena Maizani, who recorded Discépolo's songs. Tango sextets expanded their ensembles, emphasizing rhythm and bringing the music back to the dancer, lost to café tables and cinema portrayals during the '20s and early '30s. Arrangers were required for tango orchestras. Ismael Spitalnik remembered: "We had to study harmony and counterpoint and apply the new knowledge to enrich the interpretation of the tango. It was very different work from thirty years earlier ... we stood in opposition to the so-called classical musicians who looked down on us and despised us like rats" (Collier 150). Also, the "finest bandoneon player there has ever been or is ever likely to be," Anibal Carmelo Troilo, shared the spotlight, performing in the Tibidabo cabaret for sixteen years; his status in the world of tango is second only to Carlos Gardel. (Today the Buenos Aires restaurant Pichuco honors his memory.) Additionally, "commercialization, through recording companies, radio stations and music publishers, also played a part in fastening the tango's hold on Argentines of all classes" ("Popular Roots" 99). Tango became "an exotic good in the political economy of Passion: appropriation, accumulation, marketing, packaging, commercialization, distribution, and consumption of the wealth of exotic feelings, that is, of the Passion of the Other" (Savigliano qtd. in Jaeck 47). Having been half-way around the world and back, by 1935, tango entered its Golden Age.

During this era, considered the most choreographically complex in tango's history, males entered *prácticas,* men-only tango orders in which the novice first watched the dance, then learned how to follow, practicing four or five times a week. Only then could he try to lead. After another lengthy period, an older man (teacher) would take the young man to a milonga. "Naturally, no woman would dance with him in the *milonga* unless she had seen him dance and knew that he could do it. So his more experienced companions would ask a woman who was a friend, as a special favor to them, to dance with him, so the others could see. If his first *milonga* didn't go well, it would be back to the *práctica* for a few more months before he dared to try again" (Denniston 17). The whole process took over three years, with the first nine to twelve months spent learning to follow. Everyone tangoed, newspapers reserving page after page for dancing advertisements. Orchestras were booked a year in advance. Some milongas and cafés sponsored dances three times a day! María Nieves recalls, "We would dance with every-

Carlos Gardel, champion of tango (1933).

body.... We were swept away by our love for the tango, we just loved to go dancing. We didn't go out looking for sex, none of the girls in our gang did; we didn't care what the man looked like. It was a nice, beautiful, pure group of girls, interested only in the tango" (qtd. in Collier 155). (Women learned to follow by training with their father or brothers. This practice was appropriate to the woman's graduation to social dancing, for in the tango a woman must stop taking any responsibility for the safety of her movement on the floor, entering an *externalized* meditative state which allows for accuracy, balance, and a sense of stillness, conveying effortlessness and a sense of abandonment to the other.)

The serious nature of the training period paradoxically reflected the political seriousness of the age (1935–1955), for "between 1929 and 1941, the working family lived on 127 pesos per month, estimated to be 20 percent of the minimum required living wage" (Nielsen 14). Tango lyricists wrote songs of protest (as noted above) which were banned, and the minister of justice and education, Hugo Wast, even issued an edict forbidding lunfardo in tango lyrics. On the back of the working class protests, the army staged a coup in 1943, and Colonel Juan Perón "emerged as leader of the working class, settling strikes, and improving the plight of the working class" (Nielsen 14), elected president of Argentina in 1946. A fan of the tango, Perón rescinded the lunfardo edict and hob-nobbed with dancers and musicians, to include composer Hugo del Carril and lyricist Discépolo who "passionately defended Perón's government, turning the opposition's stances into radio cartoon monologues" (Nielsen 23). Perón even viewed (and used) tango as a means to increase the spirit of nationalism.

Ironically, however, a nation used to strife, competition, and melancholy, as well as the inherent sadness of the tango (a dance born of "real and profound failure, a complete frustration, so intense that it can evolve into infinite sorrow" [Soriano qtd. in Nielsen 18]) was at odds with the upbeat sentiment of the rural migrants and workers who acquired a comeuppance during the Peronist period. At least half of Argentina's tango dancers and musicians embraced the views of Communism, most notably Osvaldo Pugliese, a pianist, composer, and band leader from a working-class background (Nielsen 14). The middle and upper classes did not welcome the economic competition either, and though Perón's political experiments were progressive and sympathetic of the working class, they ultimately failed due to the social psychology of the times and the masses. Tango enthusiasts no doubt would have provided a heightened degree of support to Perón if they had foreseen the cyclone poised to twist tango into the Dark Ages.

Military juntas bombed the *Plaza de Mayo* in Buenos Aires in 1955, demanding Peróns' resignation. "Between Perón's overthrow and the fall of the last military junta in 1983, there were *sixteen* changes in government" (Nielsen 15). Tango, a symbol of nationalism and Peronist philosophy, was viewed as suspicious and dangerous by Communist leaders, its lyrics thought to incite opposition and rebellion. Denniston describes the profound effect on the tango art form:

Many prominent Tango artists found themselves either imprisoned or blacklisted for their Peronist associations—or even for the Peronist associations of their fans. And the junta actively encouraged the importation of the new popular music from the United States. Minors were not allowed into nightclubs, and this rule was actively enforced for Tango clubs, but a blind eye was turned for clubs playing Rock and Roll. So 14 and 15 year-olds, instead of learning Tango as their older brothers and sisters had, were going to Rock and Roll clubs. At various times in Buenos Aires meetings of more than two or three people were banned, and curfews were enforced, making it extremely difficult for any sort of social dance to take place. This created a climate that forced the dance underground....

In Buenos Aires practically no one learned to dance the Tango for almost thirty years [Denniston 77–79].

Tango experienced a pivotal redemption, thankfully, in 1983, when the military juntas fell and democracy returned to Argentina. Tango burst again into the national identity of Argentina as well as the international arena, boosted by the Parisian release of the show *Tango Argentina*, created by the team of Claudio Segovia and Hector Orezzoli, who chose older dancers Elvira Santamaria and Jorge Orcaizaguirre, not out of any political ideology, but because of their skill as dancers. The show portrayed the history of the tango through a sequence of dances and songs, the first dance, appropriately, performed by two men (*compadritos*) practicing to perfect their technique. The London-based *Spectator* described the show as "a flawless work of art," while the *Financial Times* noted the show was "sexual, glamorous and fateful ... this is the kind of vivid, meticulous, serious staging that we associate with Diaghilev" (Denniston 93). Japan's *Asahi Graph* devoted an entire article to the show. Everywhere the show played, people were determined to learn the tango.

Yet, how did young *porteñas* (the name Buenos Aires' citizens give themselves) learn the dance now, those "who had lived through a horrific period where pride in their national identity had been stretched to the limits" (Dennison 93). How might they again find joy in saying "*eso es lo nuestro*," 'this is ours,' for the dancers of the Golden Age remained skeptical of political retaliation. Young dancers began traveling to other countries to learn the dance, formed support groups, and trained with older dancers in a clandestine fashion. Finally, in the 1990s, described by Denniston as a "thrilling time to be a tango dancer," the new generation of dancers began mixing with those from the Golden Age, who taught from their heart, giving their best, allowing Buenos Aires' youth to dance in the milongas with those who were "part of the continuous, living tradition of tango" (Denniston 99). (Unfortunately, dancers from the Golden Age are fading away, and tango must now determine its future based upon their legacy.)

In the twenty-first century, the tango is kept alive by tourism, as well as the movie industry, international *aficionados*, celebrities (these last three elements appropriate to the history of the dance), and ballroom enthusiasts. Two of the oldest neighborhoods in Buenos Aires, La Boca and San Telmo, are "museums into themselves." Tango clubs, most notably the Casablanca, entertain visitors with dancing, drinks, historical brochures, and the opportunity to purchase CDs from classical and modern tango composers, to include the master of modern tango music, Astor Piazzolla. Tango appears on national TV several times a week in association with the reality TV ballroom dancing fad, and movies such as Al Pacino's *Scent of a Woman* and

Arnold Schwarzenegger's *True Lies* elicit sweltering reviews such as that found in the February 12, 1999, edition of *The New York Times*: "It's no slight to the lovers ... that the kissing seen here is less torrid than the dancing ... bodies tensed move in perfect unison ... the dancers need only display this dance's hypnotic blend of liquidity and fury, only revel in its dizzying complexity and split-second timing, to burn up the screen" (qtd. in Goertzen 73). Actor Robert Duvall, musician Eric Clapton, and classical celloist Yo-Yo Ma promote the dance and the music in performance venues and documentaries (Ma earned a Grammy in 1999 for his interpretation of Astor Piazzolla's works). Japan nourishes a core of *tango kichigai* (tango fanatics), and a modified version of the tango has become Finland's national folk dance, for, since its arrival in Helsinki in 1913, the "Finns do not think of the tango as Argentine, but as Finnish" (Collier 192). Certainly, modern tango is "old, new, certainly vital, and undeniably global" (Goertzen 74).

Tango, often described as the dance of life and death, has embraced and conquered both, reincarnating and reviving itself in a fashion similar to its cyclical nature, while remaining, above all (minus all the aplomb), the dance of two hearts fused into one, creator of life, of our next step! Hence, "there will never be a last tango ... the ceaseless dance that we may choose to call death, that we affirm as sensual expression, that we gauge as political or individual liberty, that we see as life, and that we cannot stop" (Collier 196).

Bibliography

Adams, Mildred. "Twenty Years of Franco." *Foreign Affairs* 37.2 (1959): 257–268.

Algranti, Leila Mezan. "Slave Crimes: The Use of Police Power to Control the Slave Population of Rio de Janeiro." *Luso-Brazilian Review* 25.1 (1988): 27–48.

Allen, Matthew Harp. "Rewriting the Script for South Indian Dance." *The Drama Review* 41.3 (1997): 63–100.

And, Metin. "The Mevlana Ceremony." *The Drama Review* 21.3 (1977): 83–94.

Andersson, Rani Henrik. *The Lakota Ghost Dance of 1890.* Lincoln: University of Nebraska Press, 2008.

Antar, Elias. "La Danse du Ventre." *Saudi Aramco World*, 4 March 2011. Accessed 30 May 2011.

Arundale, Rukmini Devi. "The Spiritual Background of Indian Dance." *A Bharata Natyam Reader.* Ed Davesh Soneji. New Delhi: Oxford University Press, (2010). 190–200.

Balasaraswati, T. "Bharata Natyam." *Presidential Address for 33rd Annual Conference Of the Tamil Isai Sangam.* Tr. S. Guhan. December, 1975, Tamil Isai Sangam, Chennai.

Balme, Christopher B. "Dressing the Hula. Iconography, Performance and Cultural Identity Formation in Late Nineteenth Century Hawaii." *Paideuma* 45 (1999): 233–255.

Barber, Theodore X. "Four Interpretations of Mevlevi Dervish Dance." *Dance Chronicle* 9.3 (1986): 328–355.

Baskervill, Charles. "Dramatic Aspects of Medieval Folk Festivals in England." *Studies in Philology* 17.1 (1920): 19–87.

Becker, Elizabeth. *When the War Was Over: Cambodia and the Khmer Rouge Revolution.* New York: Harcourt, 1986.

Beckwith, Martha W. "The Hawaiian Hula-Dance." *The Journal of American Folklore*, 29.113 (1916): 409–412.

Bejjani, Elias. "Brazilian Samba & Hezbollah's Terrorism." *Global Politician,* 1 October 2009. Accessed 1 June 2011.

Benedict, Ruth. *Patterns of Culture.* Boston: Houghton-Mifflin, 1934.

Berman, Judith. "Red Salmon and Red Cedar Bark: Another Look at the Nineteenth-Century Kwakwaka'wakw Winter Ceremonial." *BC Studies* 125 (2000): 53–98.

Bodensteiner, Kirsten. "Where Dance Reigns Over Evil." *Dance Spirit* 6.4 (2002): 53–102.

Bor, Joep. "Mamia, Ammani and other Bayaderes: Europe's Portrayal of India's Temple Dancers," *Music and Orientalism in the British Empire.* Ed. Martin Clayton and Bennett Zon. London: Ashgate, 2007.

Bordewich, Fergus. "A Flourishing of Whirling Dervishes." *New York Times,* 6 December 1987.

Box of Treasures. Dir. Chuck Olin. Documentary Educational Resources, 2010. DVD.

Brabant, Malcolm. "Egyptian Belly Dance in Crisis." *BBC News,* 30 March 2005. Accessed 30 May 2011.

Brabazon, Tara, and Paul Stock. "Bored of the Dance: Not in this Irish World." *Australian Quarterly* 71.3 (1999): 10–15.

Brandes, Stanley. "The Sardana: Catalan Dance and Catalan National Identity." *The Journal of American Folklore* 103.407 (1990): 24–41.

205

Bremer, Fredrika. *America of the Fifties: Letters of Fredrika Bremer*. New York: Oxford University Press, 1924.

Brennan, Helen. "Reinventing Tradition: The Boundaries of Irish Dance." *History Ireland* 2.2 (1994): 22–24.

_____. *The Story of Irish Dance*. Lanham: Roberts Rinehart Publishers, 2001.

Brissenden, Alan. "Shakespeare and the Morris." *The Review of English Studies* 30.117 (1979): 1–11.

Brown, Joseph Epes. *The Spiritual Legacy of the American Indian*. Canada: World Wisdom, 2007.

Browning, Barbara. *Samba: Resistance in Motion*. Bloomington: Indiana University Press, 1995.

Buck, Elizabeth. *Paradise Remade: The Politics of Culture and History in Hawai'i*. Philadelphia: Temple University Press, 1993.

Buonaventura, Wendy. *Serpent of the Nile: Women and Dance in the Arab World*. Northhampton, MA: Interlink Books, 2010.

Capoeira, Nestor. *The Little Capoeira Book*. Berkley: Blue Snake Books, 2003.

_____. *Roots of the Dance-Fight Game*. Berkeley: North Atlantic Books, 2002.

Carleton, William. "The Country Dancing-Master: An Irish Sketch." *The Irish Penny Journal* 1.9 (1840): 69–72.

Carlson, Paul H. *The Plains Indians*. College Station: Texas A&M University Press, 1998.

Carr, Darrah. "Colorful, Complex Creations Adorn Irish Dancers." *Dance Magazine*, October, 2001.

Castro, Donald. "The Soul of the People: The Tango as a Source for Argentine Social History." *Studies in Latin American Popular Culture* 9 (1990): 279–296.

Chakravorty, Pallabi. "From Interculturalism to Historicism: Reflections on Classical Indian Dance." *Dance Research Journal* 32.2 (2001): 108–119.

Chambers, Robert. *The Book of Days: A Miscellany of Anecdote, Biography, and History*. London: W&R Chambers, 1869.

Chandler, David P. "The Tragedy of Cambodian History." *Pacific Affairs* 52.3 (1979): 410–419.

Chasteen, John Charles. "The Prehistory of Samba: Carnival Dancing in Rio de Janeiro." *Journal of Latin American Studies* 28.1 (1996).

Chittick, William. *Sufism: A Short Introduction*. Oxford: One World Publications, 2000.

Codere, Helen. *Fighting with Property: A Study of Kwakiutl Potlatching and Warfare, 1792–1930*. Seattle: University of Washington Press, 1950.

Cole, Douglas. "Underground Potlatch." *Natural History* 100.10 (1991): 50–53.

Collier, Simon, et al. *Tango! The Dance, the Song, the Story*. London: Thames & Hudson, Ltd., 1995.

_____. "Popular Roots of the Argentine Tango." *History Workshop* 34 (1992): 92–100.

Colome, Delfi. "The Music of the Sardana." *Catalonia* (2000): 36–39.

Cravath, Paul. "The Ritual Origins of the Classical Dance Drama of Cambodia." *Asian Theatre Journal* 3.2 (1986): 179–203.

Dart, John. "Religious Freedom and Native Americans." *Theology Today* 38.174 (1981): 174–181.

Deaver, Sherri. "Concealment vs. Display: The Modern Saudi Woman." *Dance Research Journal* 10.2 (1978): 14–18.

Deloria, Ella. "The Sun Dance of the Oglala Sioux." *The Journal of American Folklore* 42.166 (1929): 354–413.

DeMallie, Raymond J. "The Lakota Ghost Dance: An Ethnohistorical Account." *Pacific Historical Review* 51.4 (1982): 385–405.

Denniston, Christine. *The Meaning of Tango: The Story of the Argentinian Dance*. London: Portico, 2007.

Diamond, Catherine. "Emptying the Sea by the Bucketful: The Dilemma in Cambodian Theatre." *Asian Theatre Journal* 20.2 (2003): 147–178.

Dils, Ann, and Ann Cooper Albright, eds. *Moving History/Dancing Cultures: A Dance History Reader*. Middletown, CT: Wesleyan University Press, 2001.

Dougherty, Dru, and Milton Azevedo. *Multicultural Iberia: Language, Literature and Music*. Berkley: University of California Press, 1999.

Dowling, Andrew. "The Reconstitution of Political Catalanism 1939–75." *IJIS* 14.1 (2001): 17–25.

Dox, Donnalee. "Dancing Around Orientalism." *The Drama Review* 50.4 (2006): 52–71.

Drinnon, Richard. "The Maypole of Merry Mount: Thomas Morton & the Puritan Patriarchs." *The Massachusetts Review* 21.2 (1980): 382–410.

Dunn, John. *The Relocation of the Native American Indian*. San Diego: Lucent Books, 1995.

Ellis, Clyde. "There Is No Doubt ... the Dances Should Be Curtailed": Indian Dances and Federal Policy on the Southern Plains, 1880–1930." *Pacific Historical Review* 70.4 (2001): 543–569.

Emerson, Nathaniel B. *Unwritten Literature of Hawaii: The Sacred Songs of the Hula*. Rutland, Vermont: Charles E. Tuttle Company, Inc., 1965.

Encarnación, Omar Guillermo. "Democracy and Federalism in Spain." *Mediterranean Quarterly* 15.1 (2004): 58–74.

Essien, Aniefre. *Capoeira Beyond Brazil: From A Slave Tradition to an International Way of Life*. Berkley: Blue Snake Books, 2008.

Floyd, Samuel A. "Ring Shout! Literary Studies, Historical Studies, and Black Music Inquiry." *Black Music Research Journal* 22 (2002): 49–70.

Flynn, Arthur. *Irish Dance*. Gretna, LA: Pelican Publishing Co., 1998.

Foley, Catherine. "Perceptions of Irish Step Dance: National, Global, and Local." *Dance Research Journal* 33.1 (2001): 34–45.

Forrest, John. *The History of Morris Dancing, 1458–1750*. Toronto: University of Toronto Press, Inc., 1999.

Foss, Clive. "When Turks Civilized the World." *History Today* 55.8 (2005): 10–16.

Frame, Robin. "Les Engleys Nees en Irlande: The English Political Identity in Medieval Ireland." *Transactions of the Royal Historical Society* 3 (1993): 83–103.

Fremantle, Anne. "Whirling Dervishes." *History Today* (1992): 329–334.

Friedlander, Shems. *The Whirling Dervishes*. Albany: State University of New York Press, 1992.

Fryer, Peter. *Rhythms of Resistance: African American Heritage in Brazil*. Hanover, NH: Wesleyan University Press, 2000.

Gallop, Rodney. "The Origins of the Morris Dance." *Journal of the English Folk Dance and Song Society* 1.3 (1934): 122–129.

Gilchrist, Anne G. "A Carved Morris-Dance Panel from Lancaster Castle." *Journal of the English Folk Dance and Song Society* 1.2 (1993): 86–88.

Goertzen, Chris, and Maria Azzi. "Globalization and the Tango." *Yearbook for Traditional Music* 31 (1999): 67–76.

Goldman, Irving. *The Mouth of Heaven: An Introduction to Kwakiutl Religious Thought*. Hoboken, New Jersey: John Wiley and Sons, 1975.

Guillermoprielo, Alma. *Samba*. New York: Vintage Books, 1990.

Hamera, Judith. "An Answerability of Memory 'Saving' Khmer Classical Dance." *The Drama Review* 46.4 (2002): 65–85.

Hawthorne, Nathaniel. *Twice Told Tales*. New York: Modern Library, 2001.

Hazzard-Gordon, Katrina. "Dancing Under the Lash: Sociocultural Disruption, Continuity, and Synthesis." *African Dance: An Artistic, Historical and Philosophical Inquiry*. Trenton, New Jersey: Africa World Press, Inc., 1996.

Heaney, Michael. "The Earliest Reference to the Morris Dance?" *Folk Music Journal* 8.4 (2004): 513–515.

Herrick, Robert. *Works of Robert Herrick, Volume I*. Ed. Alfred Pollard. London: Lawrence & Bullen, 1891.

Heth, Charlotte. *Native American Dance: Ceremonies and Social Traditions*. Washington: Smithsonian Institution, 1993.

Highwater, Jamake. *Ritual of the Wind.* Toronto: Methuen Publications, 1984.

Hill, Fred James. *Spain: An Illustrated History.* New York: Hippocrene Books, Inc., 2001.

Hinton, Alexander Laban. "Agents of Death: Explaining the Cambodian Genocide in Terms of Psychosocial Dissonance." *American Anthropologist* 98.4 (1996): 818–831.

"The History of Hula." Holo Mai Pele: A Mythic Hawaiian Tale of Love and Revenge. PBS. Accessed 10 November 2006.

Holloway, Thomas H. "A Health Terror: Police Repression in Nineteenth Century Rio de Janeiro." *The Hispanic American Historical Review* 69.4 (1989): 637–676.

Holm, Bill. "Traditional and Contemporary Kwakiutl Winter Dance." *Arctic Anthropology* 14.1 (1977): 5–24.

Hotson, Leslie. "Maypoles and Puritans." *Shakespeare Quarterly* 1.4 (1950): 205–7.

Hubel, Teresa. "The High Cost of Dancing: When the Indian Women's Movement Went After the Devadasis." *Intercultural Communications and Creative Practice: Dance, Music and Women's Cultural Identity.* Ed Laura B. Lengel. Westport: Praeger, 2005.

"Hula Gestures." Holo Mai Pele. PBS. Accessed 06 March 2007.

Irving, Washington. *The Complete Works of Washington Irving.* Paris: Baudry's European Library, 1854.

Jacknis, Ira. "Repatriation as Social Drama: The Kwakiutl Indians of British Columbia, 1922–1980." *American Indian Quarterly* 20.2 (1996): 274–286.

Jackson, Naomi, and Toni Shapiro-Phim. *Dance, Human Rights, and Social Justice: Dignity In Motion.* Lanham, MD: Scarecrow, 2008.

Jaeck, Lois Marie. "The Body as Revolutionary Text: The Dance As Protest Literature In Latin America." *Ciencia Ergo Sum* 10.1 (2003): 43–50.

Johnson, Dorothy M. "Ghost Dance: Last Hope of the Sioux." *Montana: The Magazine of Western History* 6.3 (1956): 42–50.

Johnston, Thomas. "The Social Context of Irish Folk Instruments." *International Review of The Aesthetics and Sociology of Music* 26.1 (1995): 35–59.

Jonaitis, Aldona, ed. *Chiefly Feasts: The Enduring Kwakiutl Potlatch.* Seattle: University of Washington Press, 1991.

Judge, Roy. "Cecil Sharp and Morris 1906–1909." *Folk Music Journal* 8.2 (2002): 195–228.

_____. "May Day and Merrie England." *Folklore* 2 (1991): 131–148.

_____. "Merrie England and the Morris 1881–1910." *Folklore* 104.1/2 (1993): 124–143.

Kaeppler, Adrienne L. "Acculturation in Hawaiian Dance." *Yearbook of the International Folk Music Council* 4.25 (1972): 38–46.

Karayanni, Stavros Stavrou. *Dancing Fear & Desire: Race, Sexuality, and Imperial Politics in Middle Eastern Dance.* Ontario: Wilfrid Laurier University Press, 2004.

Karpeles, Maud. "English Folk Dances: Their Survival and Revival." *Folklore* 43.2 (1932): 123–141.

Kersenboom, Saskia, "The Traditional Repertoire of the Tiruttani Temple Dancers." *Roles and Rituals for Hindu Women.* Ed. Julia Leslie. Delhi: Motilal Banarsidass, 1991.

Kingsley, Charles. *The Works of Charles Kingsley: Prose Idylls.* London: MacMillian & Co., 1880.

Klarr, Caroline. "Hula — Hawai'i's Own Dance." *CRM* 8 (1998): 26–7.

Knowles, Mark. *The Wicked Waltz and Other Scandalous Dances.* Jefferson: McFarland, 2009.

Kubik, Gerhard. "Drum Patterns in the Batuque of Benedito Caxias." *Latin American Music Review* 11.2 (1990): 115–181.

La Barre, Weston. *The Ghost Dance.* New York: Dell Publishing, 1970.

Lababidi, Yahia Samir. "Belly Dancing: A Dying Art?" *UNESCO,* 23 July 2009. Accessed 30 May 2011.

LaMothe, Kimerer L. "Sacred Dance: A Glimpse Around the World." *Dance Magazine,* 2001.

Laubin, Reginald and Gladys. *Indian Dances of North America.* Norman: University of Oklahoma Press, 1977.

Leacock, Seth. "Ceremonial Drinking in an Afro-Brazilian Cult." *American Anthropologist* 66.2 (1964): 344–354.

_____. "Fun-Loving Deities in an Afro-Brazilian Cult." *Anthropological Quarterly* 37.3 (1964): 94–109.

Lincoln, Bruce. "A Lakota Sun Dance and the Problematics of Sociocosmic Reunion." *History of Religions* 34.1 (1994): 1–14.

Lincoln, Jennette. *The Festival Book: May-Day Pastime and the May Pole.* New York: A.S. Barnes and Company, 1926.

Lowe, Barbara. "Early Records of the Morris in England." *Journal of the English Folk Dance and Song Society* 8.2 (1957): 61–82.

Lubliner, Coby. "The Sardana and I." *Berkeley Essays*, 11 April 2001. Accessed 12 May 2011.

Lydon, James. "Ireland and the English Crown, 1171–1541." *Irish Historical Studies* 29.115 (1995): 281–294.

Macilwaine, H.C. "The Revival of Morris Dancing." *The Musical Times* 47.766 (1906): 802–805.

Maira, Sunaina. "Belly Dancing: Arab-Face, Orientalist Feminism, and U.S. Empire." *American Quarterly* 60.2 (2008): 317–345.

Masco, Joseph. "It is a Strict Law That Bids Us Dance: Colonialism, Death, and Ritual Authority in the Kwakwaka'wakw Potlatch, 1849–1922." *Comparative Studies In Society and History* 37.1 (1995): 41–75.

"The May Pole." *The Dublin Penny Journal* 4.201 (1836): 355.

McCann, Frank D. "Last Hope of Western Tribes, Unleashed the Final Tragedy." *Montana: The Magazine of Western History* 16.1 (1966): 25–34.

McDermott, Edward. *The Merrie Days of England: Sketches of the Olden Time.* London: William Kent & Co., 1859.

"McIntosh County Shouters: Gullah-Geechee Ring Shout From Georgia." *Library of Congress.* Accessed 5 May 2011.

McPhee, Peter. A Case-Study of Internal Colonization: The Francisation of Northern Catalonia." *Review (Fernand Braudel Center)* 3.3 (1980): 398–428.

Meduri, Avanthi. "Bharatha Natyam — What Are You?" *Asian Theatre Journal* 5.1 (1988): 1–22.

Meneses, Rashaan. "The Near Extinction of Cambodian Classical Dance." *UCLA International Online,* 7 May 2004. Accessed 15 May 2011.

Mooney, James. *The Ghost Dance Religion and the Sioux Outbreak of 1890.* Chicago: University of Chicago Press, 1965.

Moses, L.G. "The Father Tells Me So: Wovoka: The Ghost Dance Prophet." *American Indian Quarterly* 9.3 (1985): 335–351.

Napper, Sheila. "Belly Wisdom: A New Body Politic." *Herizons* (2004): 24–44.

Nielsen, Christine, and Juan Mariotto. "The Tango Metaphor: The Essence of Argentina's National Identity." *International Studies of Management and Organization* 35.4 (2005): 8–36.

Nordland, Rod. "The Last Egyptian Belly Dancer." *Newsweek*, 31 May 2008. Accessed 30 May 2011.

Ó hAllmhuráin, Gearóid. "Dancing on the Hobs of Hell: Rural Communities in Clare and The Dance Halls Act of 1935." *New Hibernia Review* 9.4 (2005): 9–18.

O'Connor, Barbara. "Sexing the Nation: Discourses of the Dancing Body in Ireland in the 1930s." *Journal of Gender Studies* 14.2 (2005): 89–105.

O'Neill, Thomas. "Discoverers and Discoveries the Penal Laws and Dublin Property." *Dublin Historical Record* 37.1 (1983): 2–13.

Ohtani, Kimiko. "Bharata Natyam: Rebirth of Dance in India." *Studia Musicologica Academiae Scientiarum Hungaricae.* 33 (1991): 01–308.

Olin, Chuck, and U'mista Cultural Center, dir. *Box of Treasure.* Documentary Educational Resources, 1983. DVD.

Oumar, Arabov. "A Note on Sufism in Tajikistan: What Does It Look Like?" *Central Asian Survey* 23.3–4 (2004): 345–347.

Parrish, Lydia. *Slave Songs of the Georgia Sea Islands.* New York: Creative Age Press, 1942.

Perez, Joseph Marti i. "The Sardana as a Socio-Cultural Phenomenon in Contemporary Catalonia." *Yearbook for Traditional Music* 26 (1994): 39–46.

Powers, William K. *Oglala Religion*. Lincoln: University of Nebraska Press, 1975.

Prahlad, Prathibha. *Bharatanatyam*. Delhi: Wisdom Tree, 2004.

Pravaz, Natasha. "Imagining Brazil and the Mulata's Body: Seduction, Samba." *Canadian Woman Studies* 20.1 (2000): 48–55.

Puri, Rajika. "Bharatanatyam Performed: A Typical Recital." *Visual Anthropology* 17 (2004): 45–68.

Raibmon, Paige. "Theatres of Contact: the Kwakwaka'wakw Meet Colonialism in British Columbia and the Chicago World Fair." *Canadian Historical Review* 81.2 (2000): 157–185.

Reed, Little Rock. "Broken Treaties, Broken Promises: The US's Continuing Campaign vs. Native People." *Social Issues Resources* 68 (1992): 48.

Reed, Susan A. "The *Politics* and Poetics of Dance." *Annual Review of Anthropology* 27 (1998): 503–532.

Reid, Susan. "The Kwakiutl Man Eater." *Anthropologica* 21.2 (1979): 247–275.

Reis, João José. "Batuque: African Drumming and Dance Between Repression and Concession, Bahia, 1808–1855." *Bulletin of Latin American Research* 24.2 (2005): 201–214.

Rice, Julian. "It was Their Own Fault for Being Intractable: Internalized Racism and Wounded Knee." *American Indian Quarterly* 22.1/2 (1998): 63–82.

Ringel, Gail. "The Kawkiutl Potlatch: History, Economics, and Symbols." *Ethnohistory* 26.4 (1979): 347–362.

Rosenbaum, Art. *Shout Because You're Free: The African American Ring Shout Tradition in Coastal Georgia*. Athens: University of Georgia Press, 1998.

Rowe, Doc. *May Day: The Coming of Spring*. Swindon: English Heritage, 2006.

Rowe, Sharon M. "We Dance for Knowledge." *Dance Research Journal* 40.1 (2008): 31–44.

Samba on Your Feet. Patagonia Film Group, LLC, 2006. Film.

Savigliano, Marta. "Whiny Ruffians and Rebellious Broads: Tango as a Spectacle of Eroticized Social Tension." *Theatre Journal* 47 (1995): 83–104.

Schimmel, AnneMarie. "The Role of Music in Islamic Mysticism." *Sufism, Music, and Society in Turkey and the Middle East* (2001): 9–17.

Sellers-Young, Barbara. "Raks El Sharki: Transculturation of a Folk Form." *Journal of Popular Culture* 26.2 (1992): 141–152.

Shakespeare, William. *The Complete Works*. Ed. Peter Alexander. London: Collins, 1951.

Shannon, Jonathan. "Sultans of Spin: Syrian Sacred Music on the World Stage." *American Anthropologist* 105.2 (2003): 266–277.

"Shapiro, Sophiline: Interview." *Cambodia: Pol Pot's Shadow*. PBS, October, 2002. Accessed 15 May 2011.

Sharp, Ceci, and Herbert C. Macilwaine. *The Morris Book, Part I*. Charleston: Bibliobazaar, 2009.

Shay, Anthony, and Barbara Sellers-Young. "Belly Dance: Orientalism: Exoticism: Self-Exoticism." *Dance Research Journal* 35.1 (2003): 13–37.

Simeone, W.E. "The May Games and the Robin Hood Legend." *The Journal of American Folklore* 64.253 (1951): 265–274.

Sinclair, A.T. "Folk-Songs and Music of Cataluna." *The Journal of American Folklore* 23.88 (1910): 171–178.

Slutskaya, Natalia, and Christian De Cock. "The Body Dances: Carnival Dance and Organization." *Organization* 15 (2008): 851–868.

Smith, Milton M. "Dancing Through English Literature." *The English Journal* 9.6 (1920): 305–317.

Smyth, Jim. "Dancing, Depravity, and All That Jazz: The Public Dance Halls Act of 1935." *History Ireland* 1.2 (1993): 51–54.

Solberg, S.E. "Hawaiian Music, Poetry and Dance: Reflections on Protection, Preservation and Pride." *MELUS* 10.1 (1983): 39–63.

Soneji, Davesh. "Living History, Performing Memory: Devadasi Women in Telugu-Speaking South India." *Dance Research Journal* 36.2 (2004): 30–49.

Spirit of the Mask. Perf. Wade Davis. Gryphon Productions, 1992. Videocassette.

Spragens, John. "A Determined Survivor Revives Khmer Classical Dance." *The News Journal*, 10 January 1989. Accessed 15 May 2011.

Stein, Emma. "Cambodia's Sacred Dances." *Dance Spirit* 10.6 (2006): 128–129.

Sterne, Richard. "Puritans at Merry Mount: Variations on a Theme." *American Quarterly* 22.4 (1970): 846–858.

Stillman, Amy. "Globalizing Hula." *Yearbook for Traditional Music* 31 (1999): 57–66.

_____. "Hula Competitions: Event, Repertoire, Performance, Tradition." *The Journal of American Folklore* 109.434 (1996): 57–380.

Strickland-Anderson, Lily. "The Cambodian Ballet." *The Musical Quarterly* 12.1 (1926): 266–274.

Swisher, Clarice. *England.* Farmington Hills: Greenhaven, 2002.

Talmon-Chvaicer, Maya. *The Hidden History of Capoeira.* Austin: University of Texas Press, 2008.

Taves, Ann. "Knowing Through the Body: Dissociative Religious Experience in the African and British-American Methodist Traditions." *The Journal of Religion* 73.2 (1993): 200–222.

Taylor, J.M. "The Politics of Aesthetic Debate: The Case of Brazilian Carnival." *Ethnology* 21.4 (1982): 301–311.

Taylor, Julie. "Tango." *Cultural Anthropology* 2.4 (1987): 481–493.

Thompson, Allison. *May Day Festivals in America, 1830 to the Present.* Jefferson: McFarland, 2009.

Tillinghast, Richard. "Dervishes." *Irish Pages* 4.1 (2007): 52–157

Torrance, Robert M. *The Spiritual Quest.* Berkeley: University of California Press, 1994.

Tremlett, Giles. *Ghosts of Spain: Travels Through Spain and Its Silent Past.* New York: Walker & Company, 2006.

Turley, Darach, and Stephen Brown. "Consuming the Belly Dance." *European Advances in Consumer Research* 60 (2003): 187–192.

Twining, Mary Arnold. "'I'm Going to Sing and Shout While I Have the Chance: Music, Movement, and Dance on the Sea Islands." *Black Music Research Journal* 15.1 (1995): 1–15.

Vianna, Hermano. *The Mystery of Samba: Popular Music and National Identity in Brazil.* Chapel Hill: University of North Carolina Press, 1999.

Vila, Pablo. "Tango to Folk: Hegemony Construction and Popular Identities in Argentina." *Studies in Latin American Popular Culture* 10 (1991): 107–140.

Wadsworth, James E. "Jurema and Batuque: Indians, Africans, and the Inquisition in Colonial Northeastern Brazil." *History of Religions* 46.2 (2006): 140–162.

Warren, Nathan. *The Holidays: Christmas, Easter, and Whitsuntide.* New York: Hurd and Houghton, 1868.

Washbrook, David. "South India 1770–1840: The Colonial Transition." *Modern Asian Studies* 38.3 (2004): 479–516.

Washington, Erica Lanice. *Shabach Hallelujah! The Continuity of the Ring-Shout Tradition as a Site of Music and Dance in Black American Worship.* Bowling Green, OH: Bowling Green State University, 2005.

Welsh-Asante, Kariamu. *African Dance: An Artistic, Historic, and Philosophical Inquiry.* Trenton, NJ: African World Press, Inc., 1998.

Whelan, Frank. *The Complete Guide to Irish Dance.* Belfast: Appletree, 2000.

Willson, Margaret. "Designs of Deception: Concepts of Consciousness, Spirituality, and Survival in Capoeira Angola in Salvador, Brazil." *Anthropology of Consciousness* 12.1 (2001): 19–36.

Woodhead, Henry, ed. *Keepers of the Totem.* Alexandria: Time-Life Books, 1993.

Young, Mark, and Erik Schlie. "The Rhythm of the Deal: Negotiation as a Dance." *Negotiation Journal*, April 2011.

Index

abhinaya 8
aborigines 25
accordion 120, 165, 175
Africa 67, 84–95, 106, 110–16, 118, 120, 122, 126, 175, 178, 180–83, 186, 190–91, 194–95
Ahern, Pat 175
Alert Bay 18, 25, 27
ali'I 29
Allah 62, 64
All's Well That Ends Well (play) 148
Al-Rawi, Rosina Fawzia 124–25
ancestor 19, 23, 48, 75, 83, 85–86, 93–94, 103–5, 118, 154; myth 19–23
Angkor 49–50, 52–53, 57; *see also* Angkor Thom; Angkor Wat
Angkor National Park Heritage Site 57
Angkor Thom 48
Angkor Wat 50–51, 57
Anglo-Irish 157–58
Angolo 108, 110, 115–16, 178, 180, 185
Anusuya, Saride 12
apsaras 50–51, 56
Arabic 67, 84–85, 120
arangetram 6
Argentina 192–203
arrabals 194
arrest 111–13, 126, 130, 158, 183, 189
Arundale, Rukmini Devi 12–15
astronomy 96
Ataturk 67–68
attacks 113, 129–30, 170
auspiciousness 5
avian 23–24
awalim 119, 121
axis mundi 42–43

Bafioti 118
Bahia 104, 111–13, 181–82, 185–86, 189–90
ban 12–14, 27–28, 35, 38, 44–46, 54–55, 58, 89, 91, 101–2, 105, 122, 126, 129–31, 137–38, 153–54, 158–59, 167, 170, 172, 177–78, 181–83, 187, 191, 193, 199, 201–2
bandoneon 195–196, 200
bangles 8, 123, 125
Barcelona 99, 101, 103
Barefaced Cheek 202; *see also* Bianquet, Ovidio
barn dance 165, 168, 170
barrios 194
batter 161, 170
Battle of Little Big Horn 44
batuque 115, 177–79, 180–83, 186–87, 190–91
Baxbakalanoxsiwi 19, 22
bells 6–7, 146–52, 164
belly dancing 120, 124–25, 127–32
Beltane 133
Besouro, de Manganga 114
Betley window 152
bharata natyam 14–17
Biblical 88, 90
Big Foot 81–82
Big House 22, 28
Bimba 109–15
birth 19, 58, 118, 124, 128, 152, 200
bodies 43, 59, 63, 75, 77, 85–86, 88, 91, 111–12, 121, 128–32, 174, 183, 204
Boki 38
boleos 196
Book of Days (book) 149
Book of Sports (book) 147, 153
Border Morris 154
Brahma 5, 12, 16
Brazil 104–5, 109–17, 129, 177–91
bringing-in-the-May 133–43
British Columbia 17–18, 24, 28
brotherhood 27, 68, 96, 100–1, 130
Buenos Aires 192–203
buffalo 41–43, 72
Bull Head 81
Buonaventura 118–32
buong suong 49
Burchenal, Elizabeth 143

cabezeo 195
caboclos 179–80
cachaca 179
cadence 49, 96
Cairo 121–30
call-and-response 85, 88–89, 93, 107
candomblé 106–7, 178, 186, 189
Cannibal at the North End of the World 20
cannibalism 18–23
caper 92, 146, 148, 150, 151
capoeira 104–17
capoeiristas 104–17
Captain Cook 34
Carnival (Carnaval) 148, 177, 187–91, 199
Catalonia 96–103
Cavalier 138
cedar 22–24
ceílí 162, 167, 169, 170, 173
celestial 51, 65
Celts 133, 157, 162
ceremony 22, 24–25, 31, 80, 85, 145
chants 29–32, 36–38, 92, 107, 115
Charging Elk, Ed 83
Charles I 138, 153
Charles II 138–40, 153–54
Charleston 180
Chaucer 134
Chicago Tribune (newspaper) 79
Children of Lir 176
chimney sweeps 135–37
choreography 32–33, 49, 52, 105, 176
Christianity 35, 44, 46, 72, 78–79, 89–91, 94, 137–38, 145–47
Christmas 25, 27, 58, 82, 93, 147–48, 153
circle 5–6, 23–24, 41, 43, 47, 52, 63, 65, 74, 76–77, 83, 85, 91–92, 96–97, 100, 104, 106–7, 110, 125, 127, 135, 142, 147, 151, 157, 164, 174–75, 178, 181, 195–96
City of Lights 192
civilization 49, 51–53, 121, 157, 177
clandestine 90, 126, 203
cleansing 20
Cleveland, Ohio 193
cobla 98–99, 103
Codere, Helen 17
coins 66, 123, 125
colonialism, British 11–12; *see also* French colonialism
coming of age 18
compadritos 195, 197, 203
Congo 178, 183, 185
connection 34, 50, 84–85, 107, 109, 125, 174, 196
Connemara 163, 170, 175
contra punt 97
coor 166
copper 20–28

coronation 35, 67, 181
cosmos 22, 43, 48, 50, 60, 63, 105
costume 9, 14, 17, 40, 49, 54, 63, 68, 71–73, 94, 123–26, 128–29, 131, 146–49, 149–50, 170, 174, 179, 188–89
Cotswald Morris 154
counterclockwise 23, 85–87, 94, 196
counting 20, 24, 97
courtship 198
Cranmer, Daniel 25–26
Cranmer, Gloria 26
Creative Divine 59–60, 85, 153
Cromwell, Oliver 138, 153
Crooked Beak 19, 23, 26
Crow Dog, Leonard 82
Crow Dog, Mary 78
cuaird 165, 173
cunning 81, 104–5, 113
curts 96–97
cuts 166

Dahlin, Dondi 129
Dallas Daily Herald (newspaper) 44
damhsa 157
dance du ventre 126
dance halls 171–73, 195
dance master 7, 66, 107, 147, 159–66, 173, 175
dance steps 34, 139, 180, 195, 198
Dede, Ahmed, Remzi 68
deities 8–9, 179, 185
democracy 54, 100, 103, 177, 203
descerem as damas 180
devadasis 6–14
dew 136, 139
dhikr 64
dictatorship 67, 102
direk 64
Discépolo 199
divine 9, 49, 50, 60, 63, 65; *see also* Creative Divine
Donga 186–87, 189
Druids 33
drums 7, 32, 34, 42, 49, 59, 63–64, 66, 70, 76, 89, 92, 98, 107, 120, 124, 129, 139, 142, 145, 147, 149, 161, 163, 167, 177–83, 186, 189–90

earthquake 73
Echo of Our Song (book) 36
Egypt 118–31
El Cachafaz 200
Elegba 85
Elizabeth I 157–58, 160
encantados 178–79
Endicott, John 141
energy 5, 39, 43, 54, 84, 106–7, 124–25

entrudo 188
Esna 126
Esperance Club 155

family 12, 14, 23, 38, 46, 51–55, 66, 93, 124,
    131, 165, 172–73, 176, 186, 191, 201
favelas 186, 189–90
feadán 166
feather 40, 75–76, 166, 189
femininity 37, 52, 105
fertility 48, 123–24, 128, 152
fife 142, 149
fighting 73, 79, 104–5, 109–15, 146–47,
    177, 191
figures (dance) 139, 162
Finland 204
flamenco 163, 175–76
Flora 133, 139, 141
floviol 78
flowers 6, 9, 29, 34, 42, 50–52, 60, 70, 84,
    127, 133–36, 144, 152, 164
flute 7, 14, 59, 61–62, 64, 70, 98, 120, 135,
    166–67
fool 136, 146–52
Four-Hand Reel 169
France 9, 53, 67, 101, 103, 111, 120–21, 125–
    26, 146, 158, 159, 192, 194
francization 101
Franco, Francisco 102–3
freemasons 68
French colonialism 53
Friar Tuck 135, 149, 152

Gaelic 157, 169, 171–75
gardai 172
Gardel, Carlos 200–1
garlands 134, 136, 142
gauchos 194–95
gender 15, 162, 197
Georgia 84–94; *see also* Sea Islands
Georgia Sea Island Singers 94
ghawazee 121–22
Ghost Dance 71–83
ghost shirts 71, 75, 78
ghost stick 75
Gioseffi, Daniella 128
global 15, 34, 128, 162, 175, 192, 197, 204
goddess 9, 29–30, 32–34, 50, 53, 57, 118,
    133, 141
Golden Age 192–203
Gothic 133
gourd 32, 46, 107, 178
Great Awakening 89
Great Spirit 41, 81
Grindal, Edmund 153
Güiraldes, Ricardo 198
Gulick, Luther 143

Gullah 84

Haiti 89
hamatsa 17–28
hand gestures 6, 8, 36, 52
handkerchief 151–52, 154
Hansel & Gretel 17
harmony 50–51, 76, 100, 134, 167, 191, 200
harp 157, 166–67
Harpers Weekly 80, 135, 142
Harrison, Benjamin 80
hat 63–64, 68, 112–13, 136, 149, 160
Hatun, Destine 66
Hawaii 29–38
hawks 42, 75
Hawthorne, Nathaniel 136, 144
Headington Quarry Morris Dancers 154
heathen 80, 91, 137
hemlock 21, 23, 28
Henry VI 148
Henry VIII 136, 147, 149
Heper, Sadettin 70
heritage 37, 49, 56–58, 102, 131, 157, 174
Hi'laka 29
Hindu 6–14
hobby-horse 145, 148–49, 152
Hokhokw 19, 26
Hollins College 142
Hollywood 127, 197
holy 40–43, 65, 71, 82, 89, 99, 112, 128,
    181, 184
hornpipe 157, 161–67, 170
hu 65
Hudson Bay Co. 24
hula 29–38, 52
hymns 64, 89, 90

'ilima 30–33
improvisation 9, 108, 117, 127, 131, 152, 166,
    196
incantation 29, 79
indecency 79, 171, 181
Indian agents 25, 78, 82
Industrial Revolution 101, 154–55
initiation 19, 62, 66, 110, 185
Inquisition 182
instruments 7, 14, 17, 32, 45, 54, 59, 89, 98,
    111, 120, 130, 149, 166–67, 178
Irish dance 157–76
Irish Penny Journal (newspaper) 160
Irving, Washington 144, 153
Isabel II 98
Istanbul 58, 68–70
Iyer, E. Krishna 13–14

James II 157
Japan 37, 131, 203–4

Jayavarman VII 49
Jesus of Nazareth 73–74, 90, 92
jig 157–58, 161–65, 167, 169, 173–74
João, Don VI 111
jogo 105
Juca 113
juntas 202–3

kahea 32
Kalakaua, David 35–38
kalakeshetra 14–15
Kamehameha 34, 37
Kanahele, Pualani 38
kapa 32
kapu 33, 35
Kemal, Mustafa 67
Kempe, William 148–50
Khmer classical ballet 48–57
Kicking Bear 80–82
kicks 108–9, 115–16, 150, 163, 170–71
Kimber, William 154
kneebone 88
kohl 125
Konya 58, 64, 66, 69–70
Koran 65, 68
kru 52
kuaha 32
kunchita 7
Kwakiutl 17–25
Kwakwaka'wakw 17

Lake, Ma'iki 36
lakhon lueng 48
Lakota 39–47, 71–82
lambada 183
Latin America 191, 200
laxsa 20
leather 71, 150, 174, 197
legislation 27, 89, 159, 166, 171–72, 182
literature 119, 136, 139, 144, 171
Little Egypt 127
Little John 135
llargs 20
London 28, 70, 78, 134, 137–39, 145, 147–
	48, 150, 155, 169, 203
Long Parliament 138
Lord of MisRule 141
Louis XIV 101
lundu 183–84
lunfardo 199, 202
lyrics 7, 35–36, 87–88, 127, 174, 187, 197–
	99, 201–2

machismo 193, 199
madhoubs 68
Maia 133
Maid Marian 135, 145, 147–48

malacia 113–14
mana 29, 37
martial arts 104–5
masks 17–28, 52, 188
mawail 23
maxixe 183–84, 188–90
May Day 133–48
May Pole Alley 139
May Pole Dance 134–53
McIntosh County, Georgia 86, 93
McIntosh Shouters 92, 94–95
McKiver, Lawrence 88, 94
medicine man 40, 47, 79, 81
mele 30–36
Merrie Monarch 36–37
Merry Mount 140, 144
mestico 189–90
metaphor 31, 59–60, 66, 106, 183, 186, 200
Mevlana 58–70
Mevlevis 58–70
military 11, 24, 68, 72, 79, 102, 104, 111,
	116, 138, 153–54, 158, 182, 190, 202–3
milkmaids 135–36
milonga 195, 198, 201
minuets 157
mirth 6, 136–37, 141–42
missionaries 11, 25, 34, 35, 44–45, 73, 79–
	80, 82, 87; *see also* missionary
moon 9, 12, 23, 42, 62, 65, 75–76, 83, 96
Moors 145, 149
The Morris Book (book) 150
Morris dance 145–56
morros 186, 189
Morton, Thomas 140, 144
Mother Goose 136
mrdangam 7
Mubarak 129
Much Ado About Nothing (play) 148
mudras 6–7
mullah 177
Munster 163, 169, 175
museum 26, 68, 87, 103, 203
Muslim 11, 65, 67, 129, 177, 182
mysticism 19, 58, 64, 68, 96

naatu 7
naga 50–51, 55
namashar 8
Napoleon 111, 125, 188
Native Americans 44, 47, 82–83
Native Brotherhood 27
nature 20, 30, 38, 50–52, 59, 62, 73, 78,
	123–25, 134
Neal, Mary 155
New York City 94, 143, 193
New York Herald (newspaper) 127
ney 59

Nile 121, 126
Northwest Morris 154
nritta 8
nrtya 8

ocho 196
offering 49–52
Ohanian, Arman 128
One Bull 42–47
oppression 73, 86, 90, 95, 102, 110, 158, 175, 177, 182, 194, 198
orbit 60, 64
Orcaizaguirre, Jorge 203
Orezzoli, Hector 203
Oriental dance 120, 129
Orientalism 59, 120–29, 205, 207
Ottoman 66–70
Ouled Nail dancer 122–23

P!Esa' 22
Padstow 133, 140, 152
pageantry 37, 149
paint 9, 12, 17, 23, 40–43, 49, 56, 65, 71, 74–76, 3, 96, 103, 109, 112, 118, 135, 143, 161, 180
pampa 194
Pandanallur, Jeevaratnam 14
Pandanallur, Rajeswari 14
paraphernalia 19, 22, 41
Pardàs, Miquel 98
Paris 9, 70, 126, 138, 160, 172, 188, 192, 194, 198, 203
Parliament 138, 153–54, 158
Parrish, Lydia 93
passion 7, 63, 101, 159, 182, 197–98, 200, 202
pastinha 114–16
patterns (dance) 50, 54, 108, 125, 140, 149–51, 154, 164, 170, 196
Pavlova, Anna 13
Pele 29–30, 38
pelvis 34, 118–19, 124
penal laws 158–59
Pereiras, Zé 189
Perón, Juan 199–202
Persia 67, 118, 126, 130
Phon, Chheng 54–56
Piazolla, Astor 203–4
Picasso 28, 103
piercing 41–46
pilgrimage 66, 130, 145
pin peat 49
Pine Ridge Reservation 46, 72, 77–82
Plains Indians 39–45, 71–82
plaits 139–40
planet 64–65
Plaza de Mayo 202

pleasure 85, 185, 188, 196
Plough Monday 146
poetry 29–38, 61–64, 116, 164, 199
Pol Pot 53–57
pole *see* May Pole; Sun Pole
police 68, 70, 78, 79–81, 111–14, 126, 129, 181, 183, 187, 189–90
politics 53–55, 61, 67, 99–100, 102–3, 113–14, 129–132, 137, 153, 170, 184–86, 198, 200–4, 207
Polo, Marco 9
Porcupine, Chief 82
Portugal 145–46, 178
potlatch 22–28
power 5, 11, 19–23, 28–29, 35, 37, 42–49, 53–54, 59, 65, 67–68, 71–73, 84, 86, 93, 101–2, 105, 111–13, 122, 124–25, 129, 131, 176, 179, 190, 194, 196, 198
prácticas 200
prayer 9, 30, 32–33, 39–42, 56, 61, 63–65, 68, 72–77, 85, 88, 92, 107, 137, 178, 185
priests 133–34, 153–54, 165, 172
primitivism 91, 147, 195
Primo de Rivera, Miquel 101
primordialism 59–60, 191
prostitutes 130–31
psyche 17–18, 24
Pugliese, Osraldo 202
Pukui, Mary 36
Puritans 134–54

quadrilles 161, 164–65
quilombos 110–12

Rabia of Bashra 66
race 29–30, 91, 97, 157, 189–90
raffles 165
rains 46, 48–49, 52, 62, 73–74, 159
rakodi 9
raqs sharqi 118–31
rasa 7
rattle 21, 24, 32, 76, 180
Raven 19–23
rawhide 40–43, 174
rebirth 15, 55, 118, 152
Red Cloud 72
reel 161–73
reformers 11, 44–45
religion 5, 11–12, 14, 35, 65, 72, 78–79, 82–92, 106, 114, 177–78, 191
repertoire 6, 8–9, 32, 52, 159, 161, 166, 169–70
rhythm 6–7, 23, 30, 32, 34, 42, 50, 59, 84–89, 96, 99, 105–7, 110, 116–25, 147, 151, 163–64, 167, 170, 173, 178, 181, 185–86, 191, 195, 200
ribbons 112, 136, 139–40, 143, 149, 152–54

ring-shout 84–95
Rio de Janeiro 104, 111–13, 183, 185–86, 188–90
ritual 9–15, 16–28, 30–38, 39–46, 48–52, 60–72, 72–82, 86–90, 110, 123–31, 146, 149, 179–90
Riverdance 174–76
robam 52
Robin Hood 113, 134–35, 152
Robinson, Fred 82
roda 106–8
rodonas 96, 100
roeung 52
Rooted Woman 19–23
Rosebud Reservation 47, 72, 79–80
Royer, Daniel 79
Rumi 58–70

sacada 196
Sachs, Curt 118
sacred 5, 14, 33–38, 39–47, 49, 52, 58, 61, 70, 75, 85, 128, 133
sacrifice 24, 39–44, 138, 149, 151–52
St. Simon Island 93
salmon 20–24, 162
salons 127, 192, 198, 200
samba 177–91
sambistas 177, 184–90
sampeah kru 52
Samy, Chea 54–55
Santamaria, Elvira 203
sardana 96–103
Sardanistas 100
saut 84
Scotland 138, 167
Sea Islands 84–94
sean-nós 163, 170–71, 175
Segovia, Claudio 203
sema 64–70
senhor 179–80
sensuality 59, 106, 123, 126, 128–29, 204
Sewid, James 27–28
Shakers 73
Shakespeare, William 138, 148–49, 156
shakti 5, 15
shaman 20
Shapiro, Sophiline 52–56
Sharp, Cecil 146, 150, 154
Sheboygan, Wisconsin 193
sheikh 66–68
sheykh 63–64
shirts 71–83; *see also* ghost shirts
Shiva 5–6, 12, 15–16
shroud 60, 63, 68
Silva, Ismael 190
Sioux 45–47, 71–74, 78–83
Sitting Bull 47, 80–81

slaves 19, 22, 48, 88–93, 105, 110–11, 113, 116, 178, 181–83, 188, 197
soirees 165
solidarity 100–1
songs 17, 19, 21, 31, 42, 74–75, 77, 88, 90, 94, 107, 135, 154, 167, 178, 180–82, 199–203
soughtavan 7
Soviet Union 67
Spain 96, 101–3, 120, 146, 147, 149, 163, 178, 193–97, 207
spheres 58–60
Stack-of-Barley 164
Standing Rock 45–46, 79
Standish, Myles 141
Statutes of Kilkenny 159
sticks 32, 41, 104, 136, 146, 151–52, 154–55, 181
Stratford-on-Avon 155
streamers 139, 143
Strongbear, Francis 47
Sufi 58–59, 63–66, 70
Sultan 66–68, 70
Sun Dance 39–47
Sun Pole 42–43
supernatural 18–23, 39, 73, 84, 13, 176, 179
Sweets of May 164, 170
swords 122, 146, 152
symbolism 19–23, 31, 42–46, 50, 61–65, 68, 75–76, 86, 96–97, 100, 102, 111–12, 118, 123, 134–36, 152–53, 167, 174, 183, 189–90, 197, 202

taboo 23, 35, 38
talam 7
tamany 142
tambori 96–99
tango 192–202
Tango Argentina 203
tangomania 192
teams 146, 154–55
tekkes 68
Telethusa 119
temples 12, 29, 48–49, 51, 58
tenora 99
tep robam 52
terreiro 178
Thames 138
theatre 12, 14, 101, 105, 139, 175, 186, 199
Theosophical Society 12–14
thunderbird 24, 40
Tomahawk, Red 81
tomb 65–69
tourism 70, 127, 203
trance 49, 77, 96, 124, 178–80
Treaty of Lausanne 67

trees 6, 14–15, 24, 29, 32, 40–41, 48, 50, 52, 60–63, 76, 114–15, 133–36
Troilo, Anibal Carmelo 200
troupe 9, 49, 54, 129, 132, 147, 153
turban 63, 68
Turkey 58, 64, 67–69, 120, 123, 131, 146, 187
Twelfth Night 146–47

Ulster 163
Umista Cultural Center 26
UNESCO 56–58
U.S. government 44, 82

Vancouver Island 17, 24
Vargas, Getúlio 114–15, 190
Vatican 193
veils 63, 125
Ventura I Casas, Josep 98
Vietnam 53–55

violin 7, 26, 59, 195
vision 34, 39, 46–47, 59, 71–78, 127

wake 157, 165
Washington Post (newspaper) 79
Waves of Tory 164
West Africa 84–86, 89–90, 93–95, 118, 178
Whirling Dervishes 58–69
whistles 17, 19, 22, 41–42, 166–67
Whitsun 147, 153, 155
Whitsuntide 145, 148
Wilson, Jack 72, 74
Wokova 72–75, 78, 83
worship 5–12, 33, 85–93, 96, 118
Wounded Knee 81–83
wreaths 31, 43, 136, 144

zills 125
Zoroastrianism 65
Zumbi 104, 110